The
ranchising
andbook

Domino's Pizza is the UK's leading pizza delivery company and one of the world's most successful franchise businesses. Domino's represents a hugely exciting business opportunity for franchisees with a real passion for success – it has created 20 franchisee millionaires in 20 years of trading. Although Domino's has over 400 stores, covering 45% of UK households, there is still enormous potential for growth and Domino's has an ongoing aim to open 50 stores a year for the foreseeable future.

Domino's aims to recruit the highest quality franchisees – awarding franchises to those who demonstrate commitment to the brand and deliver the best product and customer service in the pizza delivery industry. All applicants are rigorously reviewed by Domino's Franchise Sales Team who look for strong evidence of the candidates competency in managing people and finances.

Pizza People

Antony Tagliamonti is a great example of what can be achieved through hard work and determination. He started his career as a part-time delivery driver, and now aged just 26 he is the franchisee of three stores, responsible for 100 staff, and looking forward to building his empire even further.

Anthony puts his success down to his relationships with both Domino's head office and his team members, which remain as strong as they were when he first began.

He comments, "Being in regular contact with Domino's head office keeps me involved and part of the bigger picture. This is something that I try to replicate in running my own stores. Every morning I meet with my teams and update them on sales, promotions and product news. I like to be as hands-on as possible but never undermine my managers. It is important to strike the right balance.

"The experience and knowledge that Domino's provides means that with motivation and hard work you can't go too far wrong! The support from head office and the marketing department is very reassuring, particularly in the early stages when you're still finding your feet."

The key to your successful business.

Could you employ and motivate a team of people to make and deliver quality pizzas, made with fresh ingredients to order on time, every time?

Domino's Pizza is looking for tenacious, business focused individuals whose personal energy knows no bounds.

With over 40 years in the pizza delivery business, Domino's will deliver a tried and tested business system. This includes intensive training and excellent support to help make your business part of the UK's number one pizza delivery company.

Up for it? Get in touch with the Domino's Franchise Department.

Tel: 01908 580657

For more information, visit: www.dominos.uk.com/franchise

the
Franchising
Handbook

The complete Guide to
Choosing a Franchise

Iain Murray

London and Philadelphia

An (family!

0749 445416 2373 03

fe can be accommodated and where you can be your own boss, a Jo Jingles franchise could be what you are looking for. Launched as a national franchise in 1995 the company now has a network of over 90 franchisees throughout the UK and Ireland, currently providing more than 20,000 babies and children with a fun introduction to the delights of music, singing and movement.

Potential franchisees must enjoy working with young children; have a keen interest in music and a good singing voice. The confidence to run a business matched with enthusiasm, fitness and the ability to have fun are all vital.

Franchise areas cost from £6,000 to £8,000 plus VAT, depending on size of territory and include a comprehensive start-up package with professional class programmes. An additional investment of at least £1000 in local advertising and promotions is expected in the first year of business. The company has a number of franchise areas available throughout the UK and in Ireland where there is a growing demand for classes.

Jo Jingles also run sessions in a variety of children's day nurseries and in Government funded SureStart centres. The company's interactive music and singing programmes with an educational slant help to ensure young children receive a positive start in life. It is well recognised that exposing children to music at an early age has many benefits helping to develop language, numeracy, concentration & listening skills for example.

Jo Jingles is credited with Full Membership of the British & Irish Franchise Associations.

For full details on the Jo Jingles Business Opportunity contact:
Jo Jingles Limited on Tel: **01494 778989**
Email: **headoffice@jojingles.co.uk** Visit: **www.jojingles.com**

Publisher's note

Every possible effort has been made to ensure that the information contained in this book is accurate at the time of going to press, and the publishers and author cannot accept responsibility for any errors or omissions, however caused. No responsibility for loss or damage occasioned to any person acting, or refraining from action, as a result of the material in this publication can be accepted by the editor, the publisher or the author.

First published in Great Britain and the United States in 2006 by Kogan Page Limited

Kogan Page Limited
120 Pentonville Road
London N1 9JN
United Kingdom
www.kogan-page.co.uk

525 South 4th Street, #241
Philadelphia PA 19147
USA

© Iain Murray, 2006

ISBN 0 7494 4541 6

British Library Cataloguing in Publication Data

A CIP record for this book is available from the British Library.

Library of Congress Cataloging-in-Publication Data

Murray, Iain.
 The franchising handbook : the complete guide to choosing a franchise
/ Iain Murray.
  p. cm.
 ISBN 0-7494-4541-6
 1. Franchises (Retail trade) I. Title.
HF5429.23.M87 2006
658.8'708--dc22   2006008963

Typeset by Saxon Graphics Ltd, Derby
Printed and bound by Cambrian Printers Ltd, Aberystwyth, Wales

Contents

Introduction

Unless you are very fortunate you will be among the many millions for whom work is more of a chore than a pleasure. Of course, paid employment has its compensations, not least of which is the money, but in those darker moments that intrude into every working life you are uncomfortably aware that you are, to all intents and purposes, a servant. The organization is your master and as long as you remain beholden to it you will never be free. And nor, if truth be told, will your efforts be fully appreciated or rewarded. You are, after all, working for someone else.

No surprise, then, that in those idle intervals set aside for day-dreaming, the fondest thoughts are of self-employment. Just think: no more subservience, no more taking orders, no more petty rivalries, no more conforming to other people's ideas.

Oh well, it was only a dream but nice while it lasted.

For some, however, the yearning to be free is a wake-up call. They are the determined few who slip the shackles of wage slavery and set up businesses of their own. 'Lucky them,' you say, 'but I haven't got that kind of entrepreneurial spirit, I wouldn't know where to begin and anyway I don't have a business idea.'

But do not despair; you have the answer in your hand. This book sets out with two clear aims in mind – first, to explain how you can be your own boss, and second, to show you how to set about it.

If you long to work for yourself but are wary of leaping into the dark and going it alone, franchising is for you. It is in many ways the answer to a dream. Picture someone coming along and presenting you with a business idea, ready-made, tried and tested, and what's more offering to teach you how to run it and to carry on helping you once you've got going. Picture that, and you've pictured a franchisor.

All you need do is choose the kind of business you would like to own and run and then pick the franchisor to help you make it happen. And if that sounds glib, well, it is. Although picking a business off the shelf sounds easy, it has to be done with discernment and care, because getting it wrong is worse than not having tried at all. Among the chief purposes of franchising is to avoid failure, therefore to fail to pick the right franchise in the first place is particularly inept.

But don't be put off: it won't happen if you allow yourself to be guided by this book. As you go through its pages you will see how often it sounds a word of caution. This is not to be negative or downbeat about franchising – on the contrary I truly believe it can offer a relatively smooth path into a fulfilling form of self-employment – but rather to ensure that you steer clear of the snares that lie in wait for the unwary.

Choosing and buying a franchise should be an exciting and rewarding experience, and what follows, when at last you have a business to call your own, should be better still.

Right from the outset you should see your search for a franchise as a campaign, a plan to be laid down, plotted and pursued to its conclusion with determination and vigour. The aim of this book is to give you the map and the weapons to see you through to a triumphant outcome. So no more dreaming, time to get real.

Chem-Dry is the world's largest carpet and upholstery cleaning company. It was established in the USA in 1977 and now has over 4,000 franchise licences in operation, in 46 countries.

With 19 years' experience in the UK, BFA full member Chem-Dry is one of the leading carpet and upholstery cleaning franchises serving both domestic and commercial premises. Its UK network 700 franchisees, backed by its national service centre with over 250 staff, also provides a market-leading fire and water disaster restoration service to the major insurance companies.

Chem-Dry, with its unique, patented hot-carbonating cleaning process and 96% success rate is a proven business solution. Dedicated to success, Chem-Dry invests heavily in updating products and equipment to ensure all franchisees are fully equipped with cutting-edge technology. Chem-Dry franchisees also enjoy a first-class technical and business development support service and Continuous Professional Development through the Chem-Dry Centre of Excellence, a purpose built training complex at our UK head office in East Yorkshire.

If you have the drive, energy and commitment to make our system work for you, visit **www.chemdry.co.uk** and request your Open Day pack, or call us on **01482 888195**.

David Hunt, Castle Chem-Dry, Edinburgh – bought an existing Chem-Dry business in April 2002 after serving as a Police Officer for 14 years. Like most franchisees he started from a home base and his 100% commitment to building a balanced business was justly rewarded in only his second year, when he achieved a £100k turnover. He now works from business premises and employs three technicians and an administrator.

Darren & Sharon Barker, Chem-Dry Solutions, Burstow, Surrey – joined Chem-Dry in April 2003, Darren coming from a career in Sales Management. They really have worked the system and applied their business skills, which resulted in them achieving a first year turnover in excess of £100k. They have achieved phenomenal growth ever since, taking on business premises, adding an additional franchise licence and their first technician in November 2003, their third franchise licence in April 2004, a second technician in September 2004 and a fourth franchise licence in October 2004.

Join the Elite

Did you know that every four seconds someone, somewhere in the world invites Chem-Dry to clean their home? That's over one billion square feet of carpet cleaned by Chem-Dry each year!

As the largest carpet and upholstery cleaning franchise in the World, our 26-year history of success has proved that our methods and products form a sound investment and an excellent business opportunity. With Chem-Dry you run your own independently owned and operated franchise business, with the added peace of mind that comes with knowing that you have the full support of the Master Franchise.

As an independent Chem-Dry franchisee, you can take advantage of the following:

- An established brand name which consumers trust
- The security of selling a unique, patented cleaning process that really works
- The opportunity to tap into £30 million of fire and water damage insurance work
- The backing of a full team of people offering technical and business development support
- Access to our new Centre of Excellence training facility

If you're thinking about running your own business, why not consider being part of a winning team...

Visit **www.chemdry.co.uk** and complete our **Questionnaire** to receive an **Open Day Pack**. If you don't have Internet access, call us on **01482 888195.**

1 Nothing succeeds like franchising success

The first thing the curious reader will want to know on opening this book is, does franchising work? Because if it doesn't, or if its performance is at best patchy, there is little point in pursuing the matter any further. Before going into the answer in detail, let's start on an encouraging note by looking at some success stories. The website of the British Franchise Association (BFA), an organization that lays fair claim to being the voice of British franchising, features some 50 case studies, each bearing a picture of a happy, smiling franchisee who explains in the accompanying text how his or her new business was life-transforming. Straight away, the list makes the point that franchisees come from a wide variety of backgrounds, are of varying ages, and are engaged in a huge diversity of activities.

Here are a few examples taken at random.

Iain McKillop, a qualified engineer with 30 years' telecommunications experience, came across franchising quite by accident. He had been working in Amsterdam for two years until family circumstances brought him back to his native Scotland. While updating his CV on his computer, a pop-up advertisement appeared for the business coaching and training franchise Action International. 'The timing was perfect', he says. 'Action offered everything I was looking for – the opportunity to use my business experience, own my own business, but still work within the support structure of a multinational company.'

He started business coaching in January 2004 in Glasgow and his subsequent success with clients has earned him recognition from the parent company in the shape of 'Gold Master Coach' status. 'One of the reasons I wanted to get into Action was the support offered to franchisees', he says. 'I knew that I would be investing a substantial amount of money and it was important to know I wouldn't just be abandoned once the cheque was signed. The support was second to none. We have regular monthly meetings as well as annual conferences. I have the opportunity to learn from other people's experiences every day.'

Neil Newman trained as a plumber, but it was only when he started his own Drain Doctor franchise that he really began to reap the benefits of both his experience and his hard work. Within 18 months of starting his franchise in Exeter he achieved a turnover of £264,000. He puts his success down to following the franchisor's business system. 'I've done it the Drain Doctor way and it works', he says. 'Someone else who trained at the same time as me didn't follow the system and eventually gave up the franchise.'

Drain Doctor says it is the country's largest emergency plumbing and drain repair business and rose to the top through offering reliable service of the kind customers do not always associate with plumbing. 'Many householders are fearful of calling out plumbers and other construction tradesmen because of the horror stories they have seen on television programmes', says Neil. 'It is very distressing to be the victim of shoddy workmanship but Drain Doctor has built a reputation for excellence that wins customer trust and loyalty. By providing a genuine 24-hour service with no call-out charge and no extras for working unsocial hours, we give customers the assurance that they are not going to be ripped off. Our smart vans and work clothes convey a professional image that is emphasized by our working practices.'

Neil employs his father as a manager, and his partner Anne Pulman handles all the business administration tasks. 'I couldn't manage without her', says Neil. 'Drain Doctor's head office team has also been great with the comprehensive initial training and the ongoing support it provides.'

Alan Abel is a franchising veteran. For the past 18 years he has been running a Complete Weed Control business, eliminating unwanted vegetation on behalf of a variety of industrial, commercial and local authority customers. As a former farm manager, he grew weary of seeing his hard effort not being fully rewarded. Franchising provided him with the independence he so wanted and enabled him to avoid many of the pitfalls that threaten independent small businesses. When he began his franchise in South Wales back in the 1980s, he started off with the great advantage of taking on many existing contracts and contacts established over the previous 10 years by the parent company. Since then, he says, his client list has grown tenfold and is growing still. 'Despite many years of experience I still find myself amazed at the number of new opportunities for increasing business that I come across every week.' In 1998, Alan was appointed to the board of directors of the parent company and now offers advice and support to new franchisees.

In 1993, Rosemary Conley launched her national network of diet and fitness clubs. Operating on a franchised basis, it now has more than 175 franchisees who run some 2,000 fitness classes every week for more than 80,000 members. Jillian MacGregor, franchisee in the Edinburgh West region, was the company's franchisee of the year in 2000. She won the title just a few days after giving birth to her second child, Cameron. Combining work and family life is, she says, one of the reasons why she loves what she does for a living. 'I joined the company in April 1995 and haven't looked back since. Before starting out I was keen to find out everything I could about the organization. I received excellent training and the ongoing support and assistance has helped me to make such a success of my business.'

Before signing up as a franchisee, Jillian worked as a computer programmer for British Gas. Leaving her job after 10 years gave her no regrets. 'It really was a complete change for me but it was the right decision to make and one that I would make again and again if I was asked to choose. I love the flexibility and the improved lifestyle I now have.'

Nadeem and Sam Sohail run a Benjys delivered 'vanchisee' in East London, delivering sandwiches, breads, drinks and prepared meals to a growing number of customers. Neither had any previous experience of the food or retail business. Sam says: 'Leaving our jobs and setting up a new business was a difficult decision, especially as we have two young children to consider. I used to buy my lunch from Benjys when I worked in the City, so I was already familiar with the brand.'

Nadeem adds: 'The training you receive when you first start is very thorough. Absolutely everything is covered, from how to store food at the correct temperature, to hygiene and day-to-day business management. You are also given the opportunity to shadow a franchisee and see for yourself how the van operates and what a typical day involves.'

Duncan Rice had already given up a steady job before he discovered franchising. 'I taught English and drama in schools in England since leaving South Africa in 1985. Increasingly, I felt a real uneasiness about another year of being a hamster on a treadmill; I needed to jump off, get out of the cage and into something more fulfilling. I was bogged down with paperwork, reports, marking, endless parents' meetings, departmental documentation, and the prospect of a looming inspection filled me with dread. So I resigned.' While he was contemplating his next move he saw a small ad in the *Times Educational Supplement* offering franchises in Helen O'Grady Drama Academy. It seemed an opportunity tailor-made just for him. Further investigation increased his confidence. 'I realized that the programme was child-centred and very much in accord with my belief in developing children's confidence and self-esteem through drama. Within two months, I sold my house in Cambridge and moved to Northern Ireland. All sorts of things were going through my mind. Would I earn enough money to survive? Would anybody sign up? How would the children respond to my accent? No one could have prepared me for the response I was to receive. I was besieged by calls and within two weeks nearly all my classes were full, with extensive waiting lists and a total enrolment of 250 pupils in my school. I feel the freedom of being a free agent – cages and treadmills are in the distant past now.'

After many years working with her husband in a property development business, Glynis Croft decided she would like to run her own business. She now has her own lavatory cleaning operation, or, more precisely, she is managing her own washroom maintenance company. 'I was originally introduced to franchising through my NatWest Bank', she says. 'On a cold and wet November evening I attended a franchise seminar and one of the several speakers at the event was Marilyn Keen, development director of Swisher. I had not heard of Swisher before and I must admit that the concept was not the most glamorous one I heard that evening.'

Over the next few months Glynis spend a lot of time looking at a variety of franchises and, to her surprise, through a process of elimination Swisher came out as one of the two best suited to her needs. 'During my meetings with Swisher's corporate team the franchise was very clearly explained and I found all the staff very friendly and approachable. I felt that the support would be good, and I have not been disappointed.

'Choosing a franchise was a lengthy process, but when I eventually decided on Swisher and started my business I felt confident that I was able to tackle it properly.'

Within six months she gained more than £70,000 of business and by the end of the first year her turnover was £120,000. 'Working together with my sales and service staff and with Swisher Corporate, I continue to ensure that my staff provide a high standard of service to my customers. This is already showing dividends in terms of growth through customer recommendations and various multi-site accounts.'

So what are we to take away from this cavalcade of success stories, this catalogue of dreams fulfilled? At first sight the evidence seems overwhelming: franchising is a tonic, an elixir. All you need do is swallow a dose and bingo! A new, better you rises from the dead, work-torn, downtrodden you. Liberated from the reins and bridle of wage slavery, you're free to canter through the lush fields of self-employment, relishing the intoxicating air of freedom. You're your own boss at last and all is well with the world. Too good to be true? Yes, I am afraid so. Franchising is not a panacea, nor a magic wand, nor even a modest passport to easy business success. It is not even self-employment in the true sense of the term since, as we shall see, franchisees can never be entirely their own boss, free to make their own decisions and determine their own destiny. What franchising achieves, when it is done well, is a measure of independence, a fairer means than salaried employment of matching reward to effort, and a much less risky way of setting up in business than doing so from scratch with no help at all and, perhaps more important, no original ideas of one's own.

There is much to be learnt from looking more closely at the BFA success stories outlined above. First, we have to bear in mind that the BFA is constitutionally predisposed to accentuate the positive: it wants wherever possible to promote and spread franchising. And so, like an evangelist, it eagerly entices the testaments of converts whose accounts are themselves a touch messianic. All the case studies I have quoted above, and there are many more giving much the same cheerful message, are, of course, genuine. But do they give the whole picture? Well, no. Since they form part of that grey area which is neither advertising nor unrestrained speech but is known as public relations, they tell only part of the story – the part the writers want you to hear. Like all of life, franchising has its downside, its disappointments, its setbacks, its drudgery, but no one is going to tell you about those, unless you ask them. (And, as we shall see in a later chapter, doing exactly that is one of the keys to franchising success.)

However, even allowing for the fact that the BFA's testimonies are partial, they are undoubtedly sincere and tell us a lot about what separates franchising achievement from franchising dissatisfaction.

From Iain McKillop we learn that he has business experience, qualifications and ambition, an excellent and relatively rare combination of qualities. He approached franchising with care and diligence. For its part, his chosen franchisor, Action International, gives him the continuing support and encouragement he needs to make his business a success.

Neil Newman had already trained as a plumber before investing in Drain Doctor, but note that he didn't arrive at franchising with a know-all attitude, quite the reverse: he followed the system laid down by the franchisor and, unlike another trainee who didn't, went on to make a go of it. Other points to note are that he understands the paramount importance of customer service, the need to create a good impression, and that he has enlisted the help of his family in running his business.

Alan Abel was a farm manager before becoming a Complete Weed Control franchisee, so he was plainly able to handle responsibility and had organizational skills. He was – and this is a good thing – fed up with putting in effort and finding the rewards unsatisfying. He wanted something better and was prepared to take a measured risk to achieve it. He approached the task of choosing a franchise in a careful, unhurried way. He took the measure of the people running the company, he investigated the likely market, he wanted to see whether his abilities and experience suited the business. He was fortunate in taking on a number of ready-made customers but over the following 18 years he lost none of his initial enthusiasm. He also had the sense of camaraderie that a good franchisee should engender – the feeling that he is in some way part of the club whose collective experience and knowledge is there to be shared for the benefit of all.

Jillian McGregor shows – who would dare doubt it? – that women are every bit as good as, possibly even better than, men at being franchisees. She, too, had qualifications, business experience, and that little worm in the system that kept nagging away with the tantalizing thought that there is more to life than paid employment, that the grass really is greener somewhere else. She wisely refrained from any rush: 'Before starting out I was keen to find out everything I could about the organization.'

She relishes the freedom her franchise gives her, she appreciates the support she gets from the franchisor, and she puts the satisfaction of her customers at the top of her priorities.

Nadeem and Sam Sohail are in their thirties with a young family, but they had the vision and nerve to leave paid employment and strike out on their own with a van-based franchise. They took a chance – don't believe anyone who tells you franchising is risk-free – but not without first getting a measure of the odds. Sam knew and trusted the product, Nadeem was keen to investigate the quality of training and support from the franchisor. They also started off with the great advantage of being able to offer each other mutual support. They are keen to expand their business and make the most of their new-found independence.

Duncan Rice was so fed up with his job that he handed in his notice before finding something else to do and without the thought of a franchise entering his head. By chance, which is so often the way, he looked upon Helen O'Grady Drama Academy, an opportunity that suited him down to the ground. Even so, he didn't jump straight aboard, but first satisfied himself that the company's approach to teaching children agreed with his own. Even so, he took a chance in an untried territory and it paid off.

Finally, we have the story of Glynis Croft, the nice, middle-class lady turned lavatory cleaner, or rather owner/manager of a thriving washroom maintenance concern. She did everything right. She went to a seminar, she listened and learnt, she carried out her research, and even when the answer was not quite what she expected, she pressed ahead with further investigations. Her managerial skills were what counted, along with her conviction that here was a market waiting to be exploited.

From these success stories we gain an insight into some of the essential ingredients of a sound franchise relationship. In fact, that word 'relationship' is itself significant: it is important to understand at the outset that franchising is a partnership between the franchise company and the network of franchisees who run their own operations in their own territories. Neither can do without the other. It may from time to time be a fraught relationship but the best franchises ensure that communication between the parties to the agreements is kept in good repair, so that disputes may be resolved or, better still, prevented from arising in the first place.

That disagreements might occur is implicit in the kind of people who choose to take up franchises. As we have seen, in many cases they turn to franchising because they're dissatisfied with their present lot (there may, of course, be other reasons – redundancy perhaps, or women wanting to return to work after a spell spent bringing up a family), they are weary of the work routine, they feel undervalued, they long to be in control of their own destiny. Such people are by their nature restless and might be expected to approach a new way of making a living with a questioning eye – and quite rightly so. But, for the franchise relationship to work, they must accept a measure of control and be willing to follow the system laid down by the franchise company.

Another characteristic exhibited by all the franchisees in the case studies outlined above is ambition. Well, of course, why take up a franchise and give up a steady job to change direction if you don't have ambition? But it's a particular kind of ambition that drives the successful franchisee – it's a clear-headed, driven determination based on a firm understanding that nothing is for nothing. If you're considering a franchise, the worst mistake you can make is to assume that it offers an easy shortcut to success and wealth. It does not. If anything, it will involve far longer hours, more effort and more stress than wage earning. So why do it? Because it offers greater independence than paid employment, but without the fearful sense of isolation that can dog people setting up in business for the first time entirely on their own.

Next, we note that all our successful franchisees were painstaking, diligent and thorough. They were not to be rushed into a hasty decision. They knew they were planning a potentially life-changing move, and they were in no hurry to jump before they had taken the measure of the risk and investigated the pluses and minuses. Only when they were sure that the odds were in their favour did they finally sign the papers and commit themselves.

Another important point to note is that they involved their families, sometimes taking them into the business to help share the burden. Although franchising is a kind of partnership between the franchisee and the franchise company, part of the attraction is that you are, by and large, left alone to make the most of your new business and need only call for help when you really need it. As you find your way and, especially in the early days, struggle to come to terms with the stimulating but daunting challenge of making a go of your new enterprise, you will need all the support and encouragement you can get from family and friends.

It is, therefore, best to involve your spouse or partner from the very beginning. Too many franchises fail because the franchisee underestimated the degree of commitment required and the consequent strains it would place on his or her relationship. A problem shared may not be a problem halved but it is still less of a problem than one borne alone or, worse still, dumped on to an unwilling husband or wife.

All the franchisees in the case studies had some previous business experience. Though this is not essential – one of the great attractions of franchising is that it can teach business skills – it certainly helps. Research shows that the majority of franchisees are not complete strangers to business life, and indeed a significant number have previous experience of self-employment. Do not be put off franchising because you have always worked for someone else, but do go into it with the expectation that it will be quite unlike anything you have experienced before. When you get out of bed in the morning it will not be to go to a place where you're expected to answer to the bidding of others, but to meet a schedule entirely of your own making. It can be quite a shock.

So far, we have spoken only of the franchisee's side of the bargain and touched just briefly on the interdependence of franchisee and franchisor. But you will have noticed how all the successful franchisees discussed above paid tribute to the training and support they received from the franchise company. This is arguably the single most important feature of a sound franchise relationship, especially in the early days. The very essence of franchising is that it takes people from all walks of life, and with varying degrees of experience, and gives them the opportunity to fulfil themselves as entrepreneurs, albeit of a kind that stops short of total independence. It follows that success or failure hinges on the quality of training and support provided.

This may strike you as obvious – as indeed may much more that you will read in this book – but please bear in mind that when most franchising manuals describe the way the system works, they are assuming the ideal; they take for granted that the formula applies in all cases. Sadly, this is far from the reality. Franchise companies vary enormously in quality: in fact the franchise sector is in some ways the victim of its own success. As word got about that people eager to better themselves were willing to invest in companies called franchises because it was less risky than going it alone, all manner of organizations flocked to join in the party. Many describing themselves as franchises were not franchises at all. Others, while having some of the characteristics of a franchise, were inexperienced and had not properly researched the implications of becoming franchisors. Some, though genuine and no doubt sincere, underestimated the amount of help and training franchisees need. And, inevitably, not a few were downright dishonest, passing themselves off as franchises with no aim other than to part guileless people from their money.

The road to franchising success is paved unevenly. It is easy for the unwary to trip up and to see their life savings rolling into the gutter and down the drain. But with care and preparation there is no reason why you should not successfully negotiate your way past all the obstacles and add your name to the thousands who are already enjoying the rewards of 'being in business for yourself but not by yourself'.

The aim of this book is to help you realize that goal. If you follow the guidelines laid down in succeeding chapters, if you are able to make a frank assessment of your own strengths and weaknesses, and if you have the objectivity to examine franchising opportunities with a keen and critical eye, there is every reason to assume you will achieve your objectives and reap the rewards of your drive and ambition.

But we are getting ahead of ourselves. We have yet to define franchising, let alone describe how to choose the right one for you…

Attention to Detail

THE MARKET

The UK cleaning industry is expected to continue on its growth path with contract cleaning in particular expanding alongside the business service sector, according to an industry review by Market & Business Development. "MBD anticipate year-on-year growth within the contract cleaning market in the UK", the report verifies "with overall growth of 10 per cent expected to take the market to a level of £5459 million in 2009."

This is great news for Detail Clean. Franchisees can maximise the potential of their territories by targeting both the domestic and commercial cleaning markets.

A FORMULA THAT WORKS

With seven years experience in the industry Detail Clean has developed a concept based on a consistently professional service with impeccable reliability. With a focus upon customer service Detail Clean also provides its Franchisees with a Franchisee package of the same quality standard. The market is growing enormously and we are growing the business to meet demand.

"Working couples, single people, new and expectant mothers, the elderly, people who simply don't like cleaning, the customer base for domestic cleaning is growing all the time as having a professional cleaner is no longer viewed as a status symbol restricted to a minority of households, but rather a normal part of many people's lives," says Detail Clean's Managing Director Sandra Leggett. "Combine this burgeoning market with the very valuable and recession-defying commercial cleaning market, and Detail Clean franchisees have a large and varied market at which to target their business."

In supplying its cleaning services to both domestic and commercial clients, Detail Clean is maximising the business potential of its concept, especially as Detail Clean franchisees get exclusive rights to pursue both sectors within their territories. "Our ultimate aim is to provide comprehensive and exemplary services to customers nationwide and a network of fully equipped franchisees is the best option for achieving this," reflects Sandra. "With an extensively proven pilot company-owned operation, a franchise package professionally developed with the assistance of Franchise Development Services, and our first two Franchisees launched, the momentum is with us and we are planning to partner with our first wave of franchisees during 2006."

FRANCHISEES

The first franchisee is Veronica Miller, who wanted to become involved in an industry offering tremendous growth potential and was interested in working in both sectors of the cleaning industry. "Cleaning is a multi-billion pound industry and growing," Veronica states. "I wanted to work with a franchise that had few franchisees and felt that Detail Clean would do everything they could to help me. With my existing business management skills I felt that I could bring added value to the operation."

Veronica is targeting areas of affluence in south London. "As a management franchisee you can grow this business as large as you like," she adds. "I'm aiming to grow the franchise into a multi-million pound operation. The support so far has been fantastic and I'm confident that myself and Detail Clean will work very well together."

TECHNOLOGY

The differentiator of the Detail Clean concept is its investment in state-of-the-art technology to ensure the professionalism of its staff. "We are the first domestic cleaning company in the UK to adopt a Vehicle Management System," Sandra comments. "This system remotely manages the position of every vehicle through tracking devices to allow confirmation of arrival times, reduce insurance costs, provide detailed directions for cleaning crews, and eliminate unauthorised breaks and vehicle uses."

Detail Clean has recently updated and improved its sophisticated vehicle management system, including a master system located at its head office. Using the latest software, GPS technology and the internet the system downloads all vehiclo information automatically every six minutes. The information relayed is very detailed including location, journeys, time at location, speed of vehicle and much more. This benefits our Franchisees as they can now contact the master system at our head office via our IP address to view their vehicles over the internet 24 hours a day.

ENTREPRENEURS

Detail Clean is looking for well organised, self motivated individuals with drive and ambition with good communications skills and leadership qualities who want to develop a substantial size business. To be able to achieve this Detail Clean offers generous size territories with decreasing management service fees for high achievers.

New franchisees will receive full and ongoing support, starting with three days of classroom training covering sales and marketing, recruiting and managing staff, administration and customer service. This is complemented by a further five days hands-on training at a company branch. "Franchisees are then ready to launch their businesses," Sandra continues, "and we spend six more days assisting at their office pre- and post-launch to vet, hire and train staff, begin marketing and supervise their first cleaning jobs. We're not looking for experienced cleaning managers or a high investment, rather we want honest and ambitious individuals to match our commitment to quality of service and assist in the building of this brand across the UK."

WHY DO CLIENTS TRUST A FRANCHISED BUSINESS?

Many Franchise Brands you know and trust, because you know exactly what you are going to get when purchasing their goods or services. The public and businesses alike experience additional confidence when dealing with a known name offering the expertise of a national organisation combined with the friendliness and accountability of a local firm.

This becomes even more important in the case of a Cleaning Franchise. People are understandably wary about who they invite into their houses. There is a very strong trust element involved and an established reputation is of enormous advantage.

Attention To
DETAIL

Detail Clean has built up seven years of experience in the cleaning sector and with professional advice and guidance has developed a Franchise package offering:

- *Domestic and Commercial cleaning markets*
- *Substantial Territories*
- *Decreasing Management Service fees for high achievers*
- *State of the art vehicle technology*
- *Unlimited earning potential in an ever increasing market.*
- *Seven years experience and comprehensive training to support and assist Franchisee success.*

Which allows Franchisees to tackle the full potential of their territories.

Speak to Sandra about this opportunity by calling:

01582 529429

Or email: info:@detailclean.co.uk

www.detailclean.co.uk

2   The ins and outs, the pros and cons

So what exactly is franchising? No one can be sure how or when the term used in its business sense originated, though it was almost certainly in the United States. It has been said that in Britain the tied-house system in the licensing trade, where brewers gave landlords exclusive rights to sell their beers and no other, was an early form of franchise. Some say that even earlier the relationship between baron and serf was a franchise of sorts, but the comparison is an unhappy one in the modern context and perhaps best mentioned only in passing. So, in the absence of any firm historical evidence, let us imagine how franchising began. Let us assume that a brilliant but hard-up inventor called Hiram B Hackenbacker devised a brilliant and unique method of mending socks. After patenting the system he set about raising the capital to exploit his invention but, as is so often the way, the banks failed to share his vision no matter how eloquently he pleaded, and stubbornly remained seated on their pile of cash, refusing to release so much as a bent dime for Hackenbacker's project. Did he give up? No, he didn't. With a small sum of money raised from a kindly aunt, he set up a sock-hole-mending outlet in his home town of South Bend, Indiana. Word got about, business flowed in, and as fast as socks grew holes, he was mending them. He was, however, a man of vision, and congenial though his home town was, it was too small to contain his ambition: South Bend, Indiana could not accommodate an empire within its boundaries. But how was he to expand with only the ploughed-back profits to fund him? He was in a hurry and the banks, while conceding that he might be on to something after all, still preferred to keep their cash safely at home rather than to expose it to the hazards of the outside world where it might go astray or, worse still, disappear down a sock-hole and get lost.

It was then that Hiram had his second brainwave. Why not let someone else, someone with a little money and the vision so sadly lacking in the banks, set up a second Sock-it-to-Me outlet, using exactly the same system and running it in exactly the same way? The investor would have a ready-made, proven business system and Hiram would grow his business at someone else's expense and using someone else's energy and enthusiasm. Brilliant! Soon Sock-it-to-Me outlets were popping up all over the United States. From Atlantic City to Monterey, from Minchipicoten to Miami, Sock-it-to-Me spread like a rash. Hiram had his empire, the royalties flowed in and, at the ripe age of 93, he died, a happy man, from a surfeit of cigars and seven-course meals. And that is how franchising was born. Or might have been.

When we talk about franchising today, what we mean is 'business format franchising'. The format part is essential: it means that a tried and tested system of doing business – of selling goods or services – is in place and can be replicated by others. The term 'franchise package' is often used, and it is a helpful one. For what the franchisee gets in return for his or her money – paid in the shape of an initial fee plus continuing royalties or 'management fees' – is a bundle of items, which, taken together, form all that he or she needs to operate a clone of the original pilot project.

This is what you should find in a properly assembled franchise package:

- an entire business concept explained fully and clearly in an operating manual;
- all the visible trappings of a business, such as trademarks, logos, livery of vans, colours and patterns of uniforms, plus designs for premises;
- accounting and financial systems, which these days may be computerized in an easy-to-use way;
- training in how to operate the business and help in setting it up;
- a detailed contract setting out the rights and obligations of both parties – the franchisee and the franchisor;
- continuing support once the outlet is operating;
- the legal right to operate within an exclusive territory;
- marketing, public relations and advertising support.

So that's how franchising works. And that it is capable of delivering results is beyond question. The British Franchise Association in cooperation with

NatWest Bank produces an annual survey of the sector and, although the poll has its critics who suggest that the questions might be a little more probing, this regular health check undoubtedly shows a patient in robust form with little in the way of ailment apart from an inability to feed its appetite in the shape of more and more franchisee recruits. Here are the key findings of the 2005 survey:

- The franchising sector turns over approximately £9.1 billion, operates 718 brands and employs an estimated 327,000 people.
- The number of franchise units forced to close or change direction was at its lowest level in 21 years, at just 1.7%.
- The average length of time that franchisees run their business has risen from 6.8 years in 1994 to 9.92 years in 2004, further evidence that the industry is maturing.
- Ninety-two per cent of franchisors expected to see continuing growth in their businesses in the coming year.
- Thirty-nine per cent of franchise companies said a lack of suitable franchisees was the biggest barrier to expansion.
- Another measure of the UK industry's maturity and confidence is that more than a third of the franchise companies surveyed had expanded overseas.

If the statistics are impressive, the sheer diversity of franchising is even more so. As a franchisee you could find yourself selling fast food, cleaning carpets, designing and printing stationery, installing and looking after houseplants, minding pets while their owners are away, valeting cars, managing property, dealing in second-hand goods, running an accountancy business, distributing greetings cards, fitting locks and security devices, doing a milk round, hairdressing, renting out computers, teaching children to dance and sing, running teams of domestic cleaners, recruiting executives, replacing hydraulic hoses, running a post office, conducting searches for solicitors, managing a pub, processing films, renovating windows, refilling printer cartridges, purifying cooking oils, refurbishing kitchens, training managers, removing graffiti, landscape gardening, cleaning refuse bins, or being a private eye. And those are just a few of the possibilities.

At first, the breadth of franchising activity gives the impression that there are few forms of business activity that could not successfully be adapted to the format. In truth, however, 'franchisability' is a relatively rare commodity, since to stand a reasonable chance of developing and maturing, a franchise must have four characteristics. If any one of these is missing, its chances of success are diminished. They are:

Standardization: the franchised business must lend itself to replication. This is not a matter of each outlet being broadly similar to every other – it should be as near as possible identical. It should offer the same goods or services in the same way. It should use the same brand, logo and image. It should use the same financial, marketing and accounting systems. Take McDonald's, arguably the most public face of franchising, not just in this country, but across the world. When you go into one of its restaurants, no matter whether it's in Aberdeen or Abergavenny, you know you will see the same familiar branding, the same menu, the same promotional offers, the same baseball caps on the same... well, no, the staff will not be exactly the same, even McDonald's has yet to perfect the cloning of humans, but they should all have been trained to the same standard. All this sameness is necessary because, if the franchise is to work, the franchisor must maintain control over the quality and reliability of the goods or services being sold. After all, although each franchisee owns his or her business, they are unified under the same brand. The brand is the glue that binds them and gives them combined strength. It needs only one or two outlets to fall short of the required standards or to try to do things their own way, for the entire chain to be weakened. Word-of-mouth recommendation is the most powerful sales-aid of all: but word-of-mouth condemnation spreads just as fast and can be deadly. At its worst, bad publicity in a national newspaper can bring a company to its knees. So you can see why every franchisor wants to keep a tight grip on the quality of service delivered by everyone operating under the banner of the company name.

This doesn't mean that every franchisee is hamstrung or constricted in everything he or she does. A franchise network is a bit like a horserace: if the handicapper was completely successful, all the runners would finish in a straight line in every race. They don't, because they all have different strengths and abilities. So it is with franchising. In theory every franchisee starts out with the same chance of success as every other. So why do some do so much better than others? Because they try harder, they smile more, they have the gift of giving customer satisfaction. Everyone knows the difference that the good pub landlord or landlady can make to the enjoyment of the customers. It is exactly the same with a franchise. Some people have the gift of making themselves likeable – smiling has a lot to do with it – and they have a head start in running a business. No amount of standardization will hold them back.

Unique selling proposition (USP): this is the holy grail of all business and marketing and, in truth, is just as wrapped in myth and mystery. It postulates an ideal: some special quality that marks out a product or service from all the competition and cannot be imitated. If your product has a USP, it has a monopoly and, no matter how much businesspeople may defer to the stimulating benefit of rigorous competition, what they all crave in their heart of hearts is a monopoly. And why not? It makes for an easy life. And when you're the only horse in the race, you can be sure of winning. The term USP was coined by marketers who were expressing a dream rather than a reality – a product that has such star quality that nothing could match it. Even the dreamers, however, had to recognize that uniqueness by its very definition is a rare quality and there really is precious little new under the sun. In an imperfect world the best you could hope for is to be different enough to stand out from the competition. Often this difference is expressed in branding – that bundle of qualities comprising name, logo, colour, reputation, ubiquity, recognition and reputation that is the unique property of one company and no other. But behind the brand is delivery of customer expectation: for a brand to have value it must be associated in the customer's mind with quality, service, reliability and predictability.

But although the USP is more fiction than fact, the concept nevertheless carries significance for franchising. That is because if a franchise is to succeed in the marketplace, it should have some property or quality that makes it stand out. Though this might be a special system or formula – some years ago, for example, it was unheard of for van-based operations to come to the customer's door and, using a clever technique, repair minor damage to car paintwork, but now the field is full of competing firms, all offering much the same service – more often than not what distinguishes a franchise outlet from a company-run operation is the quality of the franchisee. To take an example cited in the previous chapter, Drain Doctor is a success because it provides a plumbing service that, if not strictly speaking unique, is rare and exceptional in that it is honest, reliable and not given to ripping people off. To cite another example, it is unlikely that either Rosemary Conley Diet and Fitness Clubs or Helen O'Grady Drama Academy would enjoy the same success if their outlets were run, not by dedicated, motivated franchisees, but by salaried employees.

Ease of operation: what franchising can do better than any other way of running a business is to take people from a wide variety of backgrounds and with varying experience, skills and abilities and train them to do something quite different from what they have done in the past. It can take a farm manager and turn him into a weed-control expert, it can take a security guard and turn him into a fast-food provider, it can turn a bank manager into a printer. But it can't work miracles. Every method or skill taught by a franchise should be quite easy to learn. Though every reputable franchise offers training to new recruits, in practice the quality and duration of the induction process vary quite widely, and every aspiring franchisee should make a point of investigating just how thoroughly he or she will be schooled in the processes of running a new business.

Most well-established franchise companies have learnt from experience just how important the training process is, and the best offer not just a couple of days of cramming, but intensive in-house residential courses followed by on-the-job experience in an established outlet. The latest NatWest/BFA survey notes that the length of time taken for a new franchise to get up and running – from first contact to opening the door for business – has risen from six months in the previous year surveyed to seven months. Part of the extra time is accounted for by increased difficulty in finding a site for the new franchised unit, but an extra emphasis on sound training also explains why the process is increasingly time-consuming. Finding and recruiting suitable franchisees is itself an arduous and lengthy process. Having chosen suitable people, it makes no sense to set them up in business without equipping them as fully as possible with the knowledge and skills needed to make it work. So, the simpler the processes, the more satisfactory the likely outcome for both parties. Of course, you can't learn everything there is to know about running a business in seven months, but you can absorb enough to make a good start – and thereafter every franchisor should offer continuing back-up and support, but especially in the early days.

Gross margin on sales: the franchised outlet is like a hard-working child who has to support two demanding parents. Both the franchisee and the franchisor will want a share of the proceeds. No one could rightfully begrudge the franchisee his or her profit: after all, they put in their money; they applied themselves diligently during the training process (or certainly should have done); and, most importantly, they continue to strive daily to make their franchise a success. And rewarding though it undoubtedly is to see a business grow as a result of your effort, the success is ultimately measured in pounds and pence. You are in business to make money: everything else is secondary.

But why should the franchisor take a cut of your profit? This is a question that every franchisee is bound to ask sooner or later. If the business grows and flourishes through your hard work and dedication, should you not reap the entire benefit? The answer, regrettably perhaps, is no. Remember, it was the franchisor who came up with the business idea in the first place, who pioneered and tested it, who took the risk of setting it up. It was the franchisor, too, who recruited you, the franchisee, trained you, supported you, helped you find premises, and who probably continues to supply you with materials.

In return, the franchisor will usually (though not always) want a continuing share in your success in the shape of a regular management services fee.

Franchisees may come to bridle at this – indeed they often do once the business is established – it is human nature to forget, once success is achieved, that you didn't do it all on your own, but it's useless to complain because the services fee is there, in black and white, in the contract. You went into it with your eyes open and no matter how much you wish it were not so, you are obliged to part with a slice of your turnover until the day the agreement comes to an end.

It follows that for both parties to be satisfied, the franchise operation should generate a sufficiently large margin on sales – the difference between the cost of providing the goods or service and the price paid by the consumer – to provide a satisfactory income for the franchisee even after the management service fee has been paid.

In other words, the customer will have to pay – wittingly or unwittingly – a premium price for the product or service. This could be achieved for a number of reasons: for example, people are prepared to pay more in return for convenience – stores that cannot compete on price with Tesco but are open all hours are able to charge more. Customers will also pay extra in an emergency – so-called distress purchases – when, for example, locks need repairing or windows replacing.

In other cases the goods or services are sufficiently unusual or different (see USP above) to command a high mark-up on costs. Customers are also prepared to pay disproportionately for added value, as well as convenience. You have only to stop and think for a moment to realize that the difference between the cost of the ingredients of a sandwich or a pizza and the asking price is several hundred per cent. No wonder that, of franchising's millionaires, a large number are to be found in the fast-food business.

So, when you are assessing a franchise opportunity, bear in mind that it should be able to generate a sufficient gross return to keep both you and the franchisor happy, or at any rate as contented as the system will allow.

The different types of franchise

We have already noted the many and varied activities in which franchising is involved, a diversity that enables almost every ambitious soul who searches through the possibilities to find something to suit him or her. Fortunately, franchising also has a breadth of opportunities to suit most pockets. It is usual to categorize the industry under four headings.

Job franchise: arguably the most popular and common form of franchise, this usually involves a one-man or one-woman owner/operator, often, though not always, going to the customer in a van equipped with the tools of the trade or products for sale. The attraction of this kind of franchise is twofold: it is usually at the lower end of the investment scale, and it is often quite easy to learn how to operate. For example, selling hygiene and cleaning chemicals to business customers from a van requires product knowledge, which can be acquired over time, but is most effective when the franchisee has a personable manner and the ability to win and retain customers. In other cases, the techniques involved in running a franchise may take some time to acquire – repairing minor damage to car bodywork, for example, requires some dexterity and practice – but, once learnt, usually commands a premium price.

The job franchise is relatively inexpensive to buy into, mainly because the overheads are low. Typically, the franchisee will need a van – often the franchisor will arrange for this to be bought on easy terms – some tools, a telephone, a fax machine and a computer (for e-mail and accounting purposes) and possibly uniform clothing. There is no need to invest in premises, often the single most expensive outlay in setting up a business, since job franchisees almost always start out by working from home. This usually causes little disturbance to the domestic routine and need not disturb neighbours. If, however, the business requires the franchisee to hold stock, then suitable space, such as in a garage, should be made available. In the interests of family harmony it is always best if suppliers and materials to do with work are kept apart from the rest of the home: no one wants to make his way to the breakfast table across a pile of paint pots or bottles of cleaning materials. Since the job franchise is often run from home, it is not uncommon for a spouse to become involved in the business, perhaps taking calls from potential customers and handling other administrative tasks. On the other hand, it is not unknown for some intrepid couples to set out together and jointly roll up their sleeves for the tasks that lie ahead.

Job franchises need not stay as small owner/operator concerns. Many franchisors are keen to encourage franchisees to add more vans to their business, recruit extra operatives to help develop the business, and in time mature into fully-fledged management franchises. So people with little capital but plenty of ambition and latent management ability can set themselves on the path to running a seriously large business for a relatively low initial outlay.

Examples of job franchises include Chem-Dry carpet cleaning; Snap-on Tools, a distributor of automated hand tools; Agency Express, estate agency board contractors; Benjys mobile catering; Bin Masters, repairers of waste containers; Mobile Car Valeting; and Pirtek hydraulic hose replacement.

Management franchise: the old distinction between blue-collar and white-collar workers is a convenient shorthand for distinguishing between job franchises and management franchises. Whereas the former involves the franchisee in delivering the goods or service with his or her own hands, usually as a sole operator, at least in the early stages of the business, the latter are concerned much more with administration and almost certainly involve recruiting and training staff. As we have seen, job franchisees can mature into management franchisees, but in those businesses that are essentially managerial from the outset, the franchisor will want new recruits to have suitable experience. Though franchising is able to train newcomers to self-employment in the basic skills needed to start a new outlet, it is asking too much of a franchisor that he or she should offer a crash course in management techniques. That is not to say that management franchisees should have managed businesses in their past careers, but rather that they should have held some position of responsibility. Former teachers and ex-service personnel, for example, might have no experience of business life but they should have the interpersonal skills and organizational ability that can be adapted to owning and running a small business.

Franchisors, however, complain of a shortage of suitable candidates. In the most recent NatWest/BFA survey, franchised companies said one of their key concerns was that too few prospective franchisees had 'business acumen and experience'. In a way this is a healthy sign since it shows that franchisors do not want just to sell franchises to whoever comes along with the right amount of money, but are concerned to establish units that stand the maximum chance of success. Even so, a shortage of people with the ability to manage is proving a serious brake on the continuing expansion of franchising in the UK. So, if you have the right kind of experience, you should expect your application to be given serious consideration: after all, you are a scarce commodity.

Management franchises tend to be in the business-to-business sector of the economy. Examples are staff recruitment agencies, print, copy and publishing services, cost and management consultants, contract cleaning, computer rental, accountancy services, and management training. Many of these kinds of businesses are run from small office premises, partly because that conveys a more professional image than a home-based oper-ation and partly because it is impractical to run a business employing staff in a domestic dwelling. There are, as always, exceptions. Molly Maid, for example, is a highly successful domestic cleaning franchise, which involves the franchisee in recruiting and managing teams of part-time and usually female 'maids'. Though plainly a management fran-chise, there is no reason at all why this business should not be run effectively from home.

Examples of management franchises are Auditel, cost management consultants; Driver Hire, employment agency; Minster Services, contract cleaning; Recognition Express, name badges and signed images; and Uniglobe, business and leisure travel agency.

Retail franchise: Napoleon scornfully dismissed us Britons as a nation of shopkeepers, and he was right – not in the scorn, but in the description. Retailing is a vital component of the UK economy. According to the British Retail Consortium, the sector accounts for 25 per cent of gross domestic product and some 30 per cent of all consumer expenditure; it is worth about £250 billion a year; it employs 3 million people; and at the last count there were about 300,000 shops in the UK, 11 per cent of all enterprises. Such is the importance of retailing to the economic health of the nation that when shop sales falter, economists look at each other nervously.

Hardly surprising, then, that a buoyant sector of the economy such as fran-chising should find itself heavily involved in retailing, though not in truth as heavily as it would like to be. Although some of the best known names in franchising can be seen on the high street – Bang & Olufsen, Clarks Shoes, DP Furniture Express, Kall-Kwik Printing, In-Toto Kitchens, Vision Express, and a whole clutch of fast-food outlets such as McDonald's, Domino's Pizza, Wimpy International and Subway – measured in terms of numbers of units retail franchises are a relatively small part of the total. The reason is simple: retailing is an expensive business to get into. Premises cost a lot and the right location can be difficult to find. On top of that, there is the initial cost of shop-fitting and the continuing overheads of local business taxes.

Even so, retailing remains an attractive way of doing business – nothing quite compares with literally setting up shop and throwing your doors open to customers – and, as is the way with franchising, the path for newcomers is smoothed as far as is possible.

The franchisor will use his or her experience to help the franchisee through the most difficult initial task of all – finding a suitable site and negotiating terms with landlords – and then handle the tasks of shop-fitting, including decking out the new outlet in the company's colours, logos and so on. The choice of site need not necessarily be smack bang in the high street where the passing trade is greatest but so too are the costs of setting up. It all depends on what you're selling. A fast-food restaurant needs to be in a prime site to draw attention to itself in competition with similar outlets, but if the goods or services that you are selling are not subject to close competition – bridal dress hire, for example, or picture framing – you should be able to operate successfully from a less expensive location in a secondary site. The important thing is to make sure potential customers know where you are and how to find you. Again, the franchisor should help you get started with an initial launch campaign including PR, local advertising and leafleting. In any case, the new franchisee should benefit from trading straight away under an established brand name and in a shop whose appearance is already familiar to customers.

Retailing has elements both of a job franchise and of a management franchise, since the franchisee will almost certainly serve customers from time to time and will usually also be required to employ staff. Retailing is a special skill involving customer care, quality of service, stock control, merchandising, promotion and advertising, pricing policy and so on. But the franchisor will offer training and assistance in all of these aspects of running the business and someone at head office should always be there, at the other end of the phone, to offer advice at times of difficulty or when unseen problems arise. Retailing can be tough – as any shopkeeper will tell you – but with franchising you're not alone.

Investment franchise: this might colloquially be termed the fat cat's franchise, or, more politely, the sleeping partner's franchise. It involves the franchisee investing in a large enterprise, such as a hotel, and delegating the management to someone else. Quite often the investment is too large for any single individual, so it is common for investment franchisees to join together in a syndicate. This kind of franchise is sufficiently far removed from the business format to be outside the concern of this book, whose purpose is to help readers choose and set up a small business of their own, albeit one that may not stay small.

The pros and cons

So far, we have touched upon the reasons for considering franchising as a means of escaping the routine of paid employment and perhaps fulfilling a long-cherished dream of being your own boss. You will therefore already have some notion of what franchising sets out to do and what's in it for you. But, as you have probably already suspected, there are few roses without thorns, and it is too much to expect that franchising offers, to mix metaphors, a one-way easy street with no potholes or obstructions.

Now then is the time to outline both the advantages and disadvantages of franchising looked at from the points of view of both franchisee and franchisor.

Advantages for the franchisee

A proven, ready-made business concept that has been tried and tested
It should have an established brand name (preferably one that is well known and trusted) and corporate image. As we shall see, not every franchise opportunity matches this ideal, but that does not mean companies falling short of the perfect profile are a bad bet, still less that they are crooked. It may mean, however, that they are a greater risk. As with all enterprises, a business format franchise has to start somewhere and it follows that in the early stages it will have yet to establish a reputation or have a widely recognized corporate identity. Nevertheless, the responsible franchisor will have done his or her best to test the concept before inviting potential franchisees to invest.

Reduced risk
Following from the above, franchising sets out to attract franchisees by eliminating much of the risk normally associated with starting a new

enterprise from scratch. It does this mainly through the franchisor putting the concept to the test of the marketplace, learning lessons from the experiment, and remedying any known faults before offering clones for sale to aspiring owner/operators. The containment of risk does not stop there: once the new franchise is up and running there are still hazards waiting to trap the business beginner – hazards that can be fatal to the enterprise: for example, failing to spot cash-flow problems – but, with the franchisor keeping a watchful eye on the fledgling units and ready to help at the first sign of difficulty, risk is again reduced. Note the word 'reduced': in business, risk is never entirely eliminated. In fact, the economist's definition of profit is the reward for taking risk. The possibility of failure comes, as the saying has it, with the territory.

Combined strength

As we have seen, it is important that if a franchised business is to satisfy both parties to the agreement, it should generate a sufficiently high margin on sales to provide an adequate return not just for the franchisee but also the franchisor. One means by which this can be achieved is to offer goods or services that can command a premium price; another is to keep costs down. If both can be achieved, so much the better. An effective means of containing costs – apart from good housekeeping methods such as avoiding waste and keeping a constant eye on outgoings – is to negotiate favourable terms from suppliers for raw materials, ingredients, capital equipment such as machinery and any other bought-in items needed to run the business.

With size comes buying power, as anyone who supplies goods to the likes of Tesco will tell you. The arrangement usually works to the benefit of both parties – though the supplier whose prices are beaten down might take a different view: the seller has the benefit of a large order, which administratively is far preferable to selling the same number of goods to a variety of different customers, all of whom will have varying policies regarding payment; the buyer obtains the goods at a favourable price in return for the comfort and assurance that a large order provides.

That's fine for big companies with muscle, but quite beyond the capabilities of even well-established small businesses, let alone start-ups. But once again franchising can offset a disadvantage that might hamper the growth of a new unit.

A well-established, large franchise company should enjoy just the same buying power as any other concern of a similar size and, better still, be able to pass the benefit on to the franchise network.

An example of combined buying power working to the advantage of all involved is the Global Travel Group franchise. This combines the resources of more than 500 independent travel agents, enabling them to compete on favourable terms with the big high-street names such as Thomas Cook and Thomson. The bulk purchasing power of Global enables it to negotiate exclusive deals with the major travel operators and airlines, and as the franchise grows, so does its ability to provide enhanced commission to its franchised agents.

In other kinds of franchised business, for example fast food, the franchisor may be the sole supplier of materials to the franchisees, who ought to benefit from bulk-buying power. In some cases, however, the benefits may not be so clear-cut: if the franchise agreement specifies that the franchisee must buy his or her materials from the franchisor, it will be galling if it later transpires that the same supplies could be obtained more cheaply elsewhere. Where the franchisor stipulates that supplies can be obtained only from head office and no one else, this is a condition that should be carefully examined, preferably with the advice and help of a lawyer and after having spoken to existing franchisees about their satisfaction or otherwise with the terms of the agreement.

As we shall see later, the line is blurred between bona fide franchises and business opportunities that are not franchises at all but may nevertheless describe themselves as such. It is a common ploy of the latter to exploit 'franchisees' by compelling them to buy supplies at inflated prices. Beware.

Easier finance

Of all the favourite Aunt Sallies in English life, the high-street banks offer the most tempting targets. The charges levelled against them are familiar: they make far too much money; they are aloof and condescending; they are unwilling to help when you need them most – in this they resemble Dr Johnson's definition of a patron: one who looks with unconcern on a man struggling for life in the water, and, when he has reached ground, encumbers him with help. A bank will pursue you relentlessly if your account is overdrawn without authorization, but, should you stray into the black, will bombard you with offers of 'cheap' loans. But that is the nature of banking and there is nothing we can do about it, other than keep our dealings with them to a minimum.

Unfortunately, the prospective franchisee is unable to take such a detached view, since he or she will usually need to raise finance to help launch the business, and the banks remain the most accessible sources of help. Do not, however, approach this task with a heavy heart, for there is good news. Difficult, cautious and suspicious though the banks may be, they are alive to the benefits of wise lending and in franchising they have found something to their liking. Experience and a native caution have taught them that most new business start-ups are a bad risk. The combination of inexperience and an untested new idea, which is what most applicants for a loan lay before the sceptical eye of the local branch manager, is unattractive commercially. But franchising is different. Inexperienced though the franchisee may be, he or she will have the benefits of training and continuing support, and, far from being untested, the business idea should be proven. In short, franchises are less risky and risk is something from which bankers shrink in dread.

In fact, such was the glee with which the high-street banks discovered business format franchising that they set up dedicated units for the special purpose of lending to prospective franchisees. Do not, however, get too carried away by this apparent lowering of the banking guard. Though franchises are less risky, they are not without risk and the bank manager will want to be satisfied that the franchise you have chosen is one that meets with the approval of the bank's franchise unit, and also that you personally are a suitable and sufficiently motivated person to make your business a success.

We will show in a later chapter how you should set about this task. For the moment, however, enjoy the thought that for once the bank manager will be predisposed to giving you a sympathetic hearing.

Beginners please

The franchising sector has its own unique selling proposition – that it can take people from a variety of different backgrounds, and often with no previous experience of running a business, and transform them into successful entrepreneurs. It's a proud boast and is in many ways justified. There are countless case histories showing how a struggling and disaffected wage slave discovered franchising and, like a convert to an improving religion, emerged a better person – or at any rate one better equipped to make the most of self-employment. By providing a proven business format and training to go with it, franchising is capable of transforming beginners into accomplished businessmen and women. That is why so many people who have long hankered after the satisfaction and stimulation of running their own show but were stymied by a lack of an idea or by self-doubt, or both, turn to franchising.

But it has to be stressed that the system is not foolproof. The business format may be good and proven and the training first class, but that still leaves the vital third ingredient – the franchisee. Ambition alone is not enough, nor his or her determination, nor even those twin virtues beloved of human resources practitioners the world over – passion and commitment. Valuable though all these qualities are, they do not necessarily add up to franchising success. Just as important are a formidable capacity for hard work and that indefinable asset – a feel for business. You will not get far either without the kind of self-confidence that can withstand setbacks and disappointments and allow you to sell. In fact, the ability to sell is so important that it merits special attention later in this book.

So although franchising can take a trawlerman and turn him into a sign maker, and a headmistress and make of her an estate agent, the transformation cannot be wrought in every case for the very simple reason that each individual is different. All experienced franchisors know that hard though coming up with a good, workable business idea is, and tough though the testing phase may be, these difficulties are as nothing compared with the daunting task of recruitment. In the end the difference between a modest success and a thoroughgoing triumph depends on the quality of the franchise network. Infuriatingly, the ideal candidate may turn out to be something of a dud, while the marginal applicant goes on to be a roaring success.

Because wise and responsible franchisors – the kind who want to succeed in business rather than make money from selling franchises – take so much trouble over recruitment, it makes sense as an applicant first to assess your own abilities honestly and second to prepare yourself as thoroughly as possible for the interview. Later chapters will help you do both.

Exclusive territory

There are enough worries involved in starting a business without constantly having to look over your shoulder, fearful that some pesky competitor is going to queer your pitch. As far as is possible, franchising seeks to eliminate this danger by granting each new franchisee the right to operate in a territory exclusive to him or her. For the sake of convenience this is often a postcode area, which should supply a sufficiently large potential market for whatever it is that you are planning to sell.

Two things to bear in mind: first, the franchisor can, of course, offer exclusivity only in so far as he or she will not grant franchises for other people in the network to operate in your territory. If a competitor from a different, similar franchise sets up shop next door to you, there is nothing to be done other than to rise to the challenge. Second, not all franchise agreements offer exclusivity. A non-exclusive declaration in the franchise agreement allows the franchisor to start as many franchises as he or she considers suitable in a given territory.

Regarding territory, however, the most important consideration is its ability to support the franchise. As a prospective franchisee you should always research the area yourself, even if the franchisor has already conducted a feasibility study. This essential task should not be too difficult since most franchisees choose to operate in areas close to their home and therefore ones with which they are already familiar.

A sense of independence

The word 'sense' has more significance than you might at first suppose. The whole point of being your own boss is to be independent, to have control over your own destiny, to make your own decisions, and, most important, to reap the rewards of your having had the courage to set out on your own.

But, as I have mentioned before, franchising is not quite like that. True, it offers independence, but not total untrammelled freedom of manoeuvre. To make a success of your franchise you must follow the system laid down by the franchisor. So straight away you can see that you're not wholly independent. Also, your bookkeeping, accounts, trading records and so on must be made available for inspection by the franchisor – again detracting somewhat from the image of the freebooting entrepreneur.

The Americans have a term for franchisees – they call them 'entrepreneurs lite' – and although that might at first seem condescending, it is accurate. As a franchisee you trade in the full-blown freedom of a self-employed businessperson for the more reassuring and less risky option of having someone else to guide and help you.

So although your sense of independence will in many respects be soundly based – as a franchisee the success or failure of your business will be down to you, and that is a sure mark of being your own person – you should accept that you alone are not the author of your business. Franchisees who face up to that are going to be more content than those who wrongly come to believe that the success of their business is entirely down to them.

Disadvantages for the franchisee

Inflexibility

In business you have to adapt to survive. Companies operate in a constantly changing environment; new competitors may arrive on the scene; new technologies may mean existing systems of production are outmoded; fashions change as fast as the weather and may be just as unpredictable; the cost of raw materials may change; new legislation may impinge on the business. Not even the most successful companies are immune to sea changes in the market. McDonald's, for example, arguably the most spectacularly successful franchise of all, suffered a severe setback when some of the blame for mass obesity was nailed on its door. In short, markets never stand still but are in an ever-changing state of flux. The most successful businesses are those that are ever alert to change and quick to adapt. Unfortunately, franchising by its nature is not the most flexible of systems. It is founded on formats, carefully laid down rules, detailed manuals, and the need for uniformity throughout the network. These restrictions are a source of cohesion and strength and present few problems provided the market is fairly stable. If, however, the parameters shift, as well they might, a franchise might be slow to respond. This is plainly a disadvantage to the franchisee, who has no control over the big policy decisions that will determine the response to change. This can be particularly frustrating when, as is inevitably the case, the individual franchisees are the first to spot changes in trading conditions but, under the terms of their agreement, can do nothing on their own initiative to adjust.

The best and wisest franchise operations seek to overcome this problem by ensuring that information flows freely not only between the franchise network and the franchisor's management at head office but also among franchisees themselves. It is quite usual for franchised businesses to hold regular seminars and conferences where problems may be raised, difficulties discussed and solutions suggested. It is tempting for some franchise companies, who are fearful of dissent or rebellion in the ranks, to discourage too much fraternization among franchisees. They are mistaken:

when a network has a sense of camaraderie and pulls together, it can offset the inherent rigidities of the franchise system by providing a dynamic source of new ideas and answers to problems. It may also offset the sense of powerlessness which some franchisees feel when the requirements for central controls and monitoring seem most irksome.

When you are investigating a franchise opportunity, ask around to find out whether or not the franchisor encourages the free exchange of ideas within the company.

While inflexibility is a disadvantage, one should not exaggerate the danger. McDonald's adapted to criticism by introducing 'healthier' options in its menu and, at the time of writing, was duly recovering much of its early momentum. Other franchise operations have a readiness to respond built into them. The high-street quick-print operations, for example, were alive to the possibilities that changing technologies presented and swiftly adopted them. Colour printing, faxing, the transmission of data through the internet, all were quickly made available to customers, proof that franchising can rise to challenges as fast as any other business provided the franchisor is nimble footed.

It only takes one rotten apple

One of the irritating things about clichés such as this, apart from the fact that they grate, is that they often contain an uncomfortable truth; so here is another – a chain is only as strong as its weakest link. It is one of franchising's virtues that a network of highly motivated business owners, all striving to make the most of their brand, is a formidable business combination. A chain of franchised retail outlets, for example, is likely to offer better customer service and be run more efficiently than a managed chain, in which the person responsible for the day-to-day running of the shop has no personal stake.

But suppose something goes wrong. What if an outlet in a fast-food chain, for example, poisons its customers because some negligent employee fails to wash his hands? The bad publicity is bound to have an adverse effect throughout the company. That's damaging enough when the individual restaurants are all company-owned and run by salaried managers. Head office will have some hard work to do to recover lost ground. But if the chain is franchised, the effect will be felt by individual business owners whose trade may suffer through no fault of their own.

So it is a weakness of franchising that the reputation and profitability of an individual franchisee may be damaged because of the negligence, or worse, of someone else operating miles away in a different town. Nor is the danger confined to the actions of other franchisees – the franchisor, too, might, through his or her bad management or misjudgement, damage the brand and inflict harm on the entire franchise network.

Not quite your own boss

The importance of maintaining the integrity of the entire franchise network and as far as possible ensuring there are no weak links in the chain is a primary reason for the tight system of controls that franchisors impose on franchisees. As we have already seen, the downside of imposing all manner of restrictions, even down to day-to-day procedures in the running of each franchisee unit, can be counted a disadvantage of franchising.

The ideal is for the franchisor to maintain control over standards while at the same time allowing franchisees sufficient freedom to enjoy the sensation of running their own business. In any case, it is impossible – not to say undesirable – to prevent the individual franchisees from imposing their personality on the business (always assuming that the personality is a friendly and attractive one). The best franchisors encourage franchisees to contribute to the development of the whole operation.

A constant drain

Anyone buying the right to run a franchise will, of course, expect to pay an initial fee and it will be up to him or her to judge whether or not the asking price is worth the money. Franchises range in price from just a few thousand pounds for a job franchise to many thousands for a retail business. Later in this book we shall see how you can calculate the likely return from your investment and therefore how long it will take to recover your initial outlay. All of that is fair and reasonable, but what tends to stick in the throat of seasoned franchisees is the continued requirement to pay service fees. This can come to seem an unnecessary drain on the profitability of the outlet – particularly when it is well established and the franchisee no longer needs to call on the services of the franchisor.

But tough though it may seem, this is just as it should be: the continuing fees may be a nuisance but the fact that the franchisee is running the outlet without much help from the franchisor is a healthy sign. A franchised business will not achieve its potential if the franchisee becomes too dependent on the franchisor and fails to provide the energy and motivation that underpin the franchise way of doing business. Some franchisees come to believe that the franchisor has a duty to ensure the success of each individual outlet through continual day-to-day involvement. In truth the relationship is akin to that of a parent and child: while the franchisee is finding his or her feet and learning how to walk, the franchisor will be there to give a helping hand, but this dependency neither can nor should last for ever. The franchisor must know when to let go, and the franchisee must face up to the challenge of being his or her own person, with ultimate responsibility for success or failure.

The continuing franchise fee carries a danger that every franchise should be aware of. A franchisor may urge franchisees to increase their turnover in order to boost the amount paid in fees, which is calculated as a percentage of sales. However, the franchisee might prefer to increase profitability, which does not necessarily flow from increased turnover. This is undoubtedly a potential weakness in a franchise system and one to look out for.

An unknown quantity

One of the most difficult tasks facing a prospective franchisee is to get the measure of the franchisor. That is why much of this book is devoted to ways of trying to make that difficult assessment. Weighing up the franchisor is important for two reasons. First, the business format package may not be as good as the promotional material and verbal assurances suggest. Second, the franchisor may not be able to provide the quality of training, continued support, and other services that the franchisee needs to make a success of the business. We shall look at these aspects in more detail later.

A hard sell

Suppose you are running a franchise and, for whatever reason, you decide to dispose of it. Immediately, you will encounter restrictions that would not apply to a non-franchised business. As part of your agreement, your choice of buyer will be limited. There are good reasons for this. Assuming that the franchisor chose you carefully as the right person to run your outlet in your area (if he didn't exercise that kind of caution he is a poor franchisor), he will naturally want to ensure that your successor is equally qualified to take over from you.

In practice, however, disposing of an existing franchise is seldom difficult, always assuming that it is trading profitably. Some people who are attracted to the idea of franchising prefer to take on an existing unit with a proven trading record rather than go through the process of building up a customer base from scratch. The prospect is more attractive still if the unit is part of a franchised organization that has a well-known and respected brand.

If you decide to sell your franchise before the term of the initial agreement has run its course – illness or family difficulties are common causes for such decisions – you may be liable to pay fees to the franchisor to cover the costs of recruiting and training your replacement.

On the plus side, the outlet is legally yours to sell and, if you have succeeded in making it prosper and grow, you stand to make a good return from its sale.

Advantages for the franchisor

An army of willing investors

The biggest single reason for franchising a business idea is that the owner/founder of the operation can get his or her hands on other people's money – in a perfectly proper and legitimate way, of course. The franchisees pay the money and in return get a business that ought to have a good chance of making a reasonable return. But for the franchisor the point of tapping into the aggregated resources of a number of franchisees is that it enables him or her to expand the business more rapidly and easily than might be possible through investing savings, borrowing from the bank, or raising equity capital. Franchisees provide the capital to open new outlets, and, provided they are recruited with care, their combined effort will enable a faster geographical penetration than might otherwise be possible. This is particularly desirable when a new product is being brought to market, because national coverage is an obstacle that would-be competitors will have to overcome.

That, at any rate, is the theory. In practice, rapid expansion is neither easy nor desirable if it is at the expense of quality. It takes time to recruit and train franchisees and, especially in the early days, the franchisor is unlikely to have the resources in either staffing or money to quickly build a network of franchisees.

That said, the prospect of growing through using other people's money remains extremely attractive.

Owners work harder

Human nature being what it is, salaried employees are inclined to give of their best only when it suits them or if they are highly incentivized: at all other times the urge to skive can prove difficult to resist. But when someone owns their own business their entire attitude changes: gone is the inclination or temptation to do only the minimum required and nothing more; in comes an urge to roll up the sleeves, spit on the hands, and set to. Wisely was it said that the greatest cure for all manner of minor ailments is self-employment. The owners of businesses do not stay in bed or ring in sick unless they are genuinely unable to work.

The franchisee's inclination to work flat out at all times should, if all goes well, be to his or her benefit: it is certainly to the benefit of the franchisor. Where else could he find such energetic and devoted souls, all beavering away for the greater good of the company?

If you took an employer with a new business to grow and a franchisor in a similar position and gave them both a standing start, it is a fair bet that the franchisor's army of owner/operators will knock spots off the manager's employees, delivering better performance in increasing market share, maximizing efficiency, controlling costs and improving profitability. That is human nature.

A little local knowledge

Most, though not all, franchisees choose to operate their businesses in their own localities. This means they bring a certain amount of local knowledge to the new venture and possibly have local contacts too. Even if their initial business knowledge is slight, they will still start with the advantage of being easily able to research the local market, something we shall look at in more detail later.

Though regional differences in Britain are nothing like as marked as they used to be, it nevertheless remains the case that someone born and bred in a particular part of the country will have a better understanding of the people who make up his or her customer base than someone coming in from the outside. This form of local knowledge is another plus for the franchisor wanting to expand his business throughout the country.

Keeping a grip on things

Although a franchised network may be spread far and wide, the franchisor will maintain a greater control over the operation of each unit than might otherwise be possible. This is because each outlet sells the franchisor's products or services and no other. And the franchisor controls how the products are presented and sold and may also insist on the franchisees buying supplies and equipment from head office. With tight controls of this kind it becomes easier to increase and maintain profit margins.

But not too tight a grip

The franchisees own their own businesses and are responsible for day-to-day administrative tasks such as recruiting staff and managing payrolls. They should also be keeping a watchful eye on operating costs. Freed from these obligations – other than the need periodically to check that the franchisees are keeping on top of things – the franchisor can run a tight ship at head office. However, there are exceptions: some franchisors handle invoicing, debt collection and other paperwork because they prefer the entire energy of franchisees to be devoted to building their businesses and serving customers.

Disadvantages for the franchisor

Everything is not under control

In the franchisor's dream world he or she would have the benefits of the franchisees' drive, energy and appetite for success, and also the power to pull all the strings all the time. But franchisees are not puppets. They own their outlets and although they are not free to do just as they wish, they are nevertheless free enough not to be easily pushed around. Salaried staff, on the other hand, can be fired (provided of course that the procedures laid down in the employment laws are followed) and disciplined. The ideal franchisee is one who is prepared to follow the laid-down procedures and systems, but still has sufficient initiative to spot and exploit business opportunities.

A tricky balance

The perfect franchisee, like the perfect spouse, is an elusive being: the best will be diligent and devoted, the worst lazy and indifferent. In the franchise relationship, the most difficult kind of franchisee is the one who is lazy, but not so lazy that he or she breaks any of the terms of the agreement. This leaves the franchisor in the awkward position of having a weak link in the chain and little power to do much about it, short of buying out the offending franchisee, possibly at an inflated price.

When sweetness and light become sourness and dark

The relationship between franchisor and franchisee rests on a measure of mutual understanding and trust. As with all relationships, this is best achieved by maintaining regular, friendly contact and dealing with minor grievances before they fester and grow into something worse.

If an effort is not made by both sides, the franchisee may become disillusioned and resentful: he or she may see the franchisor's involvement as unwarranted and intrusive. Any breakdown in trust may exacerbate any rumbling discontent concerning the payment of management service charges.

From the franchisor's point of view, an unsatisfactory relationship with the franchisee may result in the latter becoming uncooperative and withholding information.

Slimmer pickings

As we have already noted, a franchised unit needs to generate a gross margin sufficient to provide a reasonable return to both the franchisee and the franchisor. It follows that without the franchisee, the franchisor would make bigger profits. This, however, is hardly a serious disadvantage, more a case of the franchisor occasionally musing on what might have been had he or she chosen to expand without recourse to franchising. The franchisor would like to have it both ways – a string of energetic entrepreneurs building the business, and all the profit, too. Reality has other ideas.

Insiders can become outsiders

Ingratitude and treachery are two regrettable aspects of the human psyche that might bubble to the surface in a franchise relationship. It must always be in the back of the franchisor's mind that a franchisee, having seen and experienced the business from the inside and mastered the know-how and systems, might depart to set up a rival company in the same business. Such, alas, is human nature, and the wise franchisor plans for the black day when a deserter appears in the midst of the network. Hence, many franchise agreements include a clause preventing a franchisee who leaves from setting up a rival operation within a specified time of his or her departure.

The whole truth

A franchisee may succumb to the temptation to 'cook the books', in other words to declare inaccurate trading figures when asked for information by the franchisor. If this goes undetected, the franchisor may receive a smaller fee income than he is entitled to under the terms of the agreement.

Other people's money and mine, too

Although the franchisees provide vital capital to build the business, it would be mistaken to imagine that the franchisor can start up on the cheap. It costs real money to launch a franchise. There are costs of pilot-testing, not to mention the risk involved, and the expense of recruiting and training franchisees. Even then, it could be some time before fee income flows in to cover all the outgoings and enable the franchisor to reach break-even point.

So, weighing up the pros and cons on both sides, it is plain that the franchise relationship is a peculiar, not to say unique, way of doing business. The franchisor owns the business idea and the systems, but not the individual outlets. The franchisee has a business to call his or her own, but not the freedom to do as he or she pleases. The franchisor controls the business, but only up to a point.

The more you look at it, the plainer it becomes that, provided the business idea is sound, success or failure hinges on the strange partnership that exists between franchisee and franchisor.

While it is true that franchising is a proven method of cutting out much of the risk normally involved in opening up a new small business, it is wrong to believe it is failsafe. Such risk as there is attaches more to the selection of franchisees than to the normal business pitfalls such as cash flow, marketability, slack consumer demand and so on (though all these, and more, are present in franchising, albeit in a reduced form).

It follows that for a franchise to fulfil its potential, the franchisor must choose the right franchisees, and the franchisees must choose the right franchise. The rest of this book sets out to help you, the prospective franchisee, to make the right choice.

Dublcheck from Strength to Strength

Dublcheck is the franchise where you don't need to be able to sell. Dublcheck obtains all the business for you, so you know exactly what turnover you will get.

You can start with a turnover of £14,400 per annum if you want to run your business hands-on whilst retaining the security of your current position, or up to £500,000 per annum if you want to run a management business.

Most people ask:
- Where will my business come from?
- How much will I make?
- How big can I grow?

Dublcheck has all the answers:
- Guaranteed Turnover
- Guaranteed Profit
- Guaranteed Growth

New franchisees choose a guaranteed initial turnover, benefit from the security of a guaranteed gross profit and are secure in the knowledge that they have the choice of a guaranteed growth option to meet their ambitions when they are ready.

Benefits of Dublcheck are:
- The commercial cleaning market is worth over £3 billion and continues to grow
- Low-cost entry
- Invoicing and cash collection
- Recession-proof utility business
- Rapid return on investment
- Low overhead requirement
- Feeling part of a team
- Training and ongoing support from head office
- A mentor franchisee to guide and assist

Dublcheck, founded in 1993 and one of the UK's fastest growing companies, according to *The Sunday Times* and Virgin Fastrack 100, is clearly the real deal in an industry full of imitators who fail to deliver.

Carol Stewart-Gill, who founded the company, still has a very active day-to-day role. "It's not easy running any business" she says. "To be successful it requires hard work and commitment, and if you put the effort in and follow the system with Dublcheck the rewards are there."

To find out more about becoming a Dublcheck franchisee with excellent financial rewards, please contact Carol Stewart-Gill on 0800 317236.

"Dublcheck gave us all the encouragement and determination to make our franchise a successful one. Your whole team from directors to receptionists are always exceedingly friendly and obliging with even the smallest problems we have had." – **Paul & Barbara Davies** *(Ex. Greengrocers)*

"I'm reminded of a television advert, something about 'does exactly what it says on the tin.' An apt description for the Dublcheck system I would say." – **I Baker** *(Former Consultant Engineer)*

"Dublcheck gives me a degree of safety, support and backing if I need it. Setting up on your own is a big step to take, but by going down this route I feel as though I have a safety net." – **P Hart** *(Former Rolls Royce Employee)*

"Dublcheck gave us all we needed to run a business and it's been successful beyond our dreams."
– **Sue Williams & Lorraine Whiteley** *(Ex. Hairdresser & Nursery Nurse)*

DUBLCHECK, YOUR PASSPORT TO SUCCESS

Ken & Pauline
Turnover: £210,000+

Les
Turnover: £55,000+

Ehi & Yinka
Turnover: £36,000+

Ann & Blas
Turnover: £30,000+

OVER 12 YEARS EXPERIENCE SETTING PEOPLE UP IN BUSINESS

BUILD YOUR BUSINESS THE EASY WAY

**No Need To Do Any Selling:
We Get The Business For You**

Carol Stewart
Founder

We Guarantee:
- **Turnover**
- **Profit**
- **Growth**

FULL TRAINING ■ SUPPORT ■ LOW INVESTMENT
Further Details: 0800 317236

Be in business for as little as **£8,750** or choose a guaranteed turnover of up to **£120,000** per annum.

With over 100 franchisees nationwide, and many more areas and opportunities available, you too could benefit from the proven Dublcheck system.

Listed by the *Sunday Times* as one of the UK's fastest growing companies. Dublcheck's unique franchise system is a proven way to build a successful business in a multibillion pound industry.

Email: franchise@dublcheck.co.uk   Web: www.dublcheck.co.uk

3 Any questions?

O wad some Pow'r the giftie gie us
To see oursels as others see us!
It wad frae mony a blunder free us,
And foolish notion.

Depending on your point of view, Robert Burns was either the poet
laureate of Scotland or the patron saint of the typographical error. Either
way, there is no doubting the wisdom of his words: it would be both a
revealing and an unsettling experience to see ourselves through the eyes
of others. Prospective franchisees, however, should attempt the next best
thing – to stand back and attempt to make a cool and objective assessment
of their own strengths and weaknesses. Far easier said than done, of
course, but to buy a franchise is to embark on a life-changing experience,
and although it is natural to assume the change will be markedly for the
better, there is, alas, the possibility that it might be for the worse. To invest
both money and considerable effort in a project that fails is, as the poet
would say, a blunder. And to kid yourself that you have all, or most of, the
attributes required of a successful franchisee is a foolish notion.
Franchising requires a peculiar combination of characteristics: you need to
be independently minded, but not too independent; you need to be able
to exercise initiative while sticking to some pretty tight rules; you need to
be fiercely ambitious for yourself, but a good team player.

So how on earth can you discover whether you have the qualities
sought by a franchisor? No one can be entirely objective about their own
abilities, and so to be asked, in the way of most franchise manuals, to
weigh up your virtues on one side of the scales and to deposit your
shortcomings on the other is to ask the impossible. Plainly what is
needed is a questionnaire that, if answered honestly, does the probing
without you realizing it, that coolly sums you up through your
responses to some cleverly constructed choices. Fortunately, such a
thing exists and we shall come to it soon. Before then, however, here are

some preliminary questions that could save you the trouble of reading any more of this book or pressing ahead with a franchise application that will almost certainly cause you only disappointment:

■ **Is your way the best way, and blow what other people might think?**
Would you be uncomfortable, or possibly downright infuriated, to be made to accept systems and procedures without modifying them to suit your own preferences? Is yours the restless kind of mind that is for ever seeking different ways of doing things?

■ **Do you have a strong streak of independence?** Asked to subordinate your wishes to those of a team of which you are part, would you feel frustrated and hampered?

■ **Do you like to mind your own business and expect others to do the same?** As we have already noted, franchisors have it written in their contract to be nosy parkers. Would your inclination, when they poke their head around your door, be to tell them to shove off?

I need hardly tell you that if you answered one or more of those questions in the affirmative you would be better off being your own boss in the full sense of that term, rather than in the diluted version that is the lot of the franchisee.

Assuming, however, that you are sufficiently biddable to accept terms and conditions designed to help you make the most of an opportunity to run a business of your own, please press on to the next stage, which will test those claims more fully. For the following 'diagnostic questionnaire' I am indebted to its author, Professor John Stanworth of the University of Westminster, a long-standing expert in franchising. It uses a 'forced choice' system; in other words, you must respond either (a), (b) or (c) – you cannot miss out any question or duck any option. Under each question you must choose one answer to the exclusion of the other two. Try it now:

Question 1 Are you regarded by those who know you as:
   (a) Generally a fairly self-contained person? (2)
   (b) Generally a rather gregarious person? (0)
   (c) Somewhere in between (a) and (b)? (1)

Question 2 Are you regarded by those who know you as:
   (a) Frequently frustrated by tasks you find boring? (0)
   (b) Able to endure a reasonable amount of boredom and frustration? (1)
   (c) Generally good at concentrating on whatever tasks face you? (2)

Question 3 Would you say that:
  (a) You possess an excess of mental and physical stamina and enjoy excellent health?   (2)
  (b) You find that you tire easily if you try to work long hours and your health is not always of the best?   (0)
  (c) You estimate that your health and stamina are about average for a person of your age?   (1)

Question 4 Would you say that:
  (a) You find mistakes and setbacks very demoralizing?   (0)
  (b) You feel that mistakes can be a very useful way of learning as long as they are not repeated?   (2)
  (c) You try to learn from your mistakes but often find it easier said than done?   (1)

Question 5 Which of the following most accurately describes you:
  (a) You set yourself targets and almost obsessively chase after them? (2)
  (b) You get fed up if you find yourself 'on the go' all the time?   (1)
  (c) You like to take life at a modest pace and respond to pressures as and when they arise?   (0)

Question 6 Would you say that:
  (a) You find it almost impossible to make tough decisions, particularly if they involve people?   (0)
  (b) You can make tough decisions when necessary but the process takes a lot out of you emotionally?   (1)
  (c) You see tough decisions as a fact of life – you don't necessarily enjoy them but, on occasion, see no alternative?   (2)

Question 7 Would you say that:
  (a) You do not suffer fools gladly and make little attempt to hide your feelings?   (0)
  (b) You have notable patience and self-control?   (2)
  (c) You are situated in between positions (a) and (b)?   (1)

Question 8 Would you say that:
  (a) Your mood is very influenced by events?   (0)
  (b) Your mood is very little influenced by events?   (1)
  (c) You tend to adopt a policy of 'taking the rough with the smooth'? (2)

Question 9 Are you regarded by people who know you as:
- (a) A person who needs to know exactly where they stand? (0)
- (b) A person who can live with uncertainty? (2)
- (c) A person who can endure a reasonable amount of uncertainty? (1)

Question 10 If you go into business would you:
- (a) Resent people who appear to be trying to tell you how to run your own business? (0)
- (b) Regard the views of others as a potential source of useful information and guidance? (2)
- (c) Be willing to listen to others when you had the time but likely to 'take it all with a pinch of salt'? (1)

Question 11 Would you say that your total personal assets and savings together:
- (a) Exceed the full by-in cost of the franchise? (2)
- (b) Exceed two-thirds of the full buy-in cost? (1)
- (c) Amount to less than two-thirds of the full buy-in cost? (0)

Question 12 Do you feel that your spouse:
- (a) Feels that how you earn your living is very much your own affair? (0)
- (b) Would prefer to see you doing something you enjoyed? (1)
- (c) Is very keen on your taking a franchise and willing to back you very strongly? (2)

Question 13 Which of the following is true of you:
- (a) There is no history of self-employment in your family involving either yourself or close relatives? (0)
- (b) Though you have not personally been self-employed previously, there is some history of self-employment in your family via close family and/or relatives? (1)
- (c) You have personally been self-employed previously? (2)

Question 14 Is your main reason for wanting to be a franchisee:
- (a) To achieve a good standard of living? (2)
- (b) Because most of the alternative options for making a living appear closed? (1)
- (c) For the independence and autonomy involved in having your own business? (0)

Question 15 Do you feel that, in taking a franchise:
- (a) You would have a tried and tested product/service that should sell itself?   (0)
- (b) No matter how good the product/service, customers still respond to sales effort?   (1)
- (c) Selling would still be a key activity?   (2)

Question 16 Is your prior work experience:
- (a) Unrelated to the franchise in question?   (2)
- (b) Very closely related to the franchise in question?   (0)
- (c) Marginally related to the franchise in question?   (1)

Question 17 In running your own business, would you:
- (a) Prefer to stay small?   (0)
- (b) Wish to grow as much as circumstances allowed?   (2)
- (c) Grow to a size where you could begin to take more time out of the business?   (1)

Question 18 Do you feel that:
- (a) To get a job done properly, you must do it yourself?   (0)
- (b) Delegation allows you to spend your time doing what you are best at?   (2)
- (c) Delegation is a necessary evil?   (1)

Question 19 Do you usually feel that it pays to:
- (a) Take a long-term view of things?   (2)
- (b) Make hay while the sun shines?   (0)
- (c) Adopt a medium-term view?   (1)

Question 20 Do you feel that:
- (a) Your future lies largely in your own hands?   (2)
- (b) You can at least influence your own future?   (1)
- (c) The individual is merely a puppet on the end of a string and can do little to influence events?   (0)

You will have noticed that the points awarded for each response are unconcealed because in a self-assessment test such as this there is nothing to be gained from cheating apart from self-delusion. The higher your tally, the better equipped you will be to make a success of franchising. A good score is in the 20–30 range. The questionnaire serves two purposes – it helps you to gauge your strengths and weaknesses and gives you a better understanding of the qualities sought by a franchisor. Prof Stanworth sums them up as follows:

Q1   the ability to cope with the isolation of self-employment;
Q2   exercise self-discipline;
Q3   work long hours under pressure;
Q4   learn from failure;
Q5   compete with self-imposed standards;
Q6   take unpopular decisions;
Q7   resist impetuous or emotional behaviour;
Q8   take a balanced view of events;
Q9   tolerate uncertainty;
Q10 accept advice;
Q11 demonstrate financial viability;
Q12 support of spouse;
Q13 enterprise background;
Q14 profit motivation;
Q15 sales orientation;
Q16 receptiveness towards franchisor's training;
Q17 growth orientation;
Q18 a favourable attitude towards task delegation;
Q19 take the long-term view;
Q20 demonstrate belief that individuals can 'make things happen'.

Here are the issues looked at in more detail:

Q1   Ability to cope with feelings of isolation – in contrast to being an employee, you have no boss, or other people in the same organization doing the same job, who can give help, advice and moral support. To put it more precisely, it is usually of little concern to anyone else whether you succeed or fail.

Q2   Ability to exercise self-discipline – in running your own business, you're responsible for a wide range of tasks. Some of these you will almost certainly find satisfying, whilst others will prove highly frustrating. There is no one but yourself responsible for allocating your time and you can, at your peril, neglect tasks such as paperwork, financial control, invoicing and chasing payment. Although all these tasks may appear to be stopping you from getting on with the 'real job' of producing and selling, no business can survive without them.

Q3   Ability to work long hours under pressure – in running your own business you are seldom off duty. Thus you require both mental and physical stamina. In the early days of a new business, there is little time for leisure activities, holidays or illness. Some advisers go as far as to recommend that anyone setting up a new business should consult their doctor first.

Q4   Ability to learn from failure – disappointments are inevitable in business and can lead to demoralization. A good businessperson, however, must possess the resilience to survive setbacks and learn from them.

Q5   Ability to compete with self-imposed standards – when working for yourself, targets and standards need to be set which act as goals re-inforcing motivation. If these goals are set too low, they have little motivating force. If they are set unrealistically high, they will not be achieved and a sense of failure and demoralization may result. Thus, modestly ambitious, though not unrealistic, goals need to be set and used as markers of achievement.

Q6   Ability to take unpopular decisions – it is impossible to remain popular at all times and any attempt to do so is likely to have costly consequences for your business.

Q7   Ability to resist impetuous or emotional behaviour – in the face of frustration, it is tempting to react in what might later be seen as a whimsical manner that is not in the longer-term interests of the business. This may be emotionally satisfying in the short term but should be resisted at all costs – emotions must be kept under control.

Q8   Ability to take a balanced view of events – it is easy to yield to the temptation of feelings of euphoria or depression in response to good or bad news. This can prove extremely stressful and wearing. A successful businessperson needs to be able, at all times, to take a balanced view of events, to take 'the rough with the smooth'.

Q9   Ability to tolerate uncertainty – in an environment dominated by large organizations, the setting up of a new business is a highly creative venture and requires a facility for surviving uncertainty. People with a low tolerance of uncertainty experience difficulties in coping with the resulting stress.

Q10 Ability to take outside advice – having gone into business to gain a certain level of independence, it often requires a determined effort to be able to seek out and act on external advice, but, again, this capacity needs to be exercised.

Q11 Ability to demonstrate financial viability – though the clearing banks tend to lend to would-be franchisees more readily than to would-be conventional small business start-ups, it needs to be remembered that all loans have to be repaid, with interest. A large financial repayment overhead in the early days of trading can impose additional pressures.

Q12 Ability to demonstrate support of spouse – most franchise outlets involve long hours of working and domestic disruption. In a large proportion of cases there is some advantage to the spouse actually working in the running and/or administration of the business. Thus, anything less than positive support can have very negative consequences.

Q13 Ability to demonstrate enterprise background – despite the desire for self-employment being quite common, relatively few make the leap from aspiration to reality. Those who have previous direct experience of self-employment or, alternatively, have had a close relative (usually a father) self-employed appear to find the transition easier. Some evidence exists to suggest that they may also be more successful as measured in terms of business growth.

Q14 Ability to demonstrate profit motivation – amongst small business-people generally, the desire for growth is of a rather low order and profit motivation is of a lower order than other goals such as independence and autonomy. Most small businesses, in fact, never employ anyone other than the owner. In the case of a franchise, however, the pressures to push for growth of profits and size of business are usually quite strong.

Q15 Ability to demonstrate sales orientation – despite national advertising and the promotion of brand awareness by the franchisor, sales skills on the part of the franchisee can still make a very substantial difference to levels of market penetration. Local advertising and good interpersonal skills and service at the customer interface can be crucial.

Q16 Ability to demonstrate receptiveness towards the franchisor's training – franchisors tend towards the view that 'starting with a clean sheet' is the best basis for a training programme rather than competing with, or attempting to displace, previous training that a potential franchisee may have already had in the field concerned.

Q17 Ability to demonstrate growth orientation – the income of the franchisor is directly related to the growth of franchisees. Thus, franchisees easily satisfied with low levels of growth may require considerable motivating.

Q18   Ability to delegate – one serious growth constraint on most small businesses is the lack of willingness or ability to delegate.

Q19   Ability to take a long-term view – in an economy suffering from endemic 'short-termism', long-term planning and goal setting is likely to pay dividends.

Q20   Ability to make things happen – people with an 'internal locus of control' tend to believe that they personally can influence their environment. This belief can become a self-fulfilling philosophy.

Perfection in a franchisee is as rare and elusive as it is in any other form of human activity, so do not be dismayed if you fall short in some of the desiderata. The attributes that count for most are a willingness and a capacity for hard work. That may sound glib, but it carries real meaning; running a franchise is not for the timid or the work shy, it requires single-mindedness and dedication of a high order, because for all that you are in partnership with a franchisor, the gap between happy fulfilment of your dream and bitter disappointment can be bridged by you, and you alone.

So, in all honesty, if, after you have weighed yourself in the balance, you find that the prospect of continuing working life as an employee doesn't seem so bad after all, it is better to forget about franchising at this stage. If, on the other hand, you genuinely believe that you have what it takes to be in charge of your destiny with no one to blame but yourself when things go wrong, read on.

A self-analysis summary

■   Will I be willing and able to put in the hours and apply the dedication that this business demands?

■   Do those near and dear to me appreciate what I am letting myself in for and the strains that it might put on them? Do I have their support?

■   What do I want from this franchise? Job satisfaction, a higher income, or long-term capital gain? Is it likely to satisfy those needs?

■   Have I got sufficient capital to cushion me while the business gets established?

■   How much can I comfortably borrow? Looking on the bleak side, if the business were to fail, how would that impact on me and my family?

▌ Is my health robust enough to stand the strain of running a business?
▌ How will I handle the responsibility of being my own boss and possibly employing other people?
▌ Are my skills and abilities likely to be best suited to this business?
▌ Do I actually like this business?

4 Searching for the perfect partner

So, you are satisfied that you have what it takes to run your own business, now for the interesting and exciting part of the journey – finding the right franchise for you. Interesting and exciting, yes, but painstaking and time-consuming too. You should be in no hurry at this stage; time spent investigating and researching opportunities will repay the effort. Not only will you learn much about what is on offer and the ways in which franchise companies promote themselves, you will also benefit from a process of careful elimination and selection. So don't be in a rush and certainly don't let anyone rush you. In other words, beware the franchisor desperate to sell you a franchise, the kind of huckster who says he has only a few golden opportunities left and when they're gone, they're gone. Let them go.

Another reason for taking your time is that there are so many franchises to choose from – over 700, in fact. Broadly speaking, they break down into some half a dozen categories, listed as follows with one or two examples of each:

- **hotels and catering** – pubs, fast-food outlets;
- **retailing** – shoes, hi-fi, golfing equipment, second-hand goods;
- **personal services** – hair and beauty, tanning salons, fitness clubs, slimming;
- **property services** – office maintenance, plumbing, carpet cleaning, furniture repair;
- **automotive** – vehicle valeting and repair, tools;
- **business services** – accountancy, quick print, cost control advice, office supplies, recruitment.

Those give only a tiny taste of what's on offer. As a franchisee you could be mowing lawns, renting videos, fitting kitchens, washing wheelie bins, teaching children to dance, selling sandwiches, pulling pints, grinding tree stumps, checking gas and electricity safety, taking portrait photographs, washing cars, training dogs, letting property, manicuring nails, selling cruises, delivering parcels, refilling ink cartridges, running a post office or caring for the elderly. As with popular journalism, so with franchising – all of human life is there.

Now it may seem banal to point this out, but you should narrow your search to the business activities that best suit your talents, capabilities and interests. Seems obvious, doesn't it? But you might be surprised by how many people pick a franchise, not because it suits them, but because it holds out the promise of the biggest financial return. To go down that road is to make a serious and potentially costly mistake. Of course you go into franchising to make money – indeed, one of your primary considerations when assessing an opportunity should be whether it will provide a return sufficient to meet your needs and wants – but you also go into business to enjoy the experience. In self-employment job satisfaction is every bit as important as it is in paid employment. When you take on a franchise you assume an obligation that may last for 10 years or more; so before signing up you should be darned sure that you are going to be doing something you like. Though making money may compensate for doing something you hate, it is more likely that if you hate what you are doing you won't make as much money as you could if you were happy in your work. Which brings me to an important aspect of running a franchise: you will have noticed from the six categories above that many franchise opportunities are in the service industries, and even those that are not will almost certainly involve dealing face-to-face with customers. So one of the most important skills you can bring to a franchise is the ability to get on with people and be personable. A great attraction of franchising is that it takes people from a variety of backgrounds, and of varying ages and experience, and equips them to turn their hand to something quite new. But whatever your past line of work, you will have a head start if you can offer service with a smile.

So how relevant is your previous work experience? Perhaps the best answer is that it should not correspond too precisely with your chosen franchise. In fact, many franchise companies prefer applicants who have no direct prior experience of the activity in which the business is involved. Why? Because they prefer to train people with fresh minds rather than inherit people with preconceptions, people who might possibly 'know too much' or think they could run the business better their way. There are exceptions – plumbing franchises, for example, prefer applicants to have plumbing training – but generally speaking the skills and attributes should be of a more non-specific kind. If, for example, you have a sales or marketing background, look for a franchise where you can put that knowledge to use. Similarly, if you have an artistic or creative bent, or if you are good with your hands, or if you are happiest working out of doors, look for an opportunity to make the most of those attributes and preferences. Also, take into account your hobbies and interests. If, for instance, you are keen on DIY, you might be interested in a kitchen-fitting business or furniture repair; if you are a keen gardener, a landscaping franchise might appeal; if you are fond of animals, one of several opportunities in the pet business might suit you. Be warned, however, that something that might be pleasurable as an occasional diversion can pall when it becomes a full-time occupation. To introduce a personal note, I am an avid cricket follower and a journalist but the idea of being a cricket correspondent does not appeal in the slightest – it would make a chore out of what was previously a form of relaxation. And – something I've touched on before – do keep at the front of your mind the need to generate a sufficient income to provide for you and anyone else who might be dependent upon you – if the franchise you choose makes the most of an existing enthusiasm or interest, all well and good, but making a living comes first.

At any rate, the first step in making your choice is to scan the 700 or so opportunities on offer and then to set about the daunting task of whittling them down to a shortlist of, say, six. So where to begin?

Fortunately, such is the significance of franchising in the British economy today that there is no shortage of information about the many opportunities on offer. I have no doubt that the first place to look is the British Franchise Association (BFA). Formed in 1977 by eight franchise companies, the association set out with two main objectives – to act as a trade association and to dissociate reputable business format franchising from the disreputable activity of pyramid selling. The BFA's twin aims of looking after its members and self-regulation benefit prospective franchisees because every member company has to meet certain criteria. That said, an untold number of franchised businesses choose not to apply for membership; these outsiders may be bona fide franchises, but you should view non-membership with some scepticism. After all, why should a company be reluctant to submit itself to scrutiny by an organization able to offer it many benefits, not least the marketing advantage that being part of the BFA confers?

LOOKING
for your ideal franchise?
FIND IT...

...online - www.DaltonsBusiness.com
The essential website.

OVER 20,000 BUSINESSES FOR SALE

Daltons
DALTONSBUSINESS.COM

Thousands
of franchises
and business
opportunities to
buy. Updated daily.

...every Thursday in
Daltons Weekly
With the best selection of
franchises and businesses for sale,
available at all good
newsagents, just £1.

Tel: 020 7955 3784   e-mail: sales@DaltonsBusiness.com

The association has full and associate members. All members must meet the following four general objectives:

1. **Viable**: They will have proved in the marketplace that their product or service is saleable, and, furthermore, saleable at a profit that will support a franchised network. This requires the production of 24 months' recent audited accounts, including trading accounts, which show that the business is capable of being run at a profit that will support a franchised network

2. **Franchiseable**: They will have proved they have the means to transfer their know-how to a new operator at arm's length. Most will have done so at their own risk through at least one managed pilot franchise operation. They must produce 12 months' recent audited accounts for a managed, arm's-length pilot franchise, or a fully fledged pilot franchise, which show a trading performance at least in line with the business plan set for it and which is supported by a developed operating system.

3. **Ethical**: The BFA has joined with its sister bodies in Europe to devise a new and expanded code of ethics which all members commit themselves to abide by. The code requires standards of conduct in advertising for franchisees and in recruiting and selecting them, and sets minimum conditions for the terms of franchise agreements. Those terms are both critical and complex.

4. **Disclosure**: All BFA members agree that they will, in advance of any lasting contractual agreement, disclose without ambiguity to prospective franchisees the information on their business which is material to the franchise agreement. Members submit their offer documents to the association as part of the accreditation procedure.

Compliance with these four requirements admits a company to associate membership. To become a full member and to refer to itself as such in its offer documents, advertising, and other published material and to use the association's logo, a company must meet the following additional requirement:

5. **Demonstrate that the franchise network has developed over time with a proven trading and franchising record.** This requires a record of franchise openings, withdrawals and disputes (which required external intervention to resolve), together with evidence of the profitability of individual units and of the network as a whole sustained over a period of 24 months.

In 1991, to encourage as many reputable companies as possible to come within its fold, the association introduced a **provisional list** comprising companies new to franchising who could demonstrate that they were taking all reasonable measures to ensure that their business was properly developed and tested.

The success of franchising in the UK inevitably attracted a host of ancillary organizations offering to provide help and advice both to prospective franchisees and to franchisors. In recognition of this burgeoning activity the BFA established a list of **professional affiliates**. Over the years this category has grown from being primarily comprised of lawyers and accountants with expertise in franchising to encompass other categories, including exhibition organizers, financial services, insurance brokers, media and communications, bankers and franchise consultants.

You will find a complete list of the BFA's members and affiliated organizations at the end of this book.

From the above, you will see that if a franchise is a member of the BFA it offers a measure of assurance that companies outside the organization cannot provide with quite the same conviction. So, if the franchise that appeals most to you is a BFA member, that is a definite plus point. It is not a guarantee of success – franchise companies can and do make mistakes – but it is a form of proof that the operation has been well run in the past. However, if you choose to go with a firm that is not a member, you should first make every effort to ensure that it meets the criteria set out by the BFA, ie that it is viable, franchiseable, ethical and willing to disclose facts and figures that help prospective franchisees to make an informed decision. You will find more on how to do that later in this book.

We have not finished with the BFA yet: a very important part of its self-imposed remit is to foster the growth of franchising by attracting new franchisors and franchisees. It sets about this in a number of ways, many of which will help you in your search for the right business for you. The following are the main sources of information provided by the association:

■ **BFA Franchisee Information Pack**: this includes a full list of BFA member companies, what they do, contact details, investment costs and more; a list of affiliate advisers, including solicitors, chartered accountants, banks, franchise consultants and insurance brokers; information about how to evaluate a franchise; the advantages and disadvantages of franchising; details of the BFA's role in franchising; information on forthcoming franchise exhibitions; the laws and ethics of franchising; copies of the *Franchise Magazine, Business Franchise Magazine* and *Franchise Link Magazine*; a copy of the video 'Your Introduction to Franchising'.

▌ **Franchisee seminars**: a regular annual programme of seminars across the country, which set out to enable you to assess whether franchising is right for you; to help you develop the skills and knowledge to assess franchise opportunities; to give you an insight into the franchisor–franchisee business relationship; and to help you understand the franchisor's requirements and assessment criteria.

▌ **Franchise exhibitions**: a company called Venture Marketing runs an annual programme of franchise exhibitions in Birmingham, Dublin, London, Manchester and Glasgow. The biggest of these events is the autumn National Franchise Exhibition at the National Exhibition Centre in Birmingham. It forms part of National Franchise Week, a programme of events across the country aimed at banging the drum for business format franchising – as we have noted earlier, despite its success the industry still has much work to do to spread the word about 'being in business for yourself but not by yourself' and seven days of organized ballyhoo is yet another means of achieving that aim. The exhibitions are, of course, trade shows, and the main aim of the companies exhibiting is to attract business, which, in the case of franchise companies, means attracting new recruits. Be prepared, therefore, to encounter an eagerness that can develop into a 'hard sell'. But don't let that put you off: franchise exhibitions are an unrivalled opportunity to meet dozens of franchisors face-to-face under one roof and quiz them about what they have to offer. You should do your homework in advance. If you have read right through this book, you will be well informed about what makes a good franchise and able to ask franchisors about matters such as the qualities they look for in a franchisee, the training they offer, the help they provide in finding you a suitable area and premises, and the finances involved. Since exhibitions are tiring events, you should draw up a list of no more than half a dozen companies that you want to see, and allow about an hour for your conversations with each. Also, there will be opportunities to meet experts such as bankers, lawyers and accountants whose advice is free while they are at the show. Try, too, to take advantage of the daily seminars where advice on choosing a franchise is freely dispensed. Most important of all, never allow yourself to be swept along by events. Impose on yourself a cooling-off period, a time for calm reflection when you get home. Go carefully through the brochures you took away, discuss the pros and cons with your partner, and then, if you are convinced an opportunity is worth pursuing, make an appointment to go and see the company.

Other sources of information

∎ **Directories, newspapers and magazines**: there are two directories, each published annually and listing details of many franchise opportunities in the UK. They are *Franchise World* (020 8767 1371) and *The UK Franchise Directory* (01603 620 301).

Three specialist magazines are *Business Franchise*, published 10 times a year, the official journal of the BFA (020 8394 5223); *Franchise World*, published every two months (0208 767 1371); and *The Franchise Magazine*, published monthly (01603 620 301).

The *Daily Express*, *Daily Mirror* and *Daily Mail* all carry regular features on franchising. These are designed to attract advertising from franchise companies, so expect them to accentuate the positive.

∎ **The banks**: most of the big high-street banks are keen to lend to franchisees and have sections specializing in franchising. Call in at the local branches of NatWest, Lloyds TSB and HSBC and pick up their brochures on franchising.

∎ **Websites**: tap the words 'franchise UK' into a search engine such as Google and you will get more than 5 million sites. Almost all, in one way or another, are trying to sell you something, but many offer useful advice and information. Four worth singling out are:
  – www.british-franchise.org
  – www.whichfranchise.com
  – www.franinfo.co.uk
  – franchisebusiness.co.uk.

Can you afford the franchise of your choice and what do you get for your money?

Since this book is all about buying a franchise, it's about time we looked more closely at what you will have to pay and what you get in return. Having come up with a business idea, pilot-tested it and decided to launch it as a franchise, the franchisor will quite reasonably expect to reap some reward for his efforts. He will achieve this in two ways: first, by charging an initial lump-sum payment – in effect a fee for joining his club – and second, by levying continuing payments in the form of royalties, sometimes called management fees – the price you pay for staying in the club. Let us look at both these in more detail.

The initial fee

Ask a franchisor what this is for and he will tell you that it is to cover the costs incurred in setting you up in business – costs such as training you, helping with finding premises, providing an operations manual, assisting and advising in staff recruitment, getting you off to a flying start with an initial publicity splurge, paying professional fees and legal costs, and possibly providing a vehicle, computer, tools and equipment. With a well-established mature franchise, the fee should cover those items and nothing more. But with newer franchises, the franchisor will probably include in initial fees a sum to help defray the costs he incurred in launching and testing the business. In so doing, the franchisor should never be greedy, since one of the worst offences in franchising is to seek to make a quick profit from selling a franchise – that is the sort of thing fly-by-night disreputable operators get up to; by contrast, bona fide franchisors seek a continuing long-term income through developing the franchise network.

So, pitching the initial fee at the right level is both important and difficult. Set it too high and potential franchisees will be put off. Set it too low and the business may be starved of funds needed to set up new outlets. As a general rule, the initial franchisee fee should be no more than 10 per cent of the franchisee's total start-up costs. If you are asked for anything more than that, question it closely (or rather get your lawyer or accountant to probe into it for you – that's what they are paid to do). Like all rules, however, general ones are there to be broken and the initial fee will vary from franchise to franchise: in some cases you could be asked for more than 10 per cent; if, for example, you choose a franchise at the lower end of the investment scale, the fee could account for a larger percentage of the total outlay in getting up and running.

Management fees

These are at once the lifeblood of a franchise operation and the biggest source of potential friction between franchisee and franchisor. Regular payments from the network of franchisees serve two purposes: they reward the franchisor for his initiative and skill in setting up the enterprise and they pay for the continuing services he provides to the franchisees. A franchise head office has many tasks to perform, including recruiting and training new franchisees, providing continuing support and advice to existing franchisees, promoting and marketing the product or service, and researching and developing new ideas. Management fees may take three forms:

- **A percentage on turnover**: this is the most usual form of continuing fees. As with initial payments, it varies from franchise to franchise, but, again, is usually about 10 per cent of the franchisee's sales. That means that a franchisee might well find as much as 30 per cent of his or her annual trading profit going in fees to the franchisor, so you can see where the friction might creep in. In the interests of harmony, therefore, it is important that the management fee is seen to be fair and allows a reasonable income for both parties.
- **A mark-up on goods supplied**: with this system, franchisees agree under the terms of their contract to buy some or all of their materials either directly from the franchisor or from a supplier nominated by him. The franchisor makes his money by charging a mark-up or getting a commission from the nominated supplier.
- **A fixed regular fee**: this is the least satisfactory arrangement because of its inflexibility. A fixed fee large enough to satisfy the franchisor could, in the early stages of a newly established franchise unit, prove burdensome to a franchisee whose business is still producing a relatively small income. In the later years, it may fail to satisfy the franchisor who finds himself reaping a dwindling proportion of the network's increasing sales.

None of these fee arrangements is without disadvantages. The percentage on turnover gives the franchisor the right to look at the franchisee's books but also presents a resentful franchisee with an incentive to be less than frank in disclosing information. A mark-up on goods restricts the franchisee to a single supplier, itself a possible cause of disquiet, and may arouse suspicions about the fairness of the sum being charged. That in turn might tempt the franchisee to go behind the back of the franchisor and obtain supplies from another source, which could adversely affect the quality of the product sold to the customer. All in all, the percentage on turnover is the best and most transparent arrangement and therefore the one most widely used.

The franchisee shelling out his or her monthly royalty might be forgiven for thinking, that's enough, not a penny more, but there could be more all the same. It is not uncommon for a franchisor to levy in addition a regular sum – again a percentage of the franchisee's turnover, though only 5 per cent or less – to cover national advertising and promotional expenditure. Unlike the royalty fees, payments into an advertising fund do not represent income for the franchisor; rather, they are used to pay for marketing activity, including consumer research, advertising, public relations, merchandising materials and brand development. These are important to developing a business and would probably not attract as much of the franchisor's attention if they had to be funded by central office without the contributions of franchisees. Incidentally, the really good franchisor will want the contributions to be more than just financial: ideally, representatives of the franchise network should be involved in deciding how best the advertising and marketing fund should be spent. That kind of participation enables everyone concerned to see the benefits that flow from a focused marketing programme and forestalls possible criticism that the advertising levy is just another annoying outgoing.

So, looking to the future, the prospective franchisee must accept that he or she will be paying money to the franchisor for as long as the agreement lasts. More immediately, there are the costs of setting-up, and in this respect a franchise is no different from any another small business start-up. You will need to spend money on leases, fixtures and fittings, stock, working capital, plant and equipment, and so on. The total sums involved in start-up costs and initial fees vary widely from franchise to franchise and from sector to sector. At the bottom end of the scale a home-based, van-operated franchise might cost less than £10,000; at the top end a fast-food restaurant several hundreds of thousands. So, as always, your ambition, at least to start with, will be constrained by your budget. Unless you have redundancy money or substantial savings, you will have to raise finance from a lender to help you get started. How much you can borrow will depend on the security you can offer and the sum that you can advance from your own pocket.

At this stage, then, you should sit down and calculate your net worth. This may sound daunting but it's not really very complicated. All it amounts to is getting a sheet of paper and totting up on one side what you own, and on the other, what you owe. Your net worth is the difference between your assets and your liabilities. Assets might include your house, car, investments, jewellery, savings, insurance (don't worry about trying to find exact amounts in pounds and pence, just write down roughly what you could sell each item for, known as 'fair market value'); liabilities might be mortgage, loans, credit card debts. If when you deduct your liabilities from your assets the outcome is a positive number, you own more than you owe, which is of course a good thing. Calculating your net worth gives you a snapshot of your financial condition, a picture that may please or alarm and usually contains some surprises, and will help you plan for the future. Also, banks and other lenders might ask for a statement of net worth. What they will certainly want to know is how much you can stump up in liquid assets, ie readily available funds such as cash, shares, bonds and bank deposits. This is because as a general rule banks will lend you up to three times your net liquid assets.

To sum up the story so far, you will have done your best to see yourself as others see you and, reasonably satisfied with the result, decided you have what it takes to be a franchisee. You will have read as much information as you can find about franchising, visited exhibitions, attended seminars, talked to experts, and sifted it all through a keen and inquiring mind. You will have worked out your net worth and totted up your liquid assets. You will probably be exhausted. But bear up, the real work is just beginning. By now you will probably have an idea of the sectors of franchising that appeal to you, and possibly some target companies worth assessing in more detail. So what are you waiting for?

Do I have what it takes?

As an afterthought to this chapter it's worth looking at the potential franchise partnership from the other party's point of view and considering what the franchisor wants to find in a prospective franchisee. This can be summed up under three main headings:

▌ **Capital**: the franchisor will want to be sure that you have sufficient net worth and liquid assets to get your business solidly grounded. Insufficient capital in a new venture always spells trouble.

▌ **Attitude**: not 'attitude' in its modern sense of determined, defiant self-assertion, but rather a positive and consistent approach to being in business for yourself. The experienced franchisor knows that a prospective franchisee will be on his or her best behaviour during the interview and will want to probe deeper to see if you really mean what you say. Expect questions such as: 'Are you dedicated?' 'Are you single-minded?' 'Are you conscientious?' 'Are you pleasant to deal with?' 'Can you set targets and meet them?' 'Are you decisive?'

▌ **All-round skill and experience**: what can you bring to the franchise in terms of leadership qualities, business experience, managerial ability, communications skills? If you have not run a business before, can you demonstrate organizational skill?

Building a future in food retail.

Benjys seeks over 100 franchisees to fulfil 2006 expansion plans and is asking candidates from all backgrounds to come forward.

The nation's best loved sandwich chain already has a total of 70 retail stores and 120 Benjys Delivered vans in the UK and plans to open a further 50 stores and 90 Benjys Delivered franchises in 2006.

Ian Rickwood, Benjys Chief Executive says: "Expansion comes at a time when our business has performed well, with continued innovation helping to achieve significant success. With the UK sandwich market worth around £3.5 billion we want to increase our share of this growing and profitable market across the nation."

Benjys Delivered is a revolutionary concept in franchising, a mobile van which turns into a fully fledged sandwich retail operation in just 30 seconds, using Formula 1 technology.

Benjys Retail is now firmly established as a household name with hungry Londoners. And our leading brand is moving beyond its base in the capital with the rapid expansion of the Benjys retail concept nationwide.

Ongoing improvements in quality, range, presentation and image means that our Benjys retail operation is not only exciting, it is also profitable, with central production and an excellent name and reputation in the market place.

Development Agents are responsible for managing and growing Benjys retail operations by recruiting suitable franchisees, identifying growth opportunities and maintaining high in-store standards. Rewards are significant - DAs take a third of the initial set-up fee from recruitment, plus ongoing commission on all purchases of Benjys branded products. Investment required for each territory is costed on an individual basis, but starts at £150,000. The Development Agent proposition represent an excellent opportunity for Senior Retail Executives.

To find out more about these franchise opportunities call our franchise hotline on:

0845 33 00 126
or visit:
www.benjys-sandwiches.com

www.benjys-sandwiches.com

– BENJYS SET FOR UK EXPANSION –

With the backing of a tried and tested business model, franchising is often the ideal route for would be entrepreneurs – less risky than new business start-ups and with many additional benefits. And, when it comes to food retail franchises, it doesn't get much better than Benjys.

With phenomenal growth achieved in 2005, Benjys has plans to expand even further in 2006. With such vast expansion on the horizon exciting opportunities are available across the UK for potential franchisees to join this franchise network at various different investment levels.

Ian Rickwood, Benjys Chief Executive says: "Expansion comes at a time when our business has performed well, with continued innovation helping to achieve significant success. With the UK sandwich market worth around £3.5 billion we want to increase our share of this growing and profitable market across the nation."

Benjys Delivered is a revolutionary concept in franchising, a mobile van which turns into a fully fledged sandwich retail operation in just 30 seconds, using Formula 1 technology. Benjys Delivered franchisees are available as individual vans or on an investment level by becoming a multiple 'vanchisee' employing drivers to run the individual routes.

Retail

Benjys is now firmly established as a household name with hungry Londoners. And the leading brand is moving beyond its base in the capital with the rapid expansion of the Benjys retail concept nationwide.

Ongoing improvements in quality, range, presentation and image means that the Benjys retail operation is not only exciting, it is also profitable, with central production, and an excellent name and reputation in the market place. The last 12 months has seen the company undergo a nation-wide expansion plan, rolling out the network of franchised shops and bringing the great value of Benjys to many UK cities.

Development Agents are responsible for managing and growing Benjys retail operations by recruiting suitable franchisees, identifying growth opportunities and maintaining high in-store standards. Rewards are significant – DAs take a third of the initial set-up fee from recruitment, plus 5% commission on all purchases of Benjys branded products. Investment required for each territory is costed on an individual basis, but starts at £150,000. The Development Agent proposition represent an excellent opportunity for Senior Retail Executives.

5 **Don't shoot the wrong beast**

Having urged you to brace yourself for the hard task of tracking down and snaring the right franchise for you, I am now going to postpone the agony by taking you on a brief but necessary digression, the aim of which is to make sure that you are hunting the right quarry. Imagine how maddening it would be to have the target in your sights, pull the trigger and find you'd shot the wrong beast. Worse than that, the wrong species. But it can happen, and the danger arises because business opportunities sometimes disguise themselves as franchises. So how do you tell them apart? And does it really matter?

The answer to the second question is, yes, of course it matters. Although every franchise is a business opportunity, not every business opportunity is a franchise, and although the two types may shade into each other at the margins – they might, for example, have in common training policies and continuing support for people who buy their schemes – they are in truth quite different propositions. The essential distinction between the two can be summed up in one word – 'relationship'. The essence of a franchise is that you, the franchisee, have a continuing relationship with the franchisor: you operate as a quasi-independent outlet of an established business and brand with, it is to be hoped, a proven good name, and you carry on doing that for as long as the agreement lasts. As the operator of a business opportunity you are much more likely to be on your own. You pay for the system, you may get some training, you might be required to continue to buy stock or materials from the vendor, but really you are left to your own devices. You don't have to follow strict guidelines or systems, you are in every sense of the term a free agent. A typical business opportunity is a distributorship of some kind. Put simply and crudely, you are given a stack of business cards and the opportunity to go out and sell whatever it is that the parent company has to sell – it could be greetings cards, CDs, novelty goods, motor components, you name it – and you make your money in commission on sales. There is nothing wrong with that. In fact, business opportunities come with several advantages: they tend to be much cheaper to buy than franchises; they give you freedom of manoeuvre; you can work from home; and there are seldom any continuing fees or royalties to be paid. On the minus side, there is rarely any continuing support once you have invested; the product you are selling may not have a recognized brand; and it is difficult to assess the success rate of the operation.

This book is about investing in a franchise, not a 'business opportunity', but if you have spotted a distributorship or agency that appeals to you, here are a few tips on how to evaluate it. Potential franchisees should read through this section too, because it sets out exactly the sort of questioning approach they will need to apply in the search for their new business:

- Does the product you will be selling look like a winner to you? Is it new or different? If so, is there likely to be a reasonable demand for it, and will you have the confidence to go out and extol it in a sceptical marketplace?

- What can you find out about the company offering the opportunity? How long has it been in business? How does its approach strike you? Is it pushy, keen to make a sale? Or is it more inclined to talk with pride about its products and to make an effort to assess you as an individual?

- Does it offer training, a measure of continued support, a sales manual? All of these are desirable and point to an organization whose main concern is to grow through selling products rather than business opportunities.

- Will you be required to buy stock? If so, how much and on what terms? Far better if you first make a firm sale and then take delivery of the order.

- How many other people are running this opportunity? Could you meet them and discuss their experience of the company? If not, why not?

The above may seem like a lot of trouble to go to when you are being asked for perhaps only a few hundred pounds in return for what might be a part-time source of pin money, but the sale of business opportunities is an unregulated market that attracts scores of unscrupulous vendors, many of whom are not averse to passing off their business packages as franchises.

So beware. If you have followed the advice in the previous chapter and drawn up your short-list from members of the British Franchise Association, you can be confident that you have the right animal in your sights. If not, bear in mind that what you want is a fully formed business system with a known brand, a number of franchisees already trading successfully, and a organized system of training, support and guidance. If any one of those components is missing, you are on the wrong trail.

Take a closer look at what catches your eye

Now, assuming that you have done some homework, sent off for the brochures, and perhaps seen at the exhibitions a few franchises you like the look of, what next? Well, first take a closer look at the business sector in which the franchise operates, and then, if that stands up to scrutiny, move on to examining in some detail the franchise company itself.

As with all types of business in a free, competitive market, franchising does best when it operates in a niche that is not too free or too competitive. In other words, it should, for one reason or another, have an edge on its rivals, or, better still, have no rivals at all. Ideally, the product or service should not lend itself to being easily copied by others; it should be capable of commanding a premium price; it should not be a short-term fad; it should enjoy repeat business; and it should be protected by trademarks or patents. In addition, it should be in a growing market and have strong public awareness.

All this, of course, is a counsel of perfection, but the more boxes you can tick from the above, the better. The whole aim of the enterprise, after all, is to sell sufficient product at a sufficiently handsome margin to bring a smile to the faces of both franchisor and franchisee. In truth, you are almost certain to face competition and the way to beat it is to offer better quality, better reliability and better service, and franchising, with its unique combination of corporate know-how and individual motivation, is well equipped to deliver all three. But that in turn depends upon the franchise being run to its optimum. The franchisor must provide the best possible training, support, marketing programmes, research and development. So, having weighed up the market and the product or service, it's time to run a rule over the franchisor and to see how well he measures up. Your preliminary inquiries should include an investigation into the financial strength and standing of the company. This may sound daunting, but it isn't. Companies House is a government agency that stores company information delivered under the Companies Act and related legislation and makes this information available to the public for a fee of a few pounds. You can visit its website, www.companieshouse.gov.uk, or call its contact centre on **0870 33 33 636**. The BFA provides information about companies that come under its aegis. The high-street banks may be able to give an opinion in confidence on the standing of a company in which you are interested, though they would of course stop short of actively recommending a particular franchise. You might also consider commissioning a company search from one of the firms specializing in this field. These inquiries are not expensive, though they may take time, but ought to be part of a well-planned and serious evaluation of a franchise, particularly one that is relatively new and unknown. You'll want to know something about the background and experience of the directors, when the company was formed, and see the information in the latest account and report. If anything you uncover gives rise to suspicion, walk away. Or if you are simply unclear about, say, an item in the balance sheet, make a note and raise it during your interview with the franchisor. This will show him that you have done your homework, are serious about understanding the business, and do not see yourself as a passive buyer. If those qualities should make the franchisor wary of recruiting you, you're better off without him. Walk away.

In fact, now is the time to emphasize that your interview with the franchisor should not be approached like a job application. You are not begging for the favour of being taken on. You are bringing to the table qualities that will make you a valuable business partner. The franchisor is providing a business format. The interview is an opportunity for each party to weigh up the other. So although you will be asked questions about your motivation, experience, background and finances, and you may even be asked to take a psychometric test, you should have plenty of questions of your own. Here is a checklist (a more detailed version is at the end of this chapter):

■ How long has the franchise been established? How thoroughly was the system pilot-tested? How many outlets are there in total? How many are company-owned? The purpose of these questions is to assess the maturity of the operation. The newer it is, the greater will be your risk in joining. Against that, you could be getting in early on what might develop into a large, flourishing enterprise. Your decision will be influenced by your impression of the franchisor and your assessment of how well you are equipped to handle risk. If you have previous experience in sales or marketing, you might well be more confident about this.

▌ Go thoroughly into the question of training. How long will your training last? What form will it take? Will it be classroom residential training? Will there be practical experience in the field with a seasoned franchisee? Once your initial training is complete, will there be continued help to further refine your skills? What will the training cover? Is it restricted to product knowledge, or does it also include subjects such as business administration, marketing, recruitment, and customer service?

▌ As important to the franchise concept as training is continuing support. Ask the franchisor about this. What kind of support can you expect? Will someone at head office always be there at the end of the phone to come to your aid should a problem arise? Will you get help in finding customers? Many franchisors see it as an important part of their role to generate new business on behalf of the franchise network, perhaps by negotiating national contracts with business customers. If, as is likely, you will be expected do to a lot of your own sales and marketing, what help can you expect from the franchisor in terms of sales manuals, promotional materials, merchandising equipment and so on? Will the help extend to having someone visit your outlet and give you the benefit of first-hand experience in the field? If all goes well, there will come a time when you no longer need to have your hand held, but in the early stages when you are still finding your feet you will be grateful for as much cosseting as you can get.

▌ Sound out the franchisor about his plans for the future. How quickly does he want to expand? How many franchisees does he propose to take on? If the operation is approaching maturity, what is he doing to stay ahead of the game? Is he investing in research and development?

▌ Ask about existing franchisees. What kind of backgrounds do they come from? Are there systems in place for them to exchange information and help each other? Have there been any failures? If so, why?

▌ Do not shrink from asking direct questions about money. If you suffer from our peculiar national reticence to discuss financial matters, now is the time to sublimate it and be bold. After all, your future livelihood might depend upon the answers. Ask the franchisor for copies of his reports and accounts for the past three years. In the case of a newer company, ask for a banker's status report. At a later stage your bank or accountant may want to take up references, so ask if these will be readily available. These questions are in no way impertinent. Remember what I said earlier – you are not a supplicant, you are a potential business partner and any franchisor who is unwilling to disclose financial information necessary for you to make an informed judgement about your future investment is not to be trusted.

∎ Ask about fees. Is a deposit required? Is it refundable? How much is the initial fee? How is the management services fee calculated? Is there an advertising levy? If so, how much, and what does it cover?

∎ Now ask specific questions about your proposed outlet. Has the franchisor prepared financial projections for it? On what basis were they calculated? From where will you obtain supplies of goods and materials? Will you be given help in drawing up a business plan to present to the bank? Has the franchisor arranged a finance package with one or more of the high-street banks?

∎ Finally, ask about the legal terms of the deal. Will you be operating in an exclusive territory? How long does the agreement last? Will it be renewable? If so, will a further fee be required? Should you for any reason find yourself unable to continue running the outlet, will you be free to assign or sell the franchise? Ask to take away a copy of the franchise agreement; it should contain the answers to these and more questions.

So that's the interview over. You will not, of course, have signed anything at this stage or committed yourself in any other way. You will have agreed to go away and think carefully over what has been said. For his part, the franchisor will want time to weigh up his impressions of you. Whether or not he decides to take the matter further and enter into more detailed discussion with you is beyond your control. What you must do next is cool off, mull over what took place at the interview and sum up your impressions. As much will depend on personal intuition as on what was actually said at the interview. Like it or not, we are all programmed by experience and by nature to form impressions of others from their manner and their appearance. You don't have to be an expert in body language to form a judgement about the sincerity and plausibility of another human being. And unless you are dealing with an accomplished confidence trickster, whose art is feigning sincerity, your impressions are important, if for no other reason than that you are considering entering into a business relationship with the person in question, and business relationships can be as testing as any other kind.

In other words, it's important that you came away from the interview feeling that you liked and could get along with the franchisor. Entering into a franchise is not like becoming an employee who may never again set eyes on the person who interviewed him or, in the case of a large organization, have any dealings with the boss. Franchisors, even of large established organizations, know the people in the franchise network by name. They know how good they are, how well they perform, how well they fit in. And the franchisees know the franchisor: how responsive he is, how willing he is to listen, how conscientious he is in managing the franchise. The franchise agreement has been likened to a marriage, the similarity being that to make a go of it both partners have to get on with each other. So, mulling over the interview, do you think you have found a partner?

Did the franchisor strike you as being a person who lived and breathed his business, who, to use that overworked word, was passionate about it? Did he come across as open and honest and convincing? Did he look you in the eye and give straight answers to your questions? Or was he ever-so-slightly shifty and evasive? Was he businesslike in the sense of setting out to discuss a proposition and freely exchange information, or more of a salesman pitching for your money? Never lose sight of the fact that a reputable franchisor invests a lot of care and time in recruitment because it is upon the quality of the franchise network that the success of the entire operation depends. It follows that a franchisor who seems hurried or carefree about taking on new franchisees is motivated by something other than building for the long term. Far more likely that he is either short of capital and not too fussy about how he improves the position or, worse still, is hoping to make a quick killing by selling franchises prior to making an even quicker exit. In this context, remember what he said when you asked about future plans and how quickly he wanted to expand. A shrewd, responsible franchisor will have given a measured response, something along the lines of growing at a pace commensurate with the resources available to support a growing network. A franchisor who sits back in his chair, waves a cigar airily and boasts of taking on the world is conning you and possibly himself.

For the sake of convenience I omitted one vital question from the list above. It is so crucial that I have left it to this stage so that it can be dealt with in more detail. It is this: **you must ask the franchisor for a complete list of the existing franchisees in the network and meet at least two of your own choosing**. I cannot over-emphasize the importance of this phase in your investigations: although, for reasons we shall see, the results may not be conclusive, it is nevertheless a serious mistake to proceed without talking to existing franchisees.

You need a complete list because you do not want to be fobbed off with stooges, franchisees who are either exceptionally good performers or who have been primed to talk to prospective franchisees, or both. The franchisor should be willing to let you have this information. He may feel, quite understandably, that franchisees are busy people who could well do without taking time out to talk to strangers, but, as I have already emphasized, recruitment is a serious business and a franchisor should accept that introducing existing franchisees to potential newcomers is a valuable and necessary part of the process. If a franchisor refuses to let you have a complete list, the chances are he has something to hide.

Choose at least two franchisees you would like to meet, and make appointments to see them. Don't be satisfied with a telephone chat: as mentioned before in the context of meeting the franchisor, you can tell a lot just from looking into someone's eyes as you talk to them. There really is no substitute for a face-to-face meeting. Take your spouse or partner along if you wish, but don't take the franchisor along, even if he tries to insist. His presence is bound to inhibit the franchisee.

The purpose of the meeting is obvious. You want to find out whether the franchisee is satisfied with the franchise, enjoys running it, and is making enough money to consider the enterprise worth while. You will want to know if the franchise measured up to expectations, if there were any unforeseen snags, and, above all, whether or not the financial forecasts were realistic. You will want to know about trading conditions: Has business been brisk? Did the franchisor help with advertising and marketing? Is it necessary to go out and drum up business? Is cash flow a problem? You will also want to know about the relationship with the franchisor: Was the training adequate? Was there good continuing support and back-up? Was the training manual a help? You will want to know what effect the business has had on the franchisee's life: Given the opportunity, would they take up the franchise again? Has it affected their family life? What do they most like about running the business? What do they most dislike? Do they feel relatively free to get on with things and run their own show or do they feel slaves to the system? Find out what they were doing before they bought the franchise, how they found out about it, why they were attracted to it, and how well they get on with the franchisor.

Assuming your conversations were frank, open and confidential, you will have acquired a 'feel' for the way the franchise works where it most counts – at the coalface. You will have formed an impression of the sense of well-being and enthusiasm in the organization (or its absence), and the efficiency with which the franchise operates (or the lack of it). If you sensed that the franchisees were less than upbeat or even downright dissatisfied, that is obviously a bad sign, but – and here is a snag – things are not always as plain as they seem. There are many reasons why a franchisee may become disgruntled. As we have noted several times already, as time passes, ambitious individuals tend to forget the debt they owe to the franchisor and wish they were truly free to do their own thing. In other instances, disappointment has less to do with any fault in the franchise system, rather it is because the franchisee was either unsuited to the business or has neglected scrupulously to follow the systems and procedures. Unfortunately there is no certain way of getting at the truth other than to bear these possibilities in mind while you are talking to the franchisees: you should be able to form an impression of their characters and how they might have shaped their attitude to the business. It is for you to decide on the strength of your meetings with both franchisor and franchisees whether the outfit is a go-ahead, happy sort of club that breathes a general sense of optimism or whether it is shrouded in a dour, shoulder-to-the-wheel atmosphere.

The impressions gained from these face-to-face meetings may not be clear-cut, but they could be decisive. Only from seeing a working franchise unit from the inside can you really imagine how it might feel to be in the place of the franchisee. If you feel that you could happily swap places with him or her, you will obviously want to take matters further. If, however, you came away feeling a sense of unease, better to strike the organization from your list and look elsewhere.

But before pressing on to the next stage, it is a good idea to pause for reflection. You have now been close up to a franchise organization and seen some of it from the inside. Was it what you expected? Could you imagine yourself throwing all your energies into a) the market in which you will be involved and b) the particular franchise that you have seen? Give some thought to the question of selling. Almost all small businesses, and franchises are no exception, require their owners to go out and find new customers. Not everyone is cut out for a task that inevitably involves a measure of rejection. Others take to it with relish. How do you think you would cope?

If your initial enthusiasm is still undimmed, if you are impressed by what you have seen and learnt, if you can't wait to roll up your sleeves and get down to it, very well, let's do just that and take a close look at what might be your very own business.

Checklist

■ How long have you been in this industry? What is the experience and background of you and your fellow directors?

■ How many franchised outlets are in your network?

■ How many company-owned outlets do you run?

■ Did you run a pilot scheme? (If not, why not?) How successful was it? Can I see the figures?

■ What is your own financial commitment to the business?

■ Have any of your franchisees failed? If so, why?

■ Have you made any mistakes? If so, what were they?

■ Are you a member of the BFA? If not, why not?

■ What are the future prospects for the industry you are in, and of your company in particular? How do you do to keep up with developments? Do you have a research and development programme?

■ Do I get exclusive rights to a territory? How do you define a territory? Will I be able to take on an additional territory?

■ If we do go ahead, how long will it be before my outlet is up and running?

■ Will I get help in finding premises and researching my local market?

■ May I have a list of all your franchisees, and am I free to contact any of my own choosing?

■ Do you have a bank reference that I can see?

■ Do you have any other references I might follow up?

■ What are the total costs of the franchise? Are they paid all in one go, or in stages? What is the timing? What do the costs cover?

■ What percentage of my sales will be taken in royalty payments? What support do I get in return? Is there an advertising levy? If so, how much, and what does it cover?

■ How much working capital will I need?

■ Do you provide profit and cash-flow projections for my proposed business? If not, can I see figures for existing operations?

■ Will you help me to obtain finance? Do you have a finance package arranged with any of the banks?

■ Do I have to buy any materials or other supplies from you?

■ How much financial information is made available to franchisees, both in terms of the profit made by you, the franchisor, and the results of other franchisees?

■ Tell me about the advertising and marketing of the product or service offered by the franchisees. Are franchisees involved in deciding marketing strategy? How are the results measured?

■ Will you help me launch my outlet? If so, how? Will I get help in arranging local advertising and promotions?

■ Do you have any examples of marketing material that I can see? For example, point-of-sale material, brochures, leaflets.

■ Do I get help with making sales? Do you provide an initial customer base? Do I need to cold-call? Do you provide sales training? Do I need to have sales experience?

■ When can I take away a franchise agreement to show my lawyer? Is the agreement negotiable? (The usual answer to this is 'no', though some specific variation may be reasonable, especially if it is a fairly new franchise.)

■ When can I see a disclosure document?

■ Do you set minimum performance levels, or a minimum fee, or a minimum purchase level for goods? What happens if I don't meet them? How secure is the franchise tenure?

■ What is the length of the franchise agreement? What happens at the end? Do I have the automatic right of renewal?

■ What if I want to sell my business? Do I have to sell it back to you, or can I sell it to a third party? What restrictions are there on my right to sell the business?

■ Do I need insurance cover of any kind? If so, are you able to arrange favourable terms?

■ If I need premises, are they bought or leased? Do you take the head lease and sublet to me, or do I lease direct? What happens if my lease is not renewed?

■ What is the procedure if I want to terminate the agreement?

■ For what reasons can you, the franchisor, terminate the agreement?

■ How long does the initial training last? Where does it take place? Who conducts it and what does it cover? Will I get practical experience in a company outlet or with an existing franchisee?

■ If during training you think I am unsuitable, what happens? If we agree to part company, would all or part of the money I had paid be refunded?

■ Is there ongoing training? If so, what form does it take and will I have to pay for it?

■ If I need to take on staff, will you train them?

■ What kind of support can I expect from your head office? Do you employ people whose sole role is to help franchisees? Will help be available whenever I need it?

■ How often will you be in contact with me? Is there a system enabling franchisees to help each other? Will my performance be monitored so that I know how well I am doing?

■ Describe a typical day in the working life of one of your franchisees. How many hours does a typical franchisee need to devote to the business?

■ Is the business seasonal? If so, when is the best time to launch a new outlet?

■ What would you say are the keys to success in the business?

■ What are the most common pitfalls/errors?

■ Will I need to employ staff? If so, how much will it cost me? Will I be able to recruit the right kind of people in my area?

■ Will the business generate sufficient income to support a family? Will my spouse be able to work in the business too?

■ Can I spend time with an existing franchisee to see if I like it?

■ Do you provide an operations manual?

■ Does head office provide administrative support in areas such as invoicing, debt collection or bookkeeping?

■ Do you provide a computerized accounting package?

■ Do you have any arrangements for keeping franchisees in touch with you and each other?

■ Describe the relationships between franchisees and between the franchise network and yourself. How are disputes resolved?

■ What is the profile of a successful franchisee in your business, and what are your requirements for qualification as a new franchisee?

6 Getting closer and getting help

Having put in a lot of hard work and research, you have now reached the critical stage where you at last feel close to attaining your objective – a business you can call your own, ready-made and brimful of advantages that give you a head start. You could be forgiven for breathing a mighty sight of relief and coasting towards the finishing line. Correction: you will neither be forgiven nor forgive yourself if you succumb to the temptation to take things easy at this time because there is still a lot of work to be done. OK, you've assessed your strengths and weaknesses and satisfied yourself that the former outweigh the latter, you've assembled enough bumph to keep the recycling industry busy for months, you've trudged around exhibitions, listened to promotional spiel until your ears hurt, and read brochures until your eyes bubbled. You've narrowed down your choice from hundreds of companies to just two or three, and you've been through an interview and talked to existing franchisees. Isn't that enough? What next? Do you need to give blood? No, but you do need to focus, almost certainly for the first time in real detail, on the business that will be yours – not the franchise in general, but your outlet in particular. Let us assume for the time being that it does not exist outside your imagination (later in this chapter we shall look at the pros and cons of buying a real, live, up-and-running outlet), in which case you must do everything you can to clothe this fictitious skeleton in some real flesh. And that means investigating the area where you plan to set up.

The property market has more clichés than an estate agent has enemies but the best known is 'location, location, location' – the three most important factors in determining the attraction and value of a house. As with most hackneyed phrases, it may be worn to shreds, but it still embodies an eternal truth, and what goes for private homes applies with equal force to small businesses. Where you set up shop might have a decisive effect on your chances of success for three reasons: first, the potential strength of the local market, second, the investment cost of buying or renting property, and third, the ease with which customers, and possibly employees, can reach you. Let us look at each of these in turn:

▌ **The local market**: you will need to look not just at the size of the local population but also its composition. If, for example, you are planning to sell premium-priced products or services, does the area look prosperous enough to support that kind of business? Upmarket fashion retailing franchises, for example, favour places such as Bath, Tonbridge, Richmond, Chelsea and Edinburgh because they know the local population is well-heeled. Though that is an extreme example, the quality of the neighbourhood is something you should take into account. Another obvious demographic consideration is the age of the local populace – the chances of making a success of selling babywear in a seaside town packed with retired gentlefolk will be slight, whereas a domestic cleaning business could be ideal for that location. On the other hand, you may not be planning to sell to private individuals at all. Many franchises are in the business-to-business sector, in which case the initial market research will concentrate on the number and variety of firms in the area. As important as the size of the territory allocated to you is the strength of the competition you might face. How many other businesses are offering a service similar to the one you propose to provide? How, in your opinion, do they shape up? Could you do better? If so, how and why? Asking and answering these questions will help you in this essential task of visualizing your business and your role in it.

▌ **Property**: choosing the right premises is something of a balancing act between the cost involved and the location. As the cliché reminds us, the better the location, the more you have to pay. The nature of the business is a determining factor. If you are in retailing, it is essential that customers can reach you – that much is obvious. Not quite so obvious, however, is the way in which the product you are offering should influence your choice of location. If, for example, you rely on high-volume passing trade – a fast-food outlet would be a good example – you want to be in a prime location and you have to accept the high costs involved as a necessary prerequisite of setting up. If on the other hand you are in a specialist, niche business – hiring bridal wear, for example – your customers will be prepared to seek you out, so a less expensive secondary location will meet your needs. Another thing you may want to look at is the proximity of competitors. Some traders do not like to have rivals too close by, but, against that, there are many instances where groups of similar businesses huddled together attract trade.

I   **Transport links:** if you are going to recruit staff, ideally they will live near your business. If they are not within walking distance, they should nevertheless be able to reach you easily, so you should look at public transport links, parking facilities and so on. Incidentally, it helps if your location is within easy reach of local amenities – staff like to be near shops and pubs. You may also want to be near your suppliers, so again transport connections will be important.

If all this sounds daunting, not to mention wearisome, take heart. Every small business feeling its way tentatively towards a launch should go through the process of researching the market and hacking through the property jungle, but you, unlike most small businesses, have an inestimable advantage in the shape of the franchisor. Chances are he's been there and done it, not once but many times. He will know about market research and will have experience in negotiating property deals. He will be able to take you by the hand and lead you safely down a path strewn with obstacles such as the size and layout of the premises, their structure and appearance, both internally and from the outside, facilities and comfort for employees and visitors (lighting, toilets and kitchen facilities), utilities, such as power and drainage, planning permission, access and parking space, initial purchase costs, including legal costs such as solicitor's fees, initial alterations, fitting out and decoration, any changes required to meet building, health and safety and fire regulations, ongoing rent and service charges, business rates, continuing maintenance and repairs, buildings and contents insurance. Phew! Aren't you glad you've got a franchisor?

So far, we have assumed that your outlet will be located near to where you live. After all, setting up a business, possibly for the first time in your life, is a sufficiently radical step without the added upheaval of moving home. The advantages of staying in your own locality are plain: you know the area, which makes local market research that much easier; franchisors like to appoint people with local knowledge; and the transition from wage earner to self-employed businessperson is much smoother when everything else in your life – your home, surroundings, family – remains relatively undisturbed. So ideally, your franchise will in a sense come to you. Normally, that is not a problem. When a franchisor sets about building his business through recruiting franchisees he will have a geographical expansion plan. In fact, it's not unusual for franchises to announce that they have a few remaining territories left and then to list the locations that need to be allocated, preferably to local people. This means of course that the younger the franchise, the greater the choice. But what if the business you have set your heart on – possibly because it is a well-known proven success – is approaching maturity, with only a few territories unfilled? You must then decide whether it is worth uprooting yourself and your family and moving to another part of the country. Much will depend on your personal circumstances: if you do not have children at school, if your ties to the local community are not strong, if your house will find a ready buyer, if you have a bold and resolute nature, then you might well decide to up sticks and make a clean break with your old life and start afresh with a new business and a new home in a new area. It's a big decision to take and, as with almost everything else involved in the franchise decision, it should be thoroughly discussed with your family.

The question of relocating opens up a whole new topic, the possibility of buying a ready-made franchise. All franchise opportunities are ready-made in so far as the business idea is fully formed, the systems tried and tested, the training and operating manuals in place and so on, but it is possible to take the process a stage further and buy a franchise outlet that is already up and running. The obvious attraction is that you don't have all the hassle involved in starting from scratch – finding premises, launching a new outlet, winning customers – instead you have an existing customer base, the goodwill built (one hopes) by the previous owner, and an immediate cash flow. However, the chances that the franchise of your choice will just happen to have an outlet for sale in your neighbourhood are slim. So, if your preference is for the added security of a franchise that is already trading successfully, you may well have to move to a different location. You will incur the costs of moving home and you will almost certainly have to pay more for a franchise re-sale than for a new start-up, but the advantages could outweigh the disadvantages. Only you can tell whether the move is worth while, but if the idea appeals to you, the following section examines re-sales in more detail.

Although buying an existing outlet cuts out the process of setting up, it is not a short cut. The franchisor will still want to assure himself that you are a suitable person to run the business and so you will have to go through the usual selection process. For your part, you will need to do all your checks, too, including, most importantly, talking to existing franchisees. So, assuming all that is out of the way, and both you and the franchisor are satisfied with each other, the next stage is to take a close look at the outlet that might soon be yours.

The first and obvious question is why is the existing franchisee selling? There could be a number of good reasons: ill health, retirement or simply a desire to cash in on a lot of hard work could be among them. But this a naughty world in which we live and you cannot take the word of a seller for granted; you must dig deeper and make a note of the responses to your inquiries, which may come in useful should any problems arise after you have taken over.

There are two possible extremes with an existing franchise: either it is in trouble and needs turning round, or it is bursting with good health. Either way, more probing is required. If the business is in trouble, you will probably be told that it is because the franchisee is at fault. Maybe he or she wasn't cut out for franchising, or couldn't put in enough effort because of ill health, or perhaps the marketing strategy was wrong, the staff unreliable; there could be all sorts of plausible reasons for arguing that the concept was sound, the location suitable, but somehow it just didn't work out. Now, if on the other hand the outlet in which you are interested is flourishing, you might think, great, there's nothing too much to worry about. However, you must still approach it with a sceptical eye. If it's doing so well, why does the present owner want to sell? There may be very good reasons, such as those mentioned above, but there may also be hidden reasons. Does the owner, for instance, know of some impending change in local conditions, such as a new road that might divert passing trade or the arrival of new competition or a rent rise in the offing? Or is there a longer-term, downward trend in the neighbourhood?

By now you will see that buying an existing franchise is not an easy option. But, provided you investigate the proposition thoroughly you should be able to reach a sound judgement as to its viability. The good news is that an existing business will have records and accounts that you will want to inspect. Ask to see these for at least the past three years. If you are not experienced at analysing accounts, and few people are, you should pass them on for examination by a qualified accountant. The figures ought to give a guide to the trend of the business: whether it is growing and, if so, how fast; or standing still; or falling back. I mentioned earlier that you should meet existing franchisees in other territories. If the rest of the network seems in good shape, that is plainly a positive sign. At any rate, these discussions should reveal whether the outlet you are looking at is typical or in some way different.

If it isn't doing as well as it should, you must endeavour to find out why. You must look at the business as if you were planning to start from scratch and ask whether the market potential is good, the location suitable, the competition beatable. If you are satisfied there is potential for future success and growth, you must go in for yet another bout of self-examination and decide whether you could make a difference, and if so, how. What would you do differently to make a go of it? What qualities would you bring that it lacked in the past? These are important questions to ask, because as a potential franchisee you will be constricted in the remedial actions you are able to take. Normally, someone acquiring an existing business will be free to attempt to increase profits by cutting costs, raising prices or attracting more custom. With a franchise, however, the options are fewer; the franchisor will in all probability exercise control over costs and prices, leaving you with no remedies other than your ability to improve efficiency and get out and sell.

Assuming that after your research you consider that the business is either going well and is set fair for the future, or it is ripe for the kind of improvements you could bring to it, the next stage is to haggle about price. With a successful going concern you may not have a lot of room for manoeuvre, but you will still want to ensure that the asking price is fair. If possible, compare it with other businesses for sale in the same locality. If you are going to borrow to pay for the business, calculate how long it will take you to repay the loan. It is important that the term of the agreement, or the remainder of the term that you are taking over, is sufficient to allow you a reasonable return on your investment, especially if you plan to make improvements that might take some time to bear fruit.

If you decide to go ahead with the purchase, you will be asked to sign a new franchise agreement on the terms currently applied by the franchisor, which may not be the same as those undertaken by the franchisee selling the business. Careful checking will be needed to see that the conditions that you are offered will not adversely affect your financial arrangements or business forecasts.

An obvious feature of a business sale is that you are buying not just a franchise, but a going concern, which might have hidden complications. There may be potential snags concerning the liabilities of the outgoing franchisee, and you will not want to be lumbered with these. Another potential pitfall concerns staff. They will automatically transfer to your employment and you will need to protect yourself against any claims they might have against the outgoing franchisee. A business transfer agreement will be drawn up, which, as the name implies, will transfer the assets of the business to you. This will include fixtures, fittings, stock and equipment, and you will need to establish whether any items are on hire purchase or lease, and if so, who will pay the costs of transferring the agreements to you.

I mentioned earlier that in business it is a sad fact that no one's word can be taken for granted, so it pays to get as much as possible in writing. When buying a franchise re-sale, this means getting the outgoing franchisee to warrant (legally pledge will turn out to be true) details such as good title to assets, no hidden defects and the validity of past performance. In the event that things later turn out not to be as represented, such warranties may give you some legal recourse. Finally, there may be an assignment of the lease of the business premises, which will involve legal costs. Who will pay these?

You will see from the above that buying a franchise re-sale is a complicated business, too complicated to be left to the likes of you and me. Long before signing anything you must engage the services of an accountant and a lawyer, and we shall have more to say about the services of these people later in this chapter. The reason I have outlined the complexities of a re-sale agreement is not to put you off the idea of buying an existing franchise – there are some great deals to be had – but rather to alert you to some of the pitfalls and to prepare you for the ground that will be covered by your expert advisers.

However, there is no getting away from the fact that finding business premises, or even taking over premises from an outgoing franchisee, is a potentially costly and irksome process. So how about avoiding it altogether and working from home? Many franchises at the lower end of the investment scale are specifically designed to be run from home, at least in the early stages while the franchisee finds his or her feet. Later, when the business is established, the franchisee feels more confident and a customer base has been acquired, it might be better to move into business premises and perhaps take on staff. In the meantime, however, working from home has many advantages. The most obvious of these is that you have lower start-up and operating costs; there are no extra rates, rents and service charges to pay. A less measurable advantage is that business life and family life can be better integrated when you work from home. This is particularly true of working mothers, there being countless examples of female franchisees who love the flexibility of being able to run, say, a health and fitness business (hiring local halls for the classes) or a domestic cleaning operation (managing teams of cleaners) while at the same time looking after their families. Men, too, can find that working from home allows them to integrate better with the family. In some cases, working from home simply means being based at home. A common arrangement is for one spouse or partner to field telephone calls, book business and so on, while the other is out in the field repairing car paintwork, erecting estate agents' signs, clearing drains or any of the hundred and one things franchisees get up to. Technology has made home working easier. The advent of telephone answering machines, mobile phones, fax machines and personal computers enables the franchisee to be in touch and to handle orders, billing and accounts with an ease that previous generations could have only dreamt of.

But (isn't there always a but?) working from home is not without possible disadvantages. If you run a van-based franchise and therefore in effect go out to work, the problems should be few. If, however, your home is your place of work, perhaps in a white-collar business such as accountancy, you might find that being close to the family is not such a joy after all. The demands of family life, especially when young children are around, may impinge on the business and cause stress to all concerned. Then there is the problem of space. If all the businesses that began life on a kitchen table were laid end to end, they would reach from here far into the distant realms of myth and legend, which is where they belong. Of course, some began in that way, but a kitchen table really is no place to do business. You need a properly equipped office or workspace, preferably as far away from domestic activities as possible. A good solution, if you can afford it, is to use a garden shed as your workplace; not, of course, the wooden shack variety that is home to garden tools, discarded prams and the like, but a purpose-built structure equipped with light, heating and power. There are many home-based entrepreneurs who say the very act of physically removing themselves from the house and 'going to work', albeit a few yards up a garden path, concentrates the mind and prepares them for the switch from household to business. Another potential disadvantage of home working is the neighbours, or more precisely the effect that your business might have on them. Normally this should not be a problem. You are unlikely to be conducting a noisy or smelly business in your front room. You might, however, receive more visitors than the average home, either customers or people delivering supplies to your door. If this extra traffic becomes excessive in the eyes of neighbours, you could be in trouble. Common sense should tell you whether or not this is likely to be a problem, and in any case the franchisor should know from experience just how far the nature of the operation can be taken without offending neighbours or attracting the attention of the local authority.

Normally people planning to set up a business in their home, or just working from home instead of commuting to an office, are warned of the dangers of isolation, the lack of informal social contacts and the opportunities to network. They are also reminded that discipline is needed to establish steady work patterns when there is no one watching over you and the kitchen with its kettle, teapot and biscuit tin is just a few tempting steps away. But, as a franchisee, none of this will worry you. You have already assessed yourself with a rigour that would command the respect of the sternest psychologist and you know that you are focused, determined, hard-working, self-reliant, organized and have bags of drive and determination. Not for you the tea break that lasts all the way to the next one.

Better than guesswork

In discussing the possibility of buying a franchise re-sale we noted that one of the great advantages is having past performance figures to go on. But suppose you are starting a new outlet, what then? Once again, franchising scores well compared with ordinary start-ups. If you were setting up on your own you would have to make projections of likely costs, sales, cash flow and so on, but these could be no better than informed guesswork. With a franchise you can do better than that. Why? Because the franchisor has removed much of the guessing from the game. At the very least he will have the accounts of the pilot-tested franchise, but usually he will have much more in the shape of facts and figures gleaned from a number of franchised outlets in different parts of the country. Using that data he will be able to provide you with a sample business plan and estimated profit and loss accounts. Now these are of course neither guarantees nor promises: your outlet might not perform as well as others have in the past; on the other hand, it might perform better than others. So much will depend on local conditions, market circumstances and, above all, on you. Even so, the franchisor's figures will be based on hard facts rather than conjecture.

We'll look more closely at the business plan later, but it's worth mentioning at this stage what an important and valuable document this is. In effect, the plan is a sales document for the business and may well tell you more about the franchise than anything you have seen or read thus far. It should cover in detail topics such as the nature of the operation, the market, the marketing plan and the premises, and, most importantly, financial projections, including profit, financing, break-even and cash flow. In drawing up these projections, the shrewd franchisor will err on the side of caution. Tempting though it might be to use the figures to 'talk up' the prospects of a new outlet, it's a foolish thing to do. For one thing, prospective lenders to the business, particularly the banks, keep detailed records and would soon put a question mark beside franchisors who persistently presented over-optimistic forecasts. And for another, the franchisee would understandably be resentful if the rosy picture painted in the business plan turned out to be of a duller hue. All in all, better to under-egg the pudding, and there is evidence to suggest that this happens in many cases. It is not at all uncommon for new franchisees to complete their first year of trading with sales triumphantly in excess of the forecast figure. In fact, this happy outcome is sufficiently widespread to suggest that franchisors are keen that newcomers should surpass expectations. It's good for morale.

The experts

As an aspiring businessperson you must come to terms with legal and financial matters. With any luck, the legal side of owning a franchise will be out of the way once the agreement is signed and you get started. The financial side, however, is what it's all about, and even if you take on a franchise in which head office undertakes to handle invoicing and accounting on your behalf (this is quite common with van-based franchises, for example, where the franchisor wants the franchisee to devote all his or her energies to serving the customer free of the distractions of bookkeeping), you will want to keep an eye on the bottom line. But however good you are with figures and no matter how canny you are when it comes to scanning paperwork, you are unlikely to have the expertise to analyse critically a franchise agreement or spot the flaws in a business plan. To do those things you will need to call in experts. This is true no matter how helpful the franchisor, simply because however honest and open he might be, he is not impartial, and now you have got this far down the road, impartiality is not merely desirable, it's essential. Both you and the franchisor are too close to the business, too bound up in its prospects and ambitions, to be able to stand back and view it objectively, no matter how hard you try. For this you need an outsider, someone who will cast a fresh and neutral eye over the figures or read skilfully between the lines. You know where this is leading – you are about to be urged to engage the services of a solicitor and an accountant.

This advice is seldom popular for the obvious reason that you are being invited to undertake yet more expense when you are already fretting about raising the money to start up in business. Worse, money spent on lawyers and accountants could end up being wasted, with nothing to show for it at the end other than a shattered dream. Well, that's one way of looking at it. Certainly, if after studying the details of the franchise your accountant or solicitor throws up his hands and declares that he would not touch the project with a bargepole, even assuming he had one to hand, your investment in time and money would have come to naught. But there's another way of looking at it, and that is that you will have had a lucky escape. Far better to spend a few hundred pounds on professional fees than lose thousands, not to mention your sense of well-being, pride and possibly your hair, in a venture that was doomed to fail from the outset.

But that is an extreme case. If you have followed the advice in this book you are unlikely to have got this far advanced in buying a duff franchise. You will be reasonably confident that you have picked a winner. But that too presents a problem if your confidence becomes such that you think you can dispense with professional advice. Believe me, it would be most unwise to do so. For there are plenty of things that can go wrong that fall well short of total business failure but are nevertheless costly and an irritating distraction from actually running the business. To take an example hinted at earlier, suppose you bought an existing franchise and later discovered that you were liable for debts incurred by the previous franchisee; you would be aggrieved, and rightly so. If only you had taken legal advice…

An accountant will, among other things, assess the feasibility of the profit and loss forecasts, advise you on the best way to raise finance, and help you to mitigate your tax liability. A lawyer will examine documents such as business transfer, property assignment and the franchise agreement, and will draw to your attention any implications of significance and advise you on any amendments that should be made to better protect your interests. Look on their fees as a form of insurance: you may not like to pay the premiums but you get peace of mind. That said, the inestimable services outlined above cannot be provided by any old accountant or lawyer; what you need is a specialist. Franchising, though well developed in this country, is nevertheless something of a mystery to most people and that includes the learned professions. So don't expect your family lawyer to have a clue about franchise contracts.

However, one of the boons of a dynamic, enterprise economy is that ambitious people are for ever seeking out gaps in markets and duly filling them, and that applies as much to the professions as it does to any other sphere of life where success and money count. Consequently, the UK has a large and growing number of solicitors and accountants who specialize in franchising. Restrict your choice to one of these. You will find them either through asking your bank (as we have seen, the big high-street banks are keen on franchising and have access to knowledge which includes the names of sound professional advisers) or by looking at the list of advisers affiliated to the BFA (see the appendix at the end of this book). A list of names, though a start, is not much help in itself. What you want is someone who not only knows his or her stuff but is also the type of person you feel you can get on with. I am not saying your franchise lawyer or accountant should become a friend, though that is always possible, just that he or she should be personable and approachable, and be in possession of the priceless ability to translate sometimes complex matters into clear and plain English. How do you find out these things? Well, you interview a few until you find one you like, or, put another way, if the first one you meet does not appeal to you, find another. It's important to appoint an adviser whom you like, because the relationship is likely to be a continuing one. Indeed, I would go further than that and say it *should* be a continuing one. As your business develops and grows, you may from time to time need legal advice; you will certainly need regular accountancy help in preparing your accounts for tax purposes. The better and longer established your relationship with your advisers, the better they will know you and your business. If you chop and change advisers, you miss out on this important advantage.

Now, what about professional fees? There is common agreement in pubs and clubs and on street corners that the professions charge too much. Everyone has his or her story of lawyers who, like taxi drivers, start a meter the moment you climb aboard and rub their hands as the total ratchets ever upwards. The truth is that professional expertise does not come cheap. What is important is to discuss in advance how fees are going to be calculated and to ask for an estimate of the likely total cost. Don't be embarrassed about this – you are a businessperson now and the language of business is money. Advisers don't like to work on a fixed-cost basis for the good reason that unexpected problems can arise and handling them takes time. The practice is to charge on an hourly basis, so you should ask how many hours are likely to be involved in handling your business and, most important, you should also ask to be kept informed if any unforeseen expenses are being incurred. Better to find out in advance than to clap your hand to your forehead when you get the final bill. Incidentally, if you are not happy with the final invoice, mention it straight away. Delaying payment will put you in the wrong and make the other party more determined than ever to extract the full amount.

Should you follow the advice of your professional advisers? Daft question, you may say. You've paid them for their opinion, it would surely be folly to ignore it. In almost all cases that would indeed be the case, but there may be times when you disagree with your advisers, or are prepared to use your judgement to take a risk that they, in their cautious profes-sional way, would prefer were avoided. In the end the decision is yours. Advisers do exactly that – they advise; they are not there to tell you what to do. However, you are paying for their judgement, experience and knowledge of your particular case and you should note carefully what they have to say. If you disagree with the advice you are given, don't be afraid to declare your misgivings and discuss the matter further.

Finally, before we leave the topic of advisers, do remember the impor-tance of being frank with them. Never withhold any information. The quality of the output you get from your advisers will be determined in part by the quality of the input you give them.

If, as is so often said, franchising is like a marriage, you are reaching the point where the church doors beckon and the altar is in sight. This is no time for second thoughts, or is it? Marriage guidance counsellors always arrive too late, when the union is in trouble and an irretrievable breakdown is a possibility. What are needed are pre-marriage counsellors, people brave or foolhardy enough to say 'Are you sure you want to go ahead with this? It's not too late to back out now, you know.'

Let the final few paragraphs of this chapter serve that purpose. Of course the aim of this book is, in part, to extol franchising and to encourage the reader to make the most of what could and should be a great opportunity to strike out afresh and take on a new and rewarding challenge. But it is also the author's purpose to help you avoid making a mistake that could be costly both in terms of money and of emotional hurt. So, before it's too late and you press on to the next stages – signing the franchise agreement and raising the money – ask yourself 'Do I want to go ahead with this?' It's not too late to back out now, you know.

I want you to mull over these questions and answer them honestly:

■ The franchise you have chosen, is it really right for you? Can you see yourself being wholeheartedly involved in providing whatever good or service is involved and, what is just as important, actually enjoying it? Does the franchise suit you and do you suit the franchise?

■ Do your researches convince you that the business is capable, in time, of generating the kind of income that will not only meet your needs but satisfy your ambitions?

■ Still on the subject of money, will you be taking on too much? In other words, do the figures add up? Knowing what you do about the amount you will have to borrow and the projected income the business will provide, does it sound manageable, or is there a danger that you might be financially stretched to the point where sleepless nights are a possibility?

■ How is your energy, mental as well as physical? And what of your appetite for work? Franchising, in common with all forms of self-employment, can be a demanding, unforgiving master. Franchisees don't skive, they don't take sickies, they don't complain of Monday morning feelings (or if they do, they quickly forget about it), they just buckle down and get on with the job in hand.

Summed up, this last-minute, pre-marriage advice is, don't be rushed. The franchisor, having gone to the trouble and expense of satisfying himself that you are a good candidate, will understandably want to press you into reaching a quick decision. Don't let him. Don't heed the sales patter 'when it's gone, it's gone' or 'only a few left'. Buying a franchise is a big decision to be taken after due reflection, not under pressure and against the clock.

Having weighed the pros and cons and satisfied yourself that the pros have it, it's time to take those first steps up the aisle, which, in the case of a franchise, means having a close look at the marriage licence.

The most common snares and pitfalls

When franchisees fail it's usually because they have overlooked the elementary precautions needed to assess a business opportunity. Avoid the following:

■ Trying to get by without advisers. This is a false economy that can later lead to bitter regret.

■ Skipping over the legal stuff. Read every document that the franchisor gives you – the franchise agreement in particular and any other documents such as leasehold papers – and of course see that your lawyer goes through them carefully. If any points need clarifying, get the answers in writing.

■ Taking the franchisor at his word. Don't accept verbal assurances. Always ask for every undertaking to be put in writing. Take notes at your meetings with the franchisor.

■ Not talking to existing franchisees. Meet several, preferably of your own choosing. Try to talk to a cross-section – franchisees in different kinds of locations, franchisees with more than one outlet, franchisees who have been in business a long time, franchisees who are still new, franchisees who are successful, franchisees who are not doing so well.

■ Not checking out failed franchises. If during your research you find that some franchise outlets have failed, dig deeper into the reasons why.

■ Not having enough working capital. Don't allow yourself to be financially stretched from the very beginning. You must have enough money to see you through to break-even.

■ Being too optimistic about your prospects. The processes of raising finance, drawing up a business plan and making forecasts of profit and loss must be realistic and should err on the side of caution.

■ Not doing market research. This is the most elementary blunder of all. Never assume a product or service is so good that buyers will inevitably materialize.

■ Underestimating the need to sell. A life in business is not for the shy or retiring and customers will not beat a path to your door unbidden.

7 Signing on the dotted line

Like all legal documents, the franchise agreement is a man-made curiosity. It is at once a piece of paper of no intrinsic worth and the priceless key to the entire franchise relationship. Like the treasure island map marked with a cross where the loot is buried, the franchise agreement contains all you need to know to make your future assured. Its importance cannot be overstated. In those few pages are the terms and conditions of the franchise and the detailed obligations of both parties. The world over, wherever business format franchising exists, the agreement is the cornerstone on which everything else is built. But in the UK, which, unlike some other countries, has no special legislation governing franchising, the legal contract is doubly important. Should there be a dispute between franchisee and franchisor it is to the terms of the agreement that the lawyers will turn and on which the resolution of the disagreement will hinge. What is not in the agreement could turn out to be as important as what is: if the franchisor makes promises, presents you with financial forecasts, or solemnly puts his hand on his heart and pledges to undertake this or that in your interest, if it isn't in the contract it's not worth the air on which the words were spent.

The franchise agreement serves four main purposes:

1. Most obviously, it puts into writing what is agreed between the two parties. The aim is to avoid future disputes, but also to help resolve them should they occur.
2. It sets out to protect both parties from the infringement of the franchisor's intellectual property, in other words his know-how, brand identity, secret formulae and so on.
3. It ensures uniformity, which is one of the most important features of franchising.
4. It lays down certain standards of operation.

For a franchise network to operate harmoniously it is important that every franchisee plays by the same rules and under the same conditions. So every franchisee should have exactly the same agreement with the franchisor. Beware, then, the franchisor who offers you special terms or conditions: it could be that he is over-eager to sell you a franchise, and over-eager salespeople are never to be trusted. And what is to say that he isn't cutting different deals across the whole network? In which case he is surely sowing the seeds of future discord and resentment.

It is quite common for the franchise agreement to come in two parts. The first is the **purchase agreement**. Essentially, this is a declaration by both parties that they are in earnest and want to go ahead with a full agreement provided certain conditions are met. The signing of the purchase agreement is the signal for both parties to get moving. You, the prospective franchisee, will approach the bank to explain the wonderful opportunity on which you are about to embark and to ask for the finance to support the project. The franchisor will set about assessing the area where you plan to open your outlet, looking for suitable premises, preparing cash-flow figures, arranging for your training and checking your references. When you sign the purchase agreement you will be asked to pay a deposit to cover the costs incurred by the franchisor in doing his bit to get you started. It is possible that these early, exploratory forays into your franchise may come to nothing. The bank might perversely fail to perceive the merit in you and your venture (though if you have done your research and shown what the lawyers call due diligence, such a disappointment is unlikely); the franchisor, having looked closely at your chosen area, might fail to see its potential. A failure at this stage, though obviously disappointing, could be for the best. After all, if, say, no suitable premises can be found at the right price, there is little point in proceeding. Or if the premises the franchisor finds are not to your liking, you would be getting off to a bad start. All in all, if these first steps reveal flaws it is better to quit than to press ahead and be sorry later. I would stress, however, that such an outcome is unlikely unless either you or the franchisor has been careless in doing the initial research or less than honest with each other. If the deal breaks down at this stage, what about your deposit – will you get it back? That will depend on the reason for the breakdown. If the franchisor cannot find a suitable site or cannot satisfy himself that your chosen area is viable, then you may be entitled to a full refund. If, on the other hand, he has found suitable premises and you, for whatever reason, don't like them and decline to go ahead, you might lose your deposit, or part of it. Either way there is potential for the kind of wrangling that benefits no one apart from the lawyers, so the purchase agreement should make plain from the outset the terms under which a refund is obtainable should things not turn out as planned.

Assuming all goes well, the franchisor's feasibility studies are encouraging and the bank manager sits up and shows some interest, the **franchise agreement** proper will be produced. The agreement will cover two phases of your transition from applicant into fully fledged franchisee.

In the **first phase**, the franchisor shoulders most of the obligations. This is when he brings his experience and muscle to bear in setting up your business. He will busy himself in helping you to raise finance and in training you. If you need business premises, he will go ahead and negotiate a property deal on your behalf and help with the shopfitting, installation of equipment and so on. If you need to employ staff, he will help with their selection and recruitment. If yours is a more modest, home-based, van-type franchise, he will help you to find a vehicle and possibly arrange for it to be painted in the company's colours. You, for your part, will pay for these setting-up costs and complete the training programme.

The **second phase** begins when you open your door and start trading. This is where the detail of the franchise agreement comes into play because it sets down the contractual obligations of both parties and, as you will see, the emphasis switches from franchisor to franchisee. That is to say, the franchisor will already have fulfilled many of his obligations to you during phase one; your obligations will be continuing for as long as the agreement lasts.

If you heed the advice in the previous chapter, you will have both the purchase agreement and the franchise agreement looked over by a lawyer and an accountant, both experienced in franchising. If, however, you decide to dispense with the services of expert advisers, don't blame me if things go wrong. Either way, you should read the documents thoroughly from front to back. They concern your future livelihood and you should do your best to understand all the legalities, issues, rights and entitlements that fall within the framework of the franchise. To help you in this, the following is a summary of the key points that the franchise agreement should cover. The details vary from franchise to franchise, but, broadly speaking, all agreements follow the same format and cover similar areas, though they will not necessarily appear in the order outlined below.

Typically the contract will outline the **nature of the franchise and its intellectual property**, ie what it does, its trademarks, copyright, methods of production, know-how and goodwill, and set out provisions for protecting those rights. It is important that these safeguards are embodied in the contract, to protect both the franchisor and the franchisee. The franchisor will want to guard against others – for example, a former franchisee – using his rights, and it is in the interests of the franchise network as a whole that intellectual property is protected. After all, one of the main reasons for buying a franchise is often that it has a well-known brand, which is a valuable asset in the marketplace. If the franchisor has not taken steps to protect that image and good reputation from imitators, it could result in a loss of business throughout the whole network.

The term, or length, of the contract will state how long the contract between franchisee and franchisor lasts, whether you have an option to renew it, and on what terms. The duration of a franchise agreement is as long as the proverbial piece of string, but it should certainly be long enough to allow the franchisee to recoup his or her initial investment and show a reasonable return, so five years is a good round figure to have in mind. Generally speaking, the longer the agreement the better. The franchisee feels more secure knowing that he or she will be in business for a long time, and the franchisor doesn't have to worry about the franchisees terminating their contracts after a short period. At the end of the term there is often an option to renew for another term. This second agreement may not be on exactly the same terms as the original one because the renewal will have to match exactly the terms being agreed by new franchisees joining the network at that time, and they may be different from those you originally agreed. The point about this is that if you do want to renew, you should once again have your lawyer cast a forensic eye over the print large and small.

Territorial rights will state what area your franchise covers and whether you have exclusive rights to operate within it. Generally speaking, non-exclusivity favours the franchisor, while exclusivity leans towards the franchisee. Some franchisors don't like offering exclusivity lest it foster complacency in a franchisee. This is in spite of the fact that franchisees are recruited because they are highly motivated, hard-working, industrious souls who will beaver away in their own interest and, in doing so, benefit the franchisor. The experienced franchisor, however, knows human nature for what it is. He suspects that within every franchisee who attains a comfort zone there lurks a tendency to luxuriate within its confines. Competition, thinks the hard-hearted franchisor, is good for the soul and keeps the franchisee on his or her toes. One way around the problem is to grant exclusivity but also to set performance targets as an alternative means of ensuring the franchisee keeps his or her shoulder to the wheel. That, however, is a problematic solution since it carries the difficulty of what exactly to do if the targets are not met. There could be disputes, and disputes mean lawyers, and lawyers mean expense. A better answer, from the franchisor's point of view, is to grant exclusive rights for a limited period only. Again, this is a point to look out for, and your lawyer should ensure that your agreement sets out the terms under which the franchisor can change your territorial rights.

Fees and charges to be paid by the franchisee: the agreement will state the **initial fees** and what you get in return. They cover the costs of setting up your franchise unit and will probably be payable in instalments as and when the money is required for items such as materials and equipment. The timing of the payments should be stated plainly in the agreement, along with exactly what you are paying for. There may be circumstances in which whole or part of the initial fee is refundable. If, for example, the franchisor decides that you are not, after all, cut out to be a franchisee – perhaps you failed to impress during the training – you may be entitled to get your money back. If, on the other hand, you have second thoughts and decide not to go ahead, you will probably forfeit some or all of any initial fees that you might have paid. **Management services fees, or royalties**, form a central part of the contract. They are the reward the franchisor receives in return for the use of the franchise name, concept and system and are also used to cover the direct and indirect costs of providing continuing services. They are usually levied as a percentage of gross sales. (A cautionary word here: though the payment of fees is often a sore point, beware the franchisor who charges exceptionally low fees and advertises the fact as a selling point. Franchises have failed because they did not have sufficient fee income to sustain the business.) The size and timing of royalties should be clearly stated in the agreement, as should the method by which they are calculated. Here again, human nature has to be taken into account (lawyers are very good at taking cognizance of human frailty and devising ways of forestalling its consequences) and some franchisors might harbour the suspicion that franchisees, in order to mitigate their royalty payments, might be less than open in declaring the full extent of their sales. To protect himself against such a contingency the franchisor may insist that he has the right to examine the franchisee's books, stock levels, invoices and so on at any time and without warning. He may also insist on all franchisees in the network adopting uniform accountancy procedures so that he may make comparisons among them that could bring to light any suspicious anomalies. A further requirement might be that the franchisee produces profit and loss accounts at regular intervals and presents annual audited statements of accounts. If the franchisor receives his income not as a royalty on sales but as a **mark-up on goods sold** to the franchisee, the agreement should stipulate the size of the mark-up and the circumstances in which it might be changed. The advertising fund was covered in an earlier chapter. It is levied to pay for promotional activity on behalf of the whole franchise network and each franchisee will be required to contribute to it. The terms and size of such contributions should be plainly stated in the agreement, along with details of how it is proposed that the money will be spent, ie how it will be divided among national advertising, local advertising, public relations campaigns and so on.

It is usual for all parties in any legal agreement to accept certain obligations to the other parties, and these form a central part of the franchise contract. Let us deal with each in turn, beginning with the obligations of the franchisor.

He will undertake to **train the franchisee** and his staff. The relevant clauses should state details such as when the training takes place, for how long, and who pays for it, though it will come as no surprise to learn that the franchisee normally foots the bill for training.

He will **supply equipment** and advise and assist the franchisee in obtaining all materials, stock and other goods needed to run the outlet, the franchisee being liable for the cost of these items.

He will be responsible for **advertising, marketing and promotional activity** using the funds paid by the network for these purposes.

He will help the franchisee to **find suitable business premises** and where necessary provide designs and advice for fitting out the property and converting it into a franchised outlet. In the case of a van-based franchise, similar considerations apply to acquiring a suitable vehicle and fitting it out. Any subsequent alterations to designs, decor, etc can be carried out only with the approval of the franchisor.

He will provide an **operations manual**. This should be comprehensive and comprehensible. It remains the property of the franchisor and the franchisee must maintain its confidentiality. Franchisees also undertake to adopt any subsequent additions or revisions, to treat the manual as holy writ and to abide by its rules.

He will provide **continuing help and advice** throughout the term of the contract. Quite how this works in practice will come down to the common sense of both parties. Though a responsible franchisor will always be ready to help out when difficulties arise or advice is sought (after all, it's in his interests to do so), he will probably draw the line at, say, persistent daily pleas for help. In other words, the amount of help you get is ultimately a matter for the franchisor to decide.

He will provide **records** such as sales reports and accounts forms to help the franchisee to keep accurate financial records. He may also provide certain **management and accounting services.**

He will undertake to **improve, enhance and develop the business system**. From the franchisee's point of view this is a good obligation to be placed on the franchisor. Every successful business needs to evolve and adapt over time and the franchisor must be dissuaded from sitting back and luxuriating in his achievements while the franchisees toil like serfs in the fields.

For his (or her) part the franchisee undertakes obligations designed to protect the franchisor's reputation and goodwill, which really comes down to maintaining standards.

He will agree to **conduct himself and his business** in such a way as not to discredit or denigrate the reputation of the business or its name.

He will **comply with the systems and methods** set out in the operations manual. The aim of this clause is to ensure as far as possible that the quality of goods and/or services provided by franchisees is the same throughout the network. This is one of the most important features of franchising. Without uniform standards of quality there is no franchise.

He will undertake to **keep the premises in a good state** of repair. An enthusiasm for order and cleanliness is not bestowed on human beings in equal measures. Some people contrive to work well and efficiently in surroundings that might appal others. Franchising, however, strives to abide by the notion that, whether or not cleanliness is next to godliness, it is certainly desirable when one is inviting the public on to the premises and, in some cases, such as places where food is served, is a statutory requirement.

He will **maintain staff numbers and standards** consistent with running an efficient outlet to the high levels of performance expected by the franchisor.

He will at all times endeavour to **protect and promote the goodwill of the business**. Goodwill is an important asset of any business and is usually built up painstakingly over a period of time. As with any reputation, however, the work of years can be undone in a careless few minutes. Just as word-of-mouth recommendation can bestow riches on a business, word-of-mouth slagging-off can do untold damage. Franchisees should be aware of this at all times.

He will undertake to allow the franchisor or his representatives free and unrestricted access to his outlet for any purpose, including checking to see the franchisee is maintaining standards, abiding by the rules and paying his dues.

You will see from the above obligations undertaken by both parties to the agreement that franchising is a pretty closely regulated and ordered relationship between franchisor and franchisee. It has to be in order to maintain standards and uniformity, which are the essence of the business format system. People who are by temperament and nature cut out for franchising are those who accept laid-down systems and methods and see the need to abide by them. Others who are more freebooting and entrepreneurial may well find the demands placed upon them within the confines of a franchise relationship too restrictive and irksome. You, however, having passed the questionnaire earlier in this book, will know what you are letting yourself in for and should have no trouble in meeting your obligations. You know that in exchange for your investment you are getting a tried and tested way of doing business and you appreciate that it is not for you, a newcomer, to question the procedures that have been shown to work.

That said, franchise relationships do occasionally break down when, for whatever reason, one party or the other wishes to terminate the contract before it has run its full term. This possibility is covered by the franchise agreement.

Termination of the contract

The agreement must state the possible grounds for termination and the parties' rights in the event that it does happen. Termination usually allows the franchisor to reclaim premises, property and rights that are legally his. The franchisee tends not to have as many rights if the contract is ended prematurely, so it is important that you understand fully the consequences of getting out early.

Under **termination by the franchisor** the agreement will probably contain something along the following lines:

The franchisor shall have the right in his absolute discretion to terminate the agreement for cause (which shall include but not be limited to a breach by the franchisee of any obligation, covenant or duty contained herein) by giving written notice to the franchisee not less than 30 days prior to the date of termination and stating the reason for termination.

If the notice of termination states that the cause for termination may be remedied then the franchisee shall have the right to remedy the same within 30 days and if all such causes are remedied to the satisfaction of the franchisor then he shall withdraw such notice.

The franchisor, therefore, assumes pretty wide powers to get rid of a franchisee who breaks the rules or in some other way transgresses. This 'nuclear option' should be invoked only if the franchisee is in serious breach of the agreement (fiddling the books, for example), but you should check the agreement carefully to make sure the franchisor is not able to terminate the contract on a whim.

Under **termination by the franchisee** the agreement may stipulate a period (say 36 months) from the starting date of the agreement after which the franchisee is free to terminate the contract. It will then set down the procedure to be followed, ie to give written notice and to surrender the lease (if any). It will also require the franchisee to pay any debts he owes to the franchisor (and to anyone else in connection with the business), to cease to represent himself as a franchisee, and to return stationery and other materials, including the operations manuals. There will also be a requirement for the franchisee to surrender any leasehold interest and any fixtures or fittings. The franchisor will pay the franchisee the market value of these assets.

Now, looking further down the line, suppose you have been running your franchise for a number of years. All has gone well, you have traded successfully, and through your efforts added value to the business. But now you have had enough. You decide that, as with all good things, it has come to an end. How do you cash in your chips? Sadly and unavoidably, we must also consider at this stage what happens should you hand in your dinner pail; for it is the unfortunate duty of lawyers to draw attention to our mortality and to provide for its consequences.

But first let's consider the happier of the two circumstances. You've built up your asset and want to retire or move on, so how do you go about selling your franchise?

The agreement sets out in detail the conditions that apply to a franchise sale. In particular, and not unexpectedly, it makes clear the franchisor's right to have a say in deciding on the suitability of a potential purchaser. Expressed legally, that will probably be put in words such as 'a respectable and responsible person with the personal capacity and financial ability to perform the obligations of a franchisee under the Franchise Agreement. Furthermore, the prospective transferee shall at his own cost take and complete the training required of all new franchisees'. Since the franchisor reserves the right to decide who shall take over the franchise, he might offer to undertake the sale on your behalf. There is something to be said for this. Franchisors are used to selling franchises and presumably good at it, and you will be saved the trouble of putting your outlet on the market yourself. You will, of course, want to be consulted as to the asking price, and, since it is your asset that is being sold, only you can agree the sale. If the franchisor disposes of the business on your behalf he will probably levy a charge for arranging the sale. Be sure to know in advance how much that will be.

A franchisee wishing to sell might under the terms of the agreement be obliged to give the franchisor the opportunity to buy back the franchise ahead of any other potential buyer. This raises the problem of how the business is to be valued. After all, if you offer it for sale on the open market, the laws of supply and demand will determine the price you get. But if there is only one buyer, namely the franchisor, who is to say what a fair price might be? The agreement should therefore state clearly the basis on which the business is to be valued.

Bear in mind that when you give up a franchise you are normally prevented under the terms of the agreement from starting a similar business in competition with the franchisor for a specified time after the sale, perhaps 18 months or more. You are also prevented from disclosing any confidential information about the franchise, such as the contents of the operations manual, pricing policy or accounting systems, after the agreement is terminated.

By and large franchisees are a healthy and happy breed (wasn't one of the sections in the self-assessment test about how fit you are?), but they are not, alas, immortal, and so the agreement must perforce stipulate what is to happen should an incumbent franchisee die. On the death of a sole franchisee, his representatives will have a specified time, often six months from the date of death, to inform the franchisor of their decision either to assign the business to any of the heirs of the franchisee or to a third party (in which case the franchisor must be satisfied that the new owners are suitable and fit people to run the business, and they for their part must go through the training programme) or to terminate the agreement and sell the business for its market value. On the death of joint franchisees, it is usual for the surviving franchisee or franchisees to succeed in all respects to the rights of the deceased franchisee.

OK, that's the legal stuff taken care of. Now we move on from contemplating death to the invigorating prospect of meeting the bank manager.

Things that you – or better still, your lawyer – should look out for in a franchise agreement

You will have to accept at the outset that the contract will be one-sided, and that side is not yours.

For example, the franchisor may:

- reserve the right to make changes to the operations manual at any time and require the franchisee to comply with the changes even though they were not in the original agreement;
- insist that if the franchisee signs on for a second term, he or she will have to sign the current form of the franchise agreement, which may be substantially different from the earlier version;
- include widely drafted cancellation clauses in favour of himself;
- reserve the sole right to decide how advertising funds are spent even though the money is provided by the franchisee network;
- reserve the right to take over the day-to-day running of an outlet if he thinks a franchisee is performing poorly.

Pointless to complain, though. The franchisor will argue, with some justification, that the franchise agreement must be strong to ensure maintenance of standards throughout the network.

All the same, some agreements may go too far in swinging the balance in favour of the franchisor. For example, he might:

- stipulate that any costs incurred in defending the use of the trademark should be met by the franchisees;
- provide for the right of the franchisor to cancel the agreement without notice if the franchisee misses or delays payment of royalties;
- omit clauses providing for ongoing support and training and development of the business;
- limit the franchisor's liability to the franchisee even if he breaches his obligations to the franchisee;

▌ allow for the franchisees' exclusive territory to be eroded in circumstances to be decided by the franchisor.

These sorts of clauses can be challenged, though often without much effect, since the franchisor will in all probability insist that one rule applies to all, and he cannot make changes to suit the qualms of an individual franchisee.

The point is that a new franchisee must read and understand what he or she is signing up to. And it is the job of a properly qualified franchise lawyer to draw his clients' attention to the full implications of everything in the agreement. If you enter an agreement open-eyed and forewarned, there is less chance of shocks later.

8 Winning over the bank

In a bygone, deferential age when every man wore a hat, the expression to 'go cap in hand' had a literal as well as metaphorical meaning. The servant standing before his master or the supplicant before a potential benefactor would remove his cap as a sign of respect and probably bow his head too. Long after hats ceased to be worn (baseball caps don't count since they are the least deferential form of headgear), we still went cap in hand to beg a favour and no more so than when meeting the bank manager. (It is no accident that the above refers entirely to men: though women continued to wear hats some time after men had stopped, it was barely thinkable that a woman should step into a bank and ask for a loan, at least not without a husband in tow.) How things have changed! In this egalitarian age, deference has gone out of the window and we can all, every one of us, male and female, stride confidently into a bank or building society and, if not quite demand a loan, at least expect a polite hearing. We have changed and so have the banks. We no longer wear cloth caps and the bankers no longer wear suits, or not all of them anyway. In fact, so keen are the banks to appear approachable and friendly that some of their senior management feel they may have gone too far. One of the big high-street banks finds it necessary to ban staff from wearing, among other things, denims, shorts, flip-flops, strapless tops, sportswear, logo-bearing T-shirts and trainers. Instead, bank employees who meet customers are asked to wear suits and ties, or, if female, dresses, suits and blouses. You can see what the bank is getting at: a request for, say, a business loan is a serious matter with, as we shall see, many solemn details to be discussed. While there is no logical reason to prevent negotiations from being conducted by a banker dressed in beachwear, it would be, to use a phrase favoured by politicians wriggling on a hook, inappropriate.

So it is fair to conclude that the banks, though less stuffy than they were, are still mindful of the seriousness of their business (it would be worrying if they weren't) and keen to retain a measure of dignity in their approach, if not always in their appearance. And potential borrowers, though no longer cap in hand, still see an interview with the bank manager as marginally preferable to a visit to the dentist. So, for all the superficial changes in banks and bankers, raising finance is still a task to be undertaken with preparation and care and with due regard for the proprieties that lie beneath the smiling surface of modern lending institutions. To secure the best outcome from your meeting you need to be smart, both in appearance and in the presentation of your case.

As a potential franchisee, however, you start off with a considerable advantage over less fortunate souls trying to start a business all on their own. Sometime back in the 1970s, British banking discovered franchising and, fairly quickly by banking standards, grew to like what it saw. Bankers are by nature and training cautious folk. They have no choice. They keep a certain amount of money in reserve to cover bad debts, but if a bank were to lend unwisely and word got out that it was in trouble there could be a panic among depositors and that would be catastrophic. If a large number of customers try to withdraw their money at once, there would not be enough in the reserves to pay them all. The very thought of such a calamity is enough to have a banker wake up in the night screaming, which is why he errs on the side of caution. Just as a digression, it might interest you know that the money the bank lends to you is in a sense 'invented' by the bank. This is how it works: Mr Jones deposits £1 with the bank. This allows the bank to 'create' another £1 to lend to Mrs Smith and charge her interest. Note that the bank does not lend Mr Jones's £1 to Mrs Smith, it keeps it in the reserves. Now, the secret genius of banking is that when Mrs Smith pays back the £1 – money, remember, that came into being only because the bank lent it to her – the bank keeps it and adds it to its reserves. And it's had the interest too! No wonder economist J K Galbraith called the system of creating money through making loans 'so simple it repels the mind'.

Anyway, less repellent to contemplate is that the banks think well of franchising. They like it because it removes some of the risk of lending to a new small business. When any old Joe walks into a bank and asks for money to help launch a new enterprise, his business idea, however brilliant, is almost certain to be untested and his record unknown. He will have a lot to prove and a lot of hurdles to jump if he is to have any chance of wringing a penny or two from the lender. The franchisee, by contrast, will be starting with a tried and tested system, and he will have satisfied the exacting standards of recruitment set by a reputable franchisor. (He may of course fall short of those standards. The franchise may be new and relatively untried, the franchisor likewise. But the banks are nothing if not canny, and they will know a franchise by its reputation, and adjust the lending criteria accordingly.) The banks were impressed by figures showing that whereas most new start-ups go the way of all flesh, most new franchise outlets succeed. It would be an exaggeration to say that they rubbed their hands in glee – banks are too serious and unemotional for that – but they warmed to franchising all the same, and in 1981 NatWest became the first to set up a central unit dedicated to franchising. Others have since followed, and today Bank of Scotland, HSBC, Lloyds TSB and the Royal Bank of Scotland all have departments specializing in franchising. They watch the industry carefully, monitoring developments, recording comings and goings and compiling records on individual franchise companies. This information is available to the branch network and obviously influences lending decisions at local level. In fact, so keen are the banks on franchising that they want everyone to know and are happy, indeed eager, to have their names linked to the industry. For instance, NatWest sponsors the annual survey of franchising, HSBC sponsors the Franchisor and Franchisee of the Year Awards, and Lloyds TSB has helped finance research into the franchising sector by the University of Westminster. All in all, then, when you step through the portals of your branch bank and announce yourself as a prospective franchisee you can expect the orange carpet treatment, which is similar to the red carpet treatment though not quite so unquestioningly warm.

There is another way in which banking has changed since the days when branch managers wore wing collars. The manager is no longer lord of all he surveys, pillar of the Rotary Club and in a job for life. These days, local bank managers come and go like dancing partners in a ladies' excuse-me, but not to worry, you won't be dealing with the latest incumbent, you will almost certainly be asked to meet a local business manager. He or she will be trained in assessing business loans and will know something about franchising. Any gaps in their knowledge will be filled by information supplied by the franchising unit. So before they meet you they will almost certainly have mugged up on the franchise company in which you plan to invest and will already have formed a view of its standing. Armed with that knowledge, they will want to discuss in detail your proposed outlet, your ability to run it, and the amount and kind of financial help you will require.

There is another reason why you can consider yourself fortunate in your dealings with the bank: so persuaded are banks that franchising is a good bet compared to other business start-ups that they are prepared to lend to prospective franchisees on advantageous terms. Whereas an independent start-up can expect to borrow no more than half of the total cost of setting up, a franchisee may be able to borrow as much as 70 per cent, provided the franchise is well established and with a sound record. Not only that, you may be charged less interest than an independent start-up and asked to produce less in the way of security to support your loan. But before showing just how generous he can be, the business manager will go through the time-honoured process of assessing you as a suitable recipient. He will consider your application under the following headings.

The borrower, otherwise known as you

The bank will want to satisfy itself that you are a fit person to be in receipt of its generosity. With all the caginess inherent in its nature it will need to be as certain as is possible that a) you can be trusted to repay the loan and b) that you are capable of making a go of the venture on which you are about to embark. To the best of its ability it will look into your background, training, qualifications, experience, and suitability to run a business. The franchisor will already have done all those things and given you the thumbs-up. The bank will take that into account but will want to go over the same ground again just to make sure that you come up to scratch.

The amount you want, or need, to borrow

As mentioned above, the bank may be willing to lend as much as 70 per cent of the cost of setting up your outlet. It won't go any higher because the payment of interest on the loan will come out of the cash flow of your business, and if in the bank's opinion you borrow too much it could place an impossible strain on the venture. That leaves you to find the remaining 30 per cent – sometimes known as 'hurt money' because it's painful to part with it. The bank is rather particular about where this money comes from; it will insist that it is from your own savings and not borrowed from some other source. This is partly because you should be seen to be shouldering some of the risk in starting and running your own business, but also because, as mentioned above, too much indebtedness could spell collapse.

The nature of the business

The business manager will have briefed himself on the franchise company. He will know what it does and how successful it has been, and will have formed an idea of its future prospects. But he will not know about the particular outlet you propose to open and will therefore probe deeply into its viability. Inevitable questions are: 'What is the likely strength of demand for the product or service in the locality where you are setting up?', 'How much will you have to sell to break even?', 'What assumptions have you made about cash flow?' The good thing about these questions is their very predictability. You know they are coming, so you can rehearse your responses beforehand. The franchisor will brief you. Expect also the obvious questions 'What is the purpose for which the money is to be used?' and 'How will the money borrowed benefit the business?' Again, you should prepare your answers and use this opportunity to exude enthusiasm and zip.

The nature of the loan

Now that you are about to be a capitalist, you need to know about capital, which, for your purposes, comes in two kinds – fixed and working. Incidentally, the definition of capital is 'wealth in the form of money or other assets owned by a person or organization or available or contributed for a particular purpose such as starting a company or investing'. So now you know.

Fixed capital is an accounting term that describes tangible property used in the operation of a business, such as buildings, machinery, fixtures, furniture and equipment. **Working capital** includes items normally consumed in the course of business operation or production. It measures how much in liquid assets a company has available to build its business. The number can be positive or negative, depending on how much debt the company is carrying. In general, companies that have a lot of working capital are more successful since they can expand and improve their operations. Companies with negative working capital may lack the funds necessary for growth.

Now for the purposes of putting the squeeze on the bank manager, the point to grasp is that the two different types of capital are usually funded in different ways. The fixed capital is financed through a **term loan**, which is a loan repaid in regular periods, usually over a period of 1–10 years, and the working capital is covered by an **agreed overdraft facility**. The best feature of an overdraft is its flexibility – you dip into the facility only as and when the need arises and pay only for the funds you use.

Depending on the nature and requirements of your business, the bank will tailor-make a combination of term loan and overdraft to fit the bill. Or, if your chosen franchise is among those that the bank has chosen to smile on, there may be an off-the-peg finance package available. Developed in cooperation with the franchisor, these packages have a number of advantages: because the bank has confidence in the franchise company, the lending process may be speeded up; the terms of the loan may be more favourable than those offered to franchises less well known to the bank; and they are the nearest thing you will get to the bank manager bowing and sweeping his hat low in a deferential and welcoming gesture.

Repaying the loan

The bank will want to know, quite simply, where the money to repay the loan is going to come from. The answer is usually from future trading profits and the bank will scrutinize the cash-flow forecast (more of which later) to reassure itself that sufficient funds will be left after allowing for all your other financial commitments. It will also be reassured if you have a contingency plan in place to mitigate any setbacks. Let the bank know that you are flexible and can cut back where appropriate during a downturn. In addition, remind them of the value of your collateral, which brings us to the next heading.

Security

No one likes to lose money but the banks positively hate it. Although lending to a new business must of necessity always be something of a gamble (though the bank would never use the word, preferring the term 'calculated risk'), the professional lender prefers the kind of bet that cannot fail. Although in theory the bank will say that security against a loan is required only after a considered evaluation of your business proposal, in practice, no matter how strong the business plan and how promising the forecasts, you will need to support your loan with collateral such as a legal charge over a residential property with sufficient equity, a life policy, commercial property, debenture or personal guarantees. So, if you have security to cover partially or fully the amount you want to borrow, offer it at the outset. It will help forestall the unease that forever lurks within the breast of a lending manager. However, before providing security it is strongly recommended that you take advice from your solicitor, who will examine and explain the legal implications and possible consequences of, say, using your family home as collateral.

What if you have no security to offer the bank? Do not despair, help may be on hand in the unlikely shape of HM Government, an institution normally associated with extracting money from businesses rather than putting it in, and in wrapping small firms in rules and regulations, rather than liberating them to flourish and grow. However, the Department of Trade and Industry has a Small Business Service, which operates a Loans Guarantee Scheme for the benefit of start-ups and young businesses that have not been able to obtain a conventional loan because they lack assets to offer as security. The bank still decides whether or not you are a good bet but takes comfort from the fact that if it lends you the money the government will guarantee up to 75 per cent of the loan. You, the borrower, pay a 2 per cent premium on the outstanding balance of the loan. The scheme will guarantee loans of up to £250,000 with terms of up to 10 years. The bank will advise you on applying for a Small Firms Loans Guarantee and, since a big chunk of your loan will be underwritten by the Treasury, your friendly bank business manager should find it in his heart to grant you a favourable interest rate.

The business plan

But long before the terms of a loan are thrashed out, the manager will have pored over your **business plan**. This document is central to your application for finance. Everything hinges on it. It will decide the difference between the bank bestowing upon you a firm, warm handshake and a beaming smile or offering you nothing more than a sorrowful shake of the head. One high-street bank says: 'We endeavour to be open and honest in our dealings with our customers and are always keen to explain how we assess business proposals. Bank managers look first and foremost at the character, ability and experience of the business owner and the cash-generating capacity of the business itself. In this respect, it is essential to stress the importance of proper planning and forecasting before any meeting with the bank manager.'

The business plan is a blueprint of your proposed enterprise. It states in a detailed, logical and methodical way the nature of the business, the potential market, the strategy by which you intend to conquer that market, and the rewards you expect to reap. In addition to being informative, the plan should also be persuasive, though care must be taken not to overstate your case. The plan serves a number of purposes: it is your principal means of winning over the bank manager; it is an invaluable help in focusing your thoughts; and it is a standard by which you can judge your progress and performance as the business develops. So this vital document is a battle plan, an advertisement for yourself and your project, and a *vade mecum* on your path to success. Given the importance of the plan, how can you, a beginner, hope to squeeze the last drop from this opportunity? You are unlikely to have compiled such a document before; you may not be used to putting your thoughts into writing; you will probably be at a loss as to where to begin. But don't worry. Yet again, the franchisor, like the Fifth Cavalry, rides to your rescue. To him, the business plan is meat and drink. He's probably prepared dozens and knows what the bank manager wants to see. That does not mean, however, that you can sit back and watch the franchisor do all the work. If he is an old hand at producing plans, the bank manager is an old hand at reading them – he will know full well that the document is not all your own work. He will want to see that you have a comprehensive grasp of the plan in all its detail and can talk about it persuasively and knowledgeably. Two copies should be provided to the bank in advance of a meeting with the business manager: one for the manager to brief himself, the other in case he needs to refer to a lending official to gain sanction for the proposed lending. The document itself should look professional. It should be printed and well laid out in a clear and concise form.

There is no standard plan. They vary according to the type of business, the proposed location, and the person applying for the loan. That said, plans have a number of features in common. Typically, they are as follows.

The business

Arguably, the most important section of the plan is the introduction, or executive summary of your ambitions and objectives. This is the bank's first impression of your business. It must be brief and clear and highlight the key points. If the introduction is muddled or lengthy, your plan will be rejected straight away. In fact, according to one bank, the majority of plans that fail to win approval get off to a bad start.

Give a description of the product or service, its background and history, and a brief outline of its potential money-making properties, including its unique selling point, assuming it has one. In this introduction, take the opportunity to blow your own trumpet a little; say why you are keen to run your own business and why you will be good at it.

The market

Self-evidently central to the viability of the whole project, for a business without a market is like an actor without an audience. This is the part of the plan that will show you have done your homework and researched the potential in your own locality. A marketing plan sets clear, realistic and measurable targets and includes deadlines for meeting them.

Points to cover include:

- the likely size of the market in terms of people and money;
- the type of customers you will be targeting – for example, private or business;.
- the growth potential;
- your position in the market, ie where you product stands vis-à-vis the competition in terms of price, quality, and image;
- your competition – where it will come from, its size and strength, and why you are confident of being able to take it on;
- your marketing aims in terms of sales and market share;
- your marketing strategy – advertising, public relations, choice of media – leaflets, brochures, telephone sales and so on. Stress the brand recognition your franchise enjoys and the strength your fledgling business will derive from it.

Sales

Though often bracketed with marketing, sales is a separate topic requiring a section of its own. A sales plan, combined with sales forecasting, frees you to spend more time developing your business rather than responding to day-to-day developments in sales and marketing. It covers matters such as pricing, profit margin, sources of supplies, and credit facilities that you might receive from suppliers.

The people

Though a bank is most at ease when the conversation is about money, every lender to a business has to make a judgement about the quality of the person who is planning to run the enterprise. Institutional investors, such as fund management companies, will tell you that the most important consideration when deciding whether or not to back a venture is the quality of its management. A high-street bank lending to a start-up must make exactly the same kind of assessment and that means weighing up your experience and abilities and those of your staff if you plan to employ people. As a prospective franchisee you may have no previous business experience at all, but that does not mean that you lack the qualities needed to make a success of your venture. Play up your strengths. List your past experience, stress any organizational or managerial skills you have, and, above all, radiate enthusiasm. It will help if you come across as an open, confident, personable type, the sort who might be expected to charm customers and promote a business. This is also an opportunity to emphasize the training that you (and your staff) will receive.

Premises and equipment

This covers the place where you intend to work – from home, a shop, an office, a small industrial outlet – and lists costs such as fitting out the premises, business rates, insurance and rent. Location is such an important factor in running a business that the bank will want to know your plans in detail. Under the heading 'equipment' you list the items you need – tools, machinery, computer and the like – and whether you will be leasing or buying.

Finance

This is the section closest to the bank's heart. It sets out in detail every aspect of your proposed business that involves money – from what you will be putting in to what you will be getting out and the links that connect the two together. The financial information you provide forms the basis on which the bank will make its lending decision, so the more clear, detailed and logical the facts and figures, the happier the manager will be. The two key components of this financial presentation are the **projected profit and loss account** and the **cash-flow forecast**.

Start with a summary containing the following:

■ The forecast profit or loss for the first year.
■ The break-even point – the point at which your sales cover your overheads. Add up all your fixed costs and you will see how much sales revenue you will need to break even. Get past that point and wow, you're in profit and on your way to making the business hum.
■ While you are building sales the costs will still need to be covered, so explain how they will be funded – how much of your own money you are putting in and how much you will need from the bank.
■ Even the most unforgiving bank manager will concede that in order to build your business you will need to sustain yourself with creature comforts such as food, clothing and shelter, so give details of the money you will need to take out of the business to provide for yourself and your family.

Profit and loss forecast

This is a statement of your predicted sales minus your direct costs (costs incurred in making the sales) and overheads (wages, rent, rates, etc). For purposes of illustration, here is a simple example:

Forecast sales	£20,000
Cost of sales (materials needed to carry out the forecast work)	£5,000
Gross profit	£15,000
Overheads	£2,000
Net profit	£13,000
Drawings (the amount drawn out for personal living expenses)	£10,000
Retained profit	£3,000

Cash-flow forecast

Cash is the lifeblood of a business. You may have an impressive profit forecast but if you don't get paid, or get paid too late to pay staff and suppliers, you are in real trouble. Sadly, it is not uncommon for a small business to have to pay for materials in advance and then to be kept waiting for months for payment from customers to whom you have sold goods or services. This lag between making payments and receiving them can spell trouble for businesses that would otherwise be trading profitably. In this cruel world, where size means strength, when it comes to paying up on time the biggest firms are usually the worst offenders. Fortunately, most franchised businesses sell either to the public or to other small businesses and therefore seldom find themselves at the mercy of large firms. Better still, many franchises get cash on delivery, thus ensuring a healthy cash flow.

Even so, cash-flow forecasting helps you to predict peaks and troughs in your cash balance; to plan borrowing; to predict how much surplus cash you're likely to have at a given time; and to make the most efficient use of your resources. Having an accurate cash-flow forecast will help ensure that you can achieve steady growth without overtrading. You will know when you have sufficient assets to take on additional business – and, just as importantly, when you need to rein back.

A cash-flow forecast is a record of when you expect to get money into your business and when you expect to pay it out. The aim is to show the bank when your need for cash is likely to be at its greatest and to plan your funding accordingly. The forecast is usually done for a year or quarter in advance and divided into weeks or months. It is best to pick periods during which most of your fixed costs – such as salaries – go out. The forecast lists:

- receipts – cash from sales, cash from debtors;
- payments – payments to suppliers, cash purchases, rent, heating, lighting, etc;
- excess of receipts over payments – with negative figures shown in brackets;
- opening bank balance;
- closing bank balance.

Appendices

These contain additional detailed reference material, examples, statistics, CVs, etc, for reference and are not central to the main presentation of your plan.

The interview

Now all that stands between you and the finance you need to get your franchise off the ground is the bank manager's innate caution. To sweep that aside you have two means at your disposal: the business plan and yourself, by which I mean your winning persona, your powers of persuasion, your plausibility, all of which will be demonstrated at the interview. What!, I hear you say, I've never made a presentation, I'll be a bag of nerves, I'll be tongue-tied. All of which may be true, but none of which cannot be overcome by preparation. It's a bit like having to make a speech at a wedding reception. It's something you dread, but, without needing to be told, you know that the answer is to work out what you are going to say and rehearse it, and to keep on rehearsing until it comes naturally. It's the same when you are preparing to meet the bank manager. Practise your presentation in front of a mirror. If possible, cajole a relative or friend into some role-playing, with him or her acting the part of the manager. What the bank is looking for is a positive approach packed with commitment and enthusiasm. If you have rehearsed well and know your stuff, you cannot fail but come across as convincing.

Here is a brief guide to help you prepare for the interview. Forgive me if some points seem obvious, but every one of the rules has been broken in the past, so it does no harm to be reminded of them:

- **Punctuality**: don't keep the bank manager waiting. Not only is it impolite, it requires an apology, which immediately puts you at a disadvantage.
- **Dress**: don't look casual, it suggests a casual approach. If you have a suit, wear it. If not, still be neat and tidy. Check that your teeth are clean. Fragments of spinach on the incisors can be off-putting to the onlooker.
- **Eye contact**: this conveys sincerity and confidence. But don't overdo it. From time to time, look the manager in the eye. Don't fix him with a manic stare.
- **Understanding**: a sound knowledge of the information in your submission will set your mind at ease.
- **Confidence**: a well-planned and documented case must be sold to your bank manager. You have researched the proposal thoroughly and believe that it will succeed, so this must be communicated to the manager.
- **Clarity**: have five or six key points in mind – the most exciting and promising features of the enterprise. Put them across with enthusiasm.
- **A balanced approach**: take the bank manager through your business plan, elaborating where you think necessary. Because you will have sent him a copy in advance, he will probably raise questions as you go. Don't be put off your stride. Answer to the best of your ability and

don't, whatever you do, make up your response on the hoof. If you don't know the answer, say so, adding that you will provide the information later. The fact that you admit to the occasional uncertainty will help allay concerns the bank manager may have about over-confidence;

▌ **Professional assistance**: take the franchisor with you. His presence will be a confidence-booster, though not a substitute for your own knowledge and understanding of the business plan.

▌ **Interview objectives**: explain in detail your reason for seeking bank funding. This will enable the bank to inform you of the most appropriate type of funding to meet your business needs. Ensure you establish the correct amount that needs to be borrowed, allowing for unexpected expenses. Borrowing too much will cost you more interest than you need to pay, and too little may mean you need to return to the bank at a later date. Your objectives should aim to clarify:

  – the type of loan required;
  – your target interest rate;
  – the cost of setting up a loan;
  – the annual administration cost;
  – security needed.

If all goes well, and provided your plan and presentation were cogent and well structured, there is every reason to predict success, the loan will be yours and at long last you will be able to embark on the exciting phase of actually setting up your franchise and opening its doors for business.

A final word on bank lending: don't restrict your application to just one bank, shop around. It is important to research interest rates with different banks, and look at the services each bank's franchise unit offers to ensure that you are getting the best deal. Look at all five of the BFA's affiliated banks – Bank of Scotland, HSBC, Lloyds TSB, NatWest and The Royal Bank of Scotland. Don't just look at the finance but also the whole package. Some banks offer a period of free banking and the terms vary from bank to bank. If your application is strong and convincing, the banks will be keen to have your custom and so you may even have room for a little negotiation. Your position will be particularly strong if you get offers of support from more than one bank.

And do bear in mind that once the bank has lent you the money, that is not the end of your relationship. The business manager will keep an eye on your progress, partly to reassure himself that all is going according to plan but also to offer support and advice should you need it. It is sound business sense to keep him onside. You may require additional financial assistance – perhaps to overcome a temporary cash-flow problem or to invest in new equipment – and it is much easier to approach someone who knows and understands your business and has followed its progress from the beginning. A good bank business manager is more than just a trained lender of money. He will also know about the problems and challenges that confront small to medium-sized businesses and will give you the benefit of his advice. Make the most of him. Or her, which brings us swiftly to the next chapter....

Dance of the seven veils – or what your bank manager will want you modestly to reveal

1. How good is your chosen franchise? Is it well established? Does it have a good track record? Is it professionally run and operating in a viable market?
2. How good are you? What are your skills and experience? Will you be running the business on your own or with help from family or staff?
3. How supportive is your franchisor? Will he provide solid initial training and continuing back-up? Give details.
4. How much do you want to borrow? What is your financial position? What do you own? How much do you owe? How will you repay the loan? What security can you offer?
5. How will the business perform? Will it generate enough cash to pay creditors, meet all loan repayments and provide an adequate income for you as franchisee?
6. How clued up are you? Have you consulted a lawyer and an accountant? Do you understand the ins and outs of the franchise agreement?
7. How unblemished is your past? Have you run a business before? If so, how did it fare? What is your credit history?

9 Ladies (or should I say women) first

Anyone who puts pen to paper these days finds himself (there I go again – that presumptuous 'himself') torn between the dictates of grammar and the politics of feminism: whether to assume that the personal pronoun is masculine and thereby embark on a sea of troubles, or to use the clumsy 'he or she' and face the slings and arrows of irritated readers, or to use 'their' and bear the whips and scorns of pedants and grammarians. It is certainly ignobler in the mind to stumble awkwardly between all three, which is why I have chosen the masculine pronoun. Now, lest it be said that that is the choice of an unreconstructed male chauvinist, it is time quickly to make amends and set the record straight. Everything in this book applies with equal validity both to men and to women. Correction: franchising, dare it be said, is in some ways better suited to women than men. Just look at the facts:

■ Women are good at organizing – at coordinating activities and people efficiently.

■ Women are good at 'multi-tasking' – at handling and coordinating more than one activity at a time.

■ Women are good at 'prioritizing' – at deciding which of the activities and people they are handling and coordinating are more important than others, and treating them accordingly.

■ Women enjoy working with others towards a common goal.

■ Women are good at networking – listening to others and building relationships.

■ Women are willing to obey rules and follow systems rather than assume they know better.

■ Women tend to place more importance on being in a friendly congenial atmosphere than on building empires.

Doesn't all of that remind you of something? Doesn't it sound uncannily like the attributes most sought after by franchise companies looking for new recruits? Yes, it would seem that whatever deity it was that created franchising, she had women in mind. In a just and well-ordered world, then, you would expect that at least half of all franchisees would be women, and possibly more than half. But that is not the way it is. According to the NatWest/British Franchise Association 2005 Survey, 31 per cent of all new franchisees are women. So why are women under-represented in a sector that seems tailor-made to suit their abilities? Two possible explanations immediately suggest themselves – sex discrimination and lack of knowledge. There is some truth in both.

There is no evidence to suggest that franchise companies deliberately discriminate against women applicants. Rather it is a sin of omission. In other words, there is an assumption that applicants will be male and therefore a tendency to reflect that in recruitment activity. In 1999, employment lawyer Shelley Nadler published a study called *Is Franchising 'Female Friendly'?* She concluded:

> Happily we did not find any overt discrimination. However, many of the franchisors surveyed indirectly (and often unwittingly) discriminated against women by:
>
> (a) requiring the kind of business experience or technical skills that were more likely to be held by men than women who may have had career breaks bringing up a family;
>
> (b) not offering part-time working arrangements or by requiring high start-up or running costs that would make part-time working unprofitable; and
>
> (c) by using images and language in recruitment packs geared almost exclusively towards men.

Nor did the BFA escape her censure. The association, she said:

> had not yet addressed the issue of Equal Opportunities – it even refers to franchisees as 'he' on over 90 occasions in its Code of Ethics (2nd Edition)! It is easy to dismiss use of terms like 'chairperson' as 'political correctness' but changing language opens people's minds and facilitates changing attitudes and ultimately changed practices. Perhaps it is time for the BFA to actively champion the role of women in franchising. Given that the lack of suitable franchisees is putting a brake on the growth of franchising in the UK, the BFA should actively encourage franchisors to prioritize the review of their recruitment policies and materials with a view to attracting more female recruits.

But that was then, and things are changing. The British Franchise Association, in conjunction with Business Link, has won funding from the European Union to promote franchising to groups under-represented in the current franchise market. The association works in partnership with CREATE (creating equal access to enterprise), funded by the European Social Fund, to encourage over-fifties, under-thirties, ethnic minorities and women into franchising. There are encouraging signs that the policy is beginning to take effect. Since 1995, the number of franchisors setting out specifically to recruit women has tripled. And the banks, including HSBC and NatWest, are promoting information specifically tailored to the needs of women wanting to finance the purchase of a franchise. In 2005 the UK's largest franchising event, the National Franchise Exhibition, featured a women's networking zone for the first time.

The second reason why too few women consider franchising as a way of getting into business is, quite simply, that too few of them know of its existence. Too few men know about it either, but with women the problem is worse because many who do come across franchising turn away because they think the opportunities are restricted either to man-in-a-van operations in male-dominated industries or to traditional female roles such as cleaning, nursing and childcare. In truth, of course, the opportunities are huge and varied and almost without exception are as well suited to women as men.

There are reasons, some good, some bad, why franchise companies stand to gain from the current pattern of female employment and therefore why they should make still greater effort to attract them. On the good side, as we have seen, there is plenty of evidence that women make excellent franchisees. As Cathryn Hayes, National Franchise Manager at HSBC, says, 'Women who have been running a home and raising a family have many of the attributes needed to run a business successfully – they are decisive, energetic, organize well and are used to doing at least three things at once! For them, franchising could be just the thing.' I doubt that Cathryn would disagree with the observation that many women who have *not* run a home or brought up a family have those same attributes, it's just that the mothers and homemakers have amply proved their credentials. The same, regrettably, is not always true of women in employment, which brings us to the bad, or disappointing, reason why franchising may be the answer for them.

Even today, sexual discrimination still exists in many industries and organizations. There are still too many glass ceilings, too many barriers to success. Judy Behl is co-founder and managing director of Scenic Blue, a landscape gardening franchise. She says:

> There is evidence to suggest that women franchisors and franchisees have often been victims of a 'corporate casualty' experience – for example, sex discrimination, redundancy, lack of promotion, inflexible working conditions, or poor maternity conditions. These experiences have often made them determined to make their mark in business. Most women I have discussed this matter with who currently work in franchising have explained their own 'corporate casualty' experiences to me. I was subject to a sex discrimination case when in a senior employed position. This experience when I was expecting my first child certainly gave me the determination never to be placed in that position again.

These are the so-called 'push' factors that force women into looking for new possibilities. It is also the case that some women who have enjoyed success as employees, often rising to positions of executive responsibility, grow weary of the corporate world in which they find themselves. They are tired of long hours, business travel, corporate politics, power struggles and competitive games. They want greater freedom and, just like many men, begin to yearn for the rewards and challenges of running their own show rather than making money for someone else.

While it is regrettable – indeed shameful – that women continue to have a raw deal in the workplace, it cannot be emphasized enough that franchising offers an exceptional opportunity for ambitious, independently minded women to go into business for themselves. Just as the qualities that women possess are suited to franchising, so is franchising suited to the demands and circumstances of women.

In the United States, the home of business format franchising, Darcie Harris founded EWF International, an organization, which is itself a franchise, that provides peer advisory groups for women business owners and executives. She says:

> Several characteristics unique to franchising make it tremendously appealing to women. By nature women are relational, they generally enjoy, in fact crave, opportunities to work with others toward a shared goal. Women like to connect at a deeper level, to feel that bond of shared experience. Experiencing something in common with others is rewarding at a deep level. Becoming a part of a franchise system meets this need. It offers women a way to be connected with like-minded souls – you're not alone. Once you sign the franchise agreement, you become a part of a community.

Research suggests that women wanting to start businesses tend to prefer opportunities that require less start-up capital, involve less risk and offer greater flexibility to work out of normal office hours. Franchising has all three.

Instead of having to come up with an idea and then develop it, with all that entails – getting the product or services right, setting prices and financial targets, devising a marketing plan and so on, and so on – all the while striving to generate sufficient cash to pay for this gestation phase, franchising short-circuits the whole process. You get developed and tested products and services, branding systems, marketing materials, operational processes, and training and support. And, since you are your own boss, you can choose to work the hours that suit you. You still have to work extremely hard to make a success of the venture, but you are not tied to a 9–5 routine; instead you fit your business schedule to allow for family life.

Franchising is a confidence-booster. Women who have taken a career break, perhaps to bring up a family, often approach a return to work with trepidation and doubt. Have developments in the workplace overtaken them? Are their skills rusty and no longer required? As for starting a business of their own, they may feel they lack either the necessary knowledge or the experience. Franchising can assuage such doubts. The combination of a tried and tested formula, training in business skills as well as operational skills, help in setting up, an operations manual, and support from head office as well as other franchisees, all add up to a package that combines the flexibility of a small business with the assurance and efficiency of a larger organization.

Once women get into business they frequently prove themselves every bit as capable as their male counterparts. In some respects they are more aware of the mechanics of running an organization. Research by the banks, for example, strongly suggests that women have a better understanding of finance than men.

The findings showed that:

- 68% of female bosses view bank borrowing as a business tool for cash-flow management, compared to 54% of men;
- more than one in five male bosses actively avoid borrowing from banks, whilst one in four of their female counterparts view bank borrowing as an inescapable fact of business life;
- four in five women bosses have a good understanding of bank term loans, compared to just two in three male bosses;

■   84% of women bosses claimed to have a good understanding of bank overdrafts, compared to 75% of men;
■   half of female-owned or managed businesses are currently part funded by a bank loan, compared to 39% of those owned or managed by men;
■   female bosses are three times less likely than their male counterparts to feel comfortable with the idea of deliberately delaying payments to suppliers to raise business finance.

All of that certainly gives the lie to the notion that women are somehow naive about the nuts and bolts of running a business. And it is yet another reason why franchise companies cannot afford to overlook the energy and talent of potential female franchisees. Fortunately they are beginning to realize this, although it has to be said that there is plenty of scope for improvement:

■   The 2005 NatWest/BFA survey found that 21% of the franchisees surveyed were women and only 9% of new franchisees were women.
■   Franchisors said they would like to see an increase in enquiries from women more than any other group.
■   Self-motivation and hard work are more important to franchisors than gender, qualifications or experience when they are looking at prospective franchisees.

It would be wrong to close this chapter without giving a few real-life examples of just how good women are at franchising, both as franchisees and as franchisors.

For 11 years Lindsey Peters was employed by a franchisee running a Rosemary Conley Diet and Fitness Club. Finally, she decided to become a franchisee herself and her only regret is she that waited so long:

> If someone had said to me 15 years ago I'd be running my own successful business, I wouldn't have believed it possible. As a woman going into business you must have the confidence to believe in yourself – you can do it. It took me a long time to believe in myself, but now I do. Being a franchisee offers you that extra level of support and know-how that you don't get when you set up on your own. The franchise has given me more security, the ability to put my daughter through university and I've just bought a beautiful new car. I absolutely love what I do with a passion and franchising has made it possible.

At the age of 25 Rebecca Morris had had enough of employment and wanted to be her own boss. She learnt about franchising from her mother, who was training and development manager at Rosemary Conley Diet and Fitness Clubs. 'I went to the franchise exhibition in Birmingham with her and looked around. I wanted the freedom and flexibility of running my own business but I was aware that my own commercial experience was lacking. I decided that a franchise would be the best option as it would provide me with a proven business model to follow and limit the risk I was about to take by entering into self-employment.'

At the exhibition she saw Expense Reduction Analysts (ERA), a franchise specializing in helping firms to find savings in costs, and was attracted to it for two reasons. 'As I was borrowing all of the costs of the franchise I wanted to keep the investment to a minimum. The set-up costs, not including the franchise fee, are minimal for ERA, which was part of the attraction. I've also been interested in getting into management consultancy as a career and so the actual day-to-day work suited my skill set.'

Rebecca paid £22,900 plus VAT to buy the franchise and had to find an additional £10,000 in working capital to see her through the first year when there is little or no income. She raised the franchise fee through the government loans guarantee scheme and her father organized a loan for the working capital.

She admits that the going was tough to begin with. 'Put simply, the problems were paying my bills! Every month was a struggle. I was moving money between accounts to try and cover what was going out. I kept my head above water by doing my best to increase my workload to increase my income.'

Today, she is one of the youngest members of the network and one of only a handful of women in the group. This, she says, is an advantage:

The fact that I am a young female helps to break down the traditional, and sometimes stale, description of a management consultant. I find that I can relate to female prospects and clients very effectively and add a refreshing edge when working with my male counterparts. I generally attend prospect meetings with a male colleague and we have found this approach to be hugely successful.

I love the fact that I now have complete control over my own success and working hours. If I choose to take a day off, I have the luxury of being able to put in a few hours the following evening to make the time up, and I am motivated by the fact that my income level is directly related to the amount of time and effort I am willing to put in to making my business a success.

Deryn Coe runs a Jo Jingles franchise teaching young children music, singing and movement, a life that could not be more different from her previous job as a successful City lawyer. 'I enjoyed international travel, meeting famous and interesting clients, and the general lifestyle that a City salary can provide', she says. But she gave it all up when she married and had children. Her husband's work took the family to California for almost six years and by the time the Coes returned to the UK their children were of school age and she was ready to go back to work. 'I looked into returning to the law,' she says, 'but soon realized that this realistically meant a return to London or a change to the type of work I would do. I wasn't ready to commute and not see my children at all, and I wasn't keen on starting again in an office environment, with all the headaches that sick children, school holidays and other school events would bring.'

She found the answer to her dilemma by accident:

I spied a Jo Jingles advert in a national children's magazine and dismissed it as a 'get-rich-quick' advert, but kept thinking about it, and eventually decided I had nothing to lose making an inquiry. I am and always have been very musical, my children have always been exposed to music, and I was always aware of its benefits having seen them blossom in the States.

I love being in control of my business, making all the decisions without recourse to a boss. It can be worrying, especially at the outset, but after three years, I haven't made too many wrong decisions, and have certainly learnt a huge amount.

I am able to combine a business with my family's needs, and I really appreciate the term-time-only structure. I can ensure that I am home when my children are, I can still take them to and from school, and yet I have an enormous amount of fun doing my classes – that's why I do it!

Jo Jingles has a wonderful support network as well – having no previous experience in running a business, I was very well instructed from the outset, and am able to access other information as and when I require it, either from head office, or from other franchisees. I have absolutely no regrets about taking on the franchise – I love doing the classes – I never get bored or unenthusiastic, and I get a kick out of being a 'small business' too. It was not difficult to break even after set-up costs, and making a profit is the icing on the cake. It's mine!

Julie Hester is the owner and director of Property Search Group, a franchise company that runs legal checks on properties for lawyers. 'I left school at 16 and took a job cleaning in my father's textile mill', she says. 'It was an endless round of sweeping up wool from the floor, and I earned about £2 an hour. At 18, I left the mill to become a policewoman on a salary of £18,000, but left after 10 years so I could be at home with my children. We certainly weren't wealthy, but the six of us survived quite comfortably on my husband's salary of £40,000.'

She set up Property Search Group in October 1997, purely to help a solicitor friend.

> Over dinner one night, he started moaning about how the local council was holding up homebuyers by taking for ever to complete basic land searches – such as whether or not a property had the right planning permission.
>
> I offered to help by doing some of the land searches for him. After all, it was only a matter of searching public records for the relevant information. He was so pleased with the results that he recommended me to other solicitors.

Within months, she was working 70 hours a week for six different solicitors. 'I'd get up at 6 am to write reports, before giving the children their breakfast and taking them to school. Then I'd spend the day researching at the library, before coming home, cooking dinner and working until the early hours.'

Within four years the business grew into a franchise with more than 100 offices across the UK, over 600 staff, and a turnover of around £25 million.

When her seven-year-old son asked her if she was a millionaire and she replied, yes, the work she'd been doing in the spare bedroom had made her a millionaire, he burst out laughing:

> He said that if I was a millionaire I'd be driving a Ferrari and would have given him the £50 he asked for to buy a new computer game.
>
> But as someone who was brought up in a frugal, working-class Yorkshire family it's hard to get my head around the idea of frivolous spending. It's been a complete whirlwind. Occasionally, my husband Gary and I find ourselves looking at each other in disbelief. After all, we were a normal family – and now we're heading up a multi-million-pound business. It's a wonderful feeling, knowing we'll never have to worry about money again.

Her business shows that franchising is capable of making riches not just for franchisors but also franchisees. Two members of Property Search Group's network, Jo Hudson and Andrea Glover, gave up promising careers and good salaries at NatWest bank to set up the franchise's first pilot scheme.

They were, they admit, guinea pigs, but by following Julie Hester's franchise formula they have built a business with a turnover approaching £1 million and a healthy profit. Their initial investment was £10,000 and they starting by working from Andrea's home. As the business grew, they found premises in the centre of Rotherham, which they have outgrown three times. But, they add, it's not all about striving to have a successful business, but also being able to take control of their own lives. They have achieved this through franchising.

Some useful websites for networking women in business

www.bpwuk.org.uk (Organization for working women.)

www.everywoman.co.uk (Network and resource provider for women business owners.)

www.motheratwork.co.uk (Webzine with practical advice and information for working mothers.)

www.thewomenscompany.com (Networking site helping women in business achieve their full potential within their local business community.)

www.topwomenuk.com (National networking group.)

www.virtualentrepreneurs.co.uk (Women's networking organization.)

www.wbda.co.uk (The Women's Business Development Agency is a non-profit-making organization dedicated to breaking down the barriers for women entering entrepreneurship.)

10 A little marriage guidance

At last, you are about to clear the final hurdle and open your very own franchised outlet. If you have been diligent and gone about choosing your franchise with care, it will have been a painstaking business. You will have pored over brochures, visited exhibitions, met franchisors, listened to sales spiel hard and soft, met existing franchisees, agonized the while about your suitability both for franchising in general and your particular choice in particular, researched your local market, drawn up a business plan, charmed the bank manager, fitted out your workplace, either in your home or in business premises, and gone through the ballyhoo of launching the venture. You will be relieved and exhausted, nervous and exhilarated. You will probably feel like taking a holiday. But – and there is no soft or easy way of saying this – you ain't seen nothing yet. Starting any small business is hard work, involving more hours than the day contains. Franchising is no different. And yet…

As we have said repeatedly throughout this book, franchising *is* different from ordinary business start-ups in a number of ways, the most significant being that it is less risky and that you, the franchisee, are not on your own. Most people setting up small businesses are liable to suffer agonizing loneliness. They know that it's their idea that prompted the venture and their ambition that saw it through to its birth. But they are also constantly and painfully aware that success or failure is entirely down to them. All right, you can always come up with excuses when a new business fails – and one in three does – you can blame the bank for lack of support, the market for failing to respond, the economy for turning sour, poor seasonal conditions, changes in fashion, malevolent fate, the culprits are endless. But in your heart you know that if defeat comes it will probably be down to you, and you alone. For a franchisee it's different. Although success or failure is ultimately in your hands, you have someone to help and even comfort you in those awful moments of doubt. Every beginner makes mistakes, but how much better to have a mentor to turn to when unexpected setbacks occur or apparently insoluble problems arise. It is this unique relationship between franchisor and franchisee that is both franchising's strength and its weakness.

The franchising relationship has been rightly described as a kind of commercial marriage. The franchisee and the franchisor meet, take to each other, resolve to form a union, formalize the relationship by taking their vows, and set off together on a path strewn with roses to live happily ever after, or, failing that, until the term of the contract doth them part. Of course, as we all know, marriages are not quite like that. Couples start off with good intentions but as time goes by their relationship may come under strain, at which point it takes willingness and compromise on both sides to make it work. Franchising tends uncannily to follow the same pattern. The relationship starts on an up, slides into a down, and, all being well, settles back into a harmonious understanding.

Part of the difficulty with the franchise relationship is that it is not a union of equal partners. It is more like a 19th-century marriage in which the husband had more rights than the wife. For in a franchise the franchisor is the senior partner. That is made clear from the outset in the franchise agreement. If a franchised business is to succeed and grow for the benefit of both franchisor and franchisees, it is essential that there are regulations and standards in place to define and protect the quality of the service or products. When a franchisee takes on a franchise it is on the understanding that he or she is licensed to carry out the business in accordance with the terms of the franchise contract. Franchisees are expected to accept that in return for being granted the rights to the business system, brand recognition and all the other advantages that the package bestows, they must maintain standards. Acceptance of, and adherence to, the rules has to apply throughout the franchise network, without exception. A single bad franchisee who decides to do his own thing, or in some other way compromises the quality or uniformity of the goods or service, can in extreme cases bring down the entire network. At the least his actions will have an adverse effect not just on his business but on that of every other franchisee. Although the franchise relationship is of necessity quite rigid, it should not be entirely inflexible. The best franchisors, as we shall see later in this chapter, encourage franchisees to come up with ideas of their own. It's just that there is a difference between contributing suggestions for consideration by the franchisor and other franchisees and going off at a tangent on your own. Franchising involves teamwork.

That tensions should arise in the franchise relationship is not surprising given that even among expert observers of the industry there is disagreement about the nature of the relationship. At one extreme, some argue that an individual franchised unit is in effect a managed outlet of the bigger business, that of the franchisor, which is truly independent. This interpretation suggests that the franchisee is in reality a manager, albeit one with a stake in the business, who has been led to believe he is an entrepreneur. Such critics do not deny that the relationship can be beneficial to both parties, but they would rather that a franchised outlet was not confused with a genuinely independent business. At the other extreme, it might be argued that a franchised outlet is a budding independent small business operating in a close relationship with a bigger business, that of the franchisor. In this respect it is no different from many small companies who depend to a large extent on a bigger firm. This would be true of, say, a small firm supplying a major supermarket chain.

These differing interpretations show that franchising is an awkward animal to pin down and categorize. On the one hand, there are what might be called product franchises, such as parcel delivery, in which franchisees distribute a product delivered to them by the franchisor. On the other hand there is business format franchising, which involves the cloning and support of a complete business system. It seems reasonable to assume that the way in which the relationship between franchisee and franchisor develops over time will to some extent depend on the type of franchise. A product franchisee may be content to own and run what is in effect a satellite of the franchisor's business, whereas the owner of a business format franchise may see himself as more independent and entrepreneurial.

So how exactly does the relationship between franchisor and franchisee change over time? Though much will depend on the personalities and characters of the people involved and every situation is different, franchising is sufficiently well established, both here and abroad, for a pattern to have been discerned. Broadly speaking, a typical franchise 'marriage' goes through the following phases:

▌ **The honeymoon**: the franchisee and franchisor embark on their new life together, each full of optimism and hope. The franchisee is excited about running his outlet and looks forward with eager anticipation to a satisfying and enriching experience. The franchisor does everything he can to encourage this enthusiasm by promising to be there whenever he is wanted.

▌ **The awakening**: it has dawned on the franchisee that not all the profit he is making is staying where he would like it, ie in his own pocket. Instead, a chunk is being creamed off by his partner in the form of royalties and advertising fees. And of course this abstraction of funds doesn't happen once, but at regular intervals, a constant reminder to the franchisee that not all the rewards of his hard work go to him. If the franchisee lets this thought fester, he will become increasingly dissatisfied and resentful and the franchise relationship may turn sour.

▌ **The self-regard**: the franchisee's business is succeeding and growing, but does he thank his partner for standing behind him? No, he does not. Instead he preens himself and takes all the credit. In fact, he thinks he could get along very well without the franchisor. The self-regard phase is liable to kick in even if the franchisee is not enjoying all the success he would like; but instead of congratulating himself he will blame the franchisor. Self-regard, you see, can admit of no fault.

▌ **The itchy feet**: the franchisee finds the relationship increasingly irksome, what with the controls, the interference, and the regular inspections. He wants the franchisor out of his hair so that he lives his own life and develop his own ideas. If this resentment is allowed to fester it can lead to a breakdown, either because the franchisee is determined to go his own way or because the franchisor would rather be rid of a potential troublemaker than attempt to mollify him.

▌ **The reconciliation**: the franchisee accepts that the rules exist for a purpose, that the franchisor is not dispensable, and that the network has to pull together or it will fall apart. This reversal of thought cannot come about by accident. A disaffected franchisee who has shown self-regard and felt itchy feet does not suddenly awake and see the folly of his ways. Reconciliation is achieved through thrashing out problems and reaching compromises. This could involve the franchisor in paying more attention to the franchisee's concerns, and the franchisee admitting that adherence to the systems is essential if standards are to be maintained.

▌ **The happy marriage**: franchisee and franchisor establish a way of working together. This best outcome is most likely when the franchisee is a grown-up realist able to put aside his self-esteem and accept the need to work in cooperation with the franchisor. For the relationship to achieve this stability it is essential that the franchisee makes a reasonable return on his investment and that the franchisor is a good listener. If the franchisee feels that he is not making enough money and that the franchisor is indifferent to his problems, the divorce court beckons. Franchisors who have successfully helped their franchisees through all the phases to this last one are rewarded with a network that is dedicated to success and content to set about what Dr Johnson called the harmless employment of making money.

There is, of course, nothing inevitable about a franchise relationship taking the course outlined above. Ideally, friction will be kept to a minimum from the outset. How is this to be achieved? First, it helps if the partners are suited from the outset. Second, as everyone knows, a successful marriage is the result of hard work. Let us look at each in turn.

This book has already indicated at some length the qualities that make a good franchisee. He should be energetic, adaptable, independently minded without being headstrong, and ambitious. A good franchisor will be constantly mindful of the fact that he owes a duty to the franchise network; they are helping to build his business and their interests and concerns should be taken seriously. If the right franchisee and franchisor are to find each other, the recruitment process must be thorough and considered, and that is most likely to be found in a mature, well-established franchise. When a franchise operation is new and struggling to find its feet, recruitment may be either hurried or amateurish. As Prof Stanworth of the University of Westminster points out, a new franchise has to construct a front-end infrastructure of managerial support some years ahead of achieving full financial break-even point:

> In effect, given the demands placed upon an infant franchise system to finance and manage the processes of franchisee recruitment and all that entails, plus induction and field support for franchisees, the new franchise company is, in effect, developing the management and administrative structure normally associated with a medium-sized business, without the income levels normally associated with this scale of business. For a small business intent on developing into a credible franchise operation, the strains normally associated with small business growth are, in fact, likely to be magnified and concentrated, rather than reduced.

Small wonder that recruitment is not always as satisfactory as it might be. The new franchisor is understandably keen to take on his first franchisees and, perhaps through inexperience or haste, is not as discerning as he ought to be. Whereas the experienced franchisor will look for signs of over-confidence that could spell trouble later, the inexperienced franchisor might mistake bumptiousness for energy. He has yet to discover that even the best franchisees may go through a phase of questioning and doubt and yet to experience the disruption that can be caused by an overweening ego.

The hard work that makes a marriage succeed can be summed up under a single heading – communication. Mutual understanding comes from listening sympathetically to the other person's point of view and acting on his or her concerns. In franchising, as we have seen, the partnership is not equal and therefore more of the onus for establishing channels of communication rests on the franchisor. When disputes arise it's often down to poor communication, with franchisees thinking the franchisor is arrogant, busy or simply not interested, and the franchisor suspecting that a dissatisfied franchisee is nagging, incompetent or simply not committed. With care, all that can be avoided. The perfect franchisor would do the following:

- Provide the modern basics for staying in touch, preferably an intranet website, a regular newsletter with information about the organization and its franchisees, an annual conference and other regular opportunities for members of the network to meet each other, and a response head office team.

- Encourage franchisees to air their grievances rather than let them fester, and act on them. This takes time and money but the return in terms of good franchisee relations is worth it. Also, encourage the network to contribute ideas and suggestions for improving the way the franchise operates. Of course, the systems are tried and tested, that is the essence of franchising, but no business is so perfect it cannot be improved. In any case, it will need to adapt to change, and the franchisees operating at the coalface are in the best position to spot where improvements can be made.

- Congratulate franchisees who perform well and from time to time let the entire network know that you appreciate their work and the contribution they make to the success of the organization. This should not be a routine reiteration of platitudes but a genuine demonstration that you are following their progress and recognize what they are achieving.

- Arrange for new franchisees to be put in touch with more experienced members of the network. As we noted earlier, women franchisees in particular value contact and exchange of information with others, but men can benefit just as much from such informal meetings.

▌ Share long-term goals and strategic thinking with franchisees. If the network is kept informed of possible changes in advance and encouraged to comment, the possibility of dissent and friction is reduced. Think small, even as you grow big. In the early days of a franchised business, when there are just a handful of new franchisees, they are close to the franchisor. They may be in contact daily, and almost certainly they will be on first-name terms. But as the franchise grows and prospers and the network expands, those first franchisees may begin to feel neglected and that early sense of belonging may turn into dissatisfaction and chippiness. The aim should be to treat each franchisee as a valued individual, however large the organization becomes.

▌ If franchisees form themselves into an association, accept the fact and work with it. Treating it in the way that a 19th-century factory owner would treat a trade union is a sure way to build resentment and provoke hostility.

▌ Where possible, encourage successful franchisees to take on a second franchise. That way, their achievements are recognized and rewarded, they are given a new challenge, their financial prospects are enhanced and their self-esteem is boosted. Some franchisors achieve a similar effect by encouraging franchisees to start from small beginnings – perhaps working from home and doing the 'job' themselves – and then, as the business becomes established, to move into an office, recruit staff and take on a more managerial role.

Not all franchisors – indeed, perhaps only a minority – are as good at communicating with franchisees as they should be, but those who make the effort are rewarded in terms of a more stable relationship with their franchisees. Time and resources spent on good relations are a sound investment because if the network becomes unsettled for whatever reason, the costs involved in resolving difficulties can be immense and the harm done irreparable.

As a prospective franchisee assessing a franchise you should find out how much importance the franchisor attaches to communication with the network. You can learn this from your conversations with existing franchisees. Ask them if the franchisor keeps in touch, whether he is a good listener, whether any conflicts have arisen and, if so, how they were resolved. The answers can be very revealing.

Pitman Training Group is an example of a franchise that places importance on relationships with its franchisees and has the systems needed to make its communications work. The company founded over 150 years ago by Sir Isaac Pitman, who invented the shorthand that bears his name, has branched out from teaching trainee secretaries and now runs courses in information technology and business skills. It began franchising in 1992 and, as a long-established company with a respected name, set up its network with admirable professionalism, as this extract from its prospectus shows:

> The first contact point for any Pitman Training Franchise Partner is Franchise Support Services. This is an expert call centre based at our head office, where a team of experienced staff answer questions from centres on course materials and contractual issues, and share information around the network.
>
> The Support Services team can be contacted by telephone, fax or e-mail. They also offer an e-service solution 'Ask Isaac' should you wish to find out more out of normal office hours or just browse through their amazing online FAQ database.
>
> In the field, a team of experienced and proactive Senior Sales Managers provide a wide range of trading partnerships to the network including national contracts and agreements in training that increases revenue earning potential for each centre.
>
> Our Business Development provides staff training and other issues that will catapult your business into success.
>
> The Pitman Training Group Management team monitor shifts in government policy, which directly impact on the training market. Franchise Partners are regularly updated on changes in the rules and the effect these might have.
>
> Pitman Training seeks to involve the network in as many ways as possible. The Pitman Training Management Board is made up of elected franchise partners and senior Pitman Training managers in equal numbers, meeting to discuss strategic issues facing the business. In addition, our training centres within Regional Support Groups meet with Pitman Training representatives twice yearly to exchange ideas and gain an update of new and forthcoming developments. A central marketing fund invests a contribution from every course sold into national marketing initiatives, chosen by the elected franchise partners.

That is the way it should be done.

If throughout this book I have given the impression that franchising is a hard slog, it is because I wish to dispel the notion that low-risk means easy. While it is true that buying and running a proven business format is a safer way of becoming self-employed than starting from scratch, it is not the whole story. Examined more closely, the claims made on behalf of franchising by those wishing to sell franchises are, to be blunt, misleading, though not always intentionally so. Much of the fault lies with that enemy of the truth – statistics. Or rather their interpretation. The problem dates back to the early 1980s in the United States, the home of franchising, when the Department of Commerce compiled a report called 'Franchising in the Economy'. Of its many findings, one has stuck in the memory, and that is that 95 per cent of all franchises are still in business after five years. Understandably, this was seized on by the industry, both here and in the United States, and has since become a sacred article in the canon of franchising. It is not, however, true. The Department of Commerce was wrong. Critics have since argued that the data were incomplete and inaccurate. In particular, no account was taken of the fact that many franchise failures are concealed by a change of ownership; in other words, the franchisee failed but the business was sold on to someone else and did not itself fail. However, the fact that a business may roll on, leaving you pick yourself up from the wayside, is small consolation. There are other reasons for doubting the validity of the 95 per cent success claim. The Department of Commerce researchers questioned only bona fide franchise companies, so their findings took no account of the failures suffered by people who invested in dubious operations passing themselves off as franchises. Though this might be seen as no more than a matter of terminology, it underlines the importance of investigating a franchise proposition thoroughly and knowing in advance what constitutes a properly formed business format. Another reason for suspecting the findings is that the study had the weakness inherent in many surveys, and that is that the respondents were self-selecting. Franchisors with a happy story to tell are more inclined to sit down and fill in a questionnaire than those with troubles they would rather not admit to.

Even more doubt was cast by the research of an American academic, Timothy Bates, who examined figures from the US Census Bureau Business Owners' Database and concluded that 34.9 per cent of franchise businesses failed, compared to 28 per cent of non-franchise businesses. If true, these figures do not merely nail the notion that franchising enjoys an abnormally high success rate, they turn it on its head. Prof Bates suggests that the difference in performance was due in part to franchises being over-represented in high-risk retailing and under-represented in services. He also says that franchise failures may often be explained by the recruitment of inadequate franchisees and by the high level of franchisor fees and royalties, which place a considerable burden on new business outlets.

Though the above findings are American, they should concern industry pundits on this side of the Atlantic who still subscribe to the almost bullet-proof stability of franchising. In any case, we have some thought-provoking research of our own. Prof John Stanworth surveyed a large sample of UK franchised businesses and concluded that there was a high attrition rate. At best, he said, one franchise company in four could be described as an unqualified success story over a 10-year period, and around half were complete failures.

Those who have studied the industry dispassionately now believe that only 25 to 30 per cent of new franchise start-ups survive for 10 years and as many as half fail to reach their fourth anniversary.

So do these rather sobering facts, here in Chapter 10, debunk the implicit message of the previous nine? Not really. They merely act as a powerful corrective to the trumpeting sounds made by franchisors eager to pull in new recruits. Yes, franchises fail more often than the advertisers would have you believe, but such flops are usually for one of two reasons – either the rules were not followed or the franchise was not really a franchise at all but a business opportunity trying to sneak in under the franchise umbrella.

The message is plain – the riskier a franchise proposition is, the more likely its promoters are to invoke the myth of low risk. As a rule, newer franchises involve greater risk, and they make up the bulk of the more heavily promoted opportunities. So the more you are reminded that franchising is safe, the warier you should be. As a potential franchisee, you must discount the marketing hyperbole and concentrate on ensuring as far as possible that your chosen franchise is a business that suits your skills and abilities and has a good chance of meeting your aspirations.

Enough of the downside, let us conclude with a couple of success stories chosen from the hundreds to be found up and down the country. Chosen, it should be added, not at random but by the careful selection of a panel of judges. Both are past winners of the BFA Franchisee of the Year competition sponsored by HSBC.

John Passfield and Roy Sharpe own a Countrywide Grounds Maintenance franchise, a business that specializes in maintaining a range of sites including commercial grounds, private gardens, parks and sports pitches. They started off owning separate outlets in the Midlands but in 1997 joined forces to secure a lucrative five-year contract with Severn Trent Water that neither had the resources to fulfil alone. Their joint venture, Countrywide Central, was such a success that they decided to merge all their franchise operations, enabling them to exploit economies of scale and build a firmer platform for future growth. They went on to buy four more franchise areas, and now run three operational depots with 40 mobile teams and 120 trained employees. Their turnover is in excess of £3 million per year. Passfield and Sharpe say their success would not have been possible without the support of their franchisor, who helped them with the complexities of risk assessment, health and safety, environmental policies, training and quality control.

After 14 years as a pub manager, Jon Bassett wanted to be his own boss and was ready for a new challenge. Luckily for him, his desire for a change coincided with the decision of his employers, Mitchells & Butlers, to launch a franchise. It was exactly what he needed: the opportunity to work for himself and still use the skills and systems he was used to. Even better, he stayed in the same pub, the Queen's Vaults in Cardiff, which in three days made the transition from a managed pub into a franchise. Jon took over the existing systems, recruited staff who had worked for him previously and introduced performance-related pay.

Surrounded by stiff competition, Jon needed to build customer loyalty. Using M&B purchasing power he put together competitive food and drink offers and developed a strong sports and machines theme, which gave the pub a specific identity. And while working to attract new business, he made sure the small group of regulars were not alienated. The results were impressive. Within 12 weeks, he recovered his initial franchise set-up cost of £30,000, and in the first year his return on investment was almost 500 per cent. He has since taken on a second business franchise, the Golden Egg, on Kilburn High Road, London, and again increased sales.

Both these examples show that franchising need not be a straitjacket. Nor is franchisee discontent an inevitability. Passfield and Sharpe bought business systems, learnt how to operate them, and applied their own ambition and enterprise to developing them. Note, however, that they pay generous tribute to the franchisor who gave them invaluable help in building their combined enterprise.

This is what Countrywide says about the support it offers to its network:

Franchisees benefit from ongoing accounts, marketing, telesales and many after-sales support services to ensure that the emphasis for the franchisee is to manage their business and service their customers. Every franchisee completes a two–three-week training course that is held at the head office in

Wilmslow, Cheshire and also time out working alongside existing franchisees. The training programme covers the setting-up processes of the franchisee's business, accounting, sales, marketing, health & safety, grounds maintenance, employment, etc, etc.

Head office negotiates national contracts and the franchisees benefit as soon as they service that contract. There is also the added benefit that the customer will have a central invoicing procedure generated from Head Office (saving the franchisees time) as well as the quality standards expected of an ISO (International Organization for Standardization) accredited company.

Countrywide takes great pride in the very high levels of service its franchisees enjoy. And it all stems from one single premise: the more successful you become, the more successful we become.

Jon Bassett didn't need training. He already had the skills to run his own pub and, even more important, the ideas and enterprise to make it work. Converting from a manager to a franchisee gave him the freedom and incentive to release his drive and energy and to reap the rewards. Like Passfield and Sharpe he received help where needed from the franchisor, but in his case head office at Mitchells & Butlers just needed to stand back and let him get on with it.

It is interesting to note that in turning to franchising M&B was reverting to a form of tenancy agreement in the licensing trade which in this country is one of the earliest forms of franchising, dating back to the 1800s. In the 1960s and 1970s, there was a shift from tenanted to managed pubs. Salaried managers, however, lack the pride and drive of tenants, who directly reap the rewards of their success. That many brewers, including M&B, should have 'discovered' franchising as a means of restoring the advantages of an older way of running pubs is, in effect, the wheel turning full circle. To its credit, M&B set about franchising with commendable professionalism, as this extract from its brochure confirms:

We will provide you, the franchisee, with a comprehensive support package that gives you a flying start with your business, and every chance to make a success of it. With established business formats, retail offers and IT systems, you'll benefit from central purchasing, with a vast choice of leading drinks brands, support from experienced Business Managers, 5 weeks' induction training and much more.

Our specialist business know-how has been developed and refined over a number of years. Included in our business start-up pack are detailed operating manuals on our extensive experience. Essentially, what we will provide is a sophisticated support infrastructure to aid you in the running of your business, offering significant back of house economies of scale and efficiencies.

We recognize your desire to develop and build your business, and our experienced Operations Managers will keep in regular personal contact, helping you to achieve your goals and maximize your rewards. Whether you have experience of the pub franchise or are a complete novice, then we'll help you to develop a wide range of skills. You'll learn every aspect of how to run a pub, from pulling your first pint and learning all about customer care, to ensuring you know all the key areas of legislation that effect your business. The highly structured training involves hands-on experience to become fully versed in our proven way of doing things, and also time in the classroom, obtaining the necessary qualifications that are required to hold a licence.

The above examples of hard-working, successful franchisees whose franchisors are conscientious and have made considerable efforts to get their franchise right are not exceptional. There are hundreds of similar cases up and down the country. But never allow the good to blind you to the bad. Almost everything you read about the industry is in some sense promotional and designed to emphasize the positive. The aim of this book has been to help and encourage the reader to find the right franchise, but also to warn throughout that there is no smooth ride to riches and that the road to franchising success is paved with pitfalls and dogged by footpads. Sidestep them and you will reach your goal.

Appendix

British Franchise Association

Full members

Established franchisors with a proven trading and franchising record. To qualify as a member, franchisors are required to submit a completed application form, including disclosure document, franchise agreement, prospectus, accounts, etc; and proof of a correctly constituted pilot scheme successfully operated for at least one year, financed and managed by the applicant company. In addition, evidence of successful franchising over a subsequent two-year period with at least four franchisees is required.

Abacus Care
Nursing and care service provider
Ormskirk Business Park
71/73 New Court Way
Ormskirk
Lancashire, L39 2YT
Tel: 01695 585400
Fax: 01695 585401
Contact:
Mr Nigel Fielding
Tel: 01695 585400
Fax: 01695 585401
headoffice@abacuscare.com

Agency Express Ltd
Specialist estate agency board contractors
The Old Church
St Matthews Road
Norwich, NK1 1SP
Contact:
Mr Stephen Watson

Tel: 01603 620044
Fax: 01603 613136
enquiries@agencyexpress.co.uk

Alphagraphics
Rapid response print, copy and publishing stores
Thornburgh Road
Eastfield
Scarborough, YO11 3UY
www.alphagraphics.co.uk
Contact:
Ms Beverley Bolton
Tel: 01723 502222
b.bolton@alphagraphics.co.uk

Amtrak Express Parcels Limited
Overnight parcels collection and delivery
Northgate Way
Northgate
Aldridge

Walsall
West Midlands, WS9 8ST
Tel: 01922 74474
Fax: 01922 745058
Contact:
Ms Sharron O'Hanlon
Tel: 01922 747031
Fax: 01922 745058
Sarah.Jobson@amtrak.co.uk

ANC
Express parcel delivery
Parkhouse East Industrial Estate
Chesterton
Newcastle-under-Lyme
Staffordshire, ST5 7RB
Tel: 01782 563322
www.anc.co.uk
Contact:
Mr John Hamill
Tel: 01782 563322
Fax: 01782 563633
franchise@anc.co.uk

Apollo Window Blinds Ltd
Manufacturers and retailers of
window blinds
Unit 102, BMK Industrial Estate
Wakefield Road
Liversedge
West Yorkshire, WF15 6BS
www.apollo-blinds.co.uk
Contact:
Ms Karen Musson
Tel: 01924 413010
Fax: 0871 9892981
karen.apollo1@amoblinds.co.uk

Auditel
Cost management consultants
St Paul's Gate
Cross Street
Winchester
Hampshire, SO23 8SZ
Tel: 01962 863915

www.era-auditel.net
Contact:
Mr Nick Tubb
Tel: 01962 863915
recruitment@auditel.net

Autosmart
Sale of vehicle cleaning products
Lynn Lane
Shenstone
Staffordshire, WS14 0DH
Contact:
Mr Steve Tulk
Tel: 01543 481616
Fax: 01543 481549
franchising@autosmart.co.uk

Bang & Olufsen
Retail television and hi-fi
630 Wharfedale Road
Winnersh Triangle
Wokingham
Berkshire, RG41 5TP
Contact:
Mr D Mottershead
Tel: 0118 969 2288
UKfranchise@bang-olufsen.dk

Barking Mad Ltd
Home from home pet care
The Hayloft
Hutton Roof
Carnforth
Lancashire, LA6 2PG
Tel: 015242 73301
Contact:
Mrs Lee Southern
Tel: 015242 73301
leesouthern@barkingmad.uk.com

BB's Coffee & Muffins Limited
Specialist coffee, muffins and
baguette retail outlet
Charter House
Brent Way

Brentford
Middlesex, TW8 8ES
Tel: 020 8758 1234
Fax: 020 8568 6868
Contact:
Mr N Sidhu
Tel: 020 8758 1234
Fax: 020 8568 6868
franchise@bbscoffeeandmuffins.com

Belvoir Lettings
Property management and
residential letting
Belvoir House
60a London Road
Grantham
Lincoln, NG31 6HR
Tel: 01476 570000
Fax: 01476 584902
www.belvoirfranchise.com
Contact:
Recruitment Department
Tel: 01476 570000
Fax: 01476 584902
franchising@belvoirlettings.com

BIGFISH
Office printer supplies and printer
repairs
Caslon Court
Pitronnerie Road
St Peter Port
Guernsey, GY1 2RW
www.bigfishfranchise.com
Contact:
Ms Helen Vernon
Tel: 02392 489653
Fax: 02392 472582
helen.vernon@bigfishhooked.com

**Blazes Fireplace and Heating
Centres Limited**
Retail sale and installation of fires,
fireplaces and central heating
23 Standish Street

Burnley
Lancashire, BB11 1AP
www.blazes.co.uk
Contact:
Mr M Eyre
Tel: 01282 831176
info@blazes.co.uk

Budgens Stores Ltd
Food retail – convenience store
Musgrave House, Widewater Place
Moorhall Road, Harefield
Uxbridge, Middlesex, UB9 6PE
Contact:
Mr Charles Mills
Tel: 0870 0500158
franchise@budgens.co.uk

Calbarrie Ltd
Portable Appliance Testing and
Safety Testing
Castle House
Dawson Road
Mount Farm
Bletchley, Milton Keynes, MK1 1QY
Contact:
Mr Spencer Pettit
Tel: 0870 839 2806,
Mob: 07771 525414
Fax: 0870 839 2802
spencer.pettit@calbarrie.com

Card Connection
Greeting card publisher and
distributor
Park House
South Street
Farnham
Surrey, GU9 7QQ
www.card-connection.co.uk
Contact:
Ms Mary Blackburn
Tel: 01252 892 354
**mary-blackburn@
card-connection.co.uk**

Card Line Greetings Ltd
Distribution of greetings cards
Units 4–5, Hale Trading Estate
Lower Church Lane
Tipton
West Midlands, DY4 7PQ
www.cardline.co.uk
Contact:
Mr M Crapper
Tel: 0121 522 4407
info@cardline.co.uk

Carewatch Care Services Ltd
Provision of domiciliary care
services
First Floor
1 Queen's Square
Brighton, BN1 3FD
Contact:
Mr Patrick Thompson
Tel: 01273 208111
Fax: 01273 204111
pthompson@carewatch.co.uk

Cartridge World
Refill printer cartridges
Unit A3
Hornbeam Square West, Hornbeam
Park
Harrogate
North Yorkshire, HG2 8PA
Contact:
Mr Duncan Berry
Tel: 01423 878520
Fax: 01423 878521
duncan@cartridgeworld.org

Cash Converters
Buying and selling high-quality
second-hand goods
Cash Converters House
Westmill Road
Ware
Hertfordshire, SG12 0EF

Contact:
Mr Mark Lemmon
Tel: 01920 485696
Fax: 01920 485695
emma.daynes@cashconverters.net

Cash Generator
Second-hand goods, instant cash
provider, cheque changer
63/64 Oakhill Trading Estate
Worsley Road North
Walkden, M28 3PT
www.cashgenerator.net
Contact:
Mr B C Lewis
Tel: 01204 574444
Fax: 01204 577711
info@cashgenerator.co.uk

Castle Estates
Residential property management
and lettings agent
Castle House
Dawson Road
Mount Farm
Bletchley, Milton Keynes, MK1 1QY
www.franchise.castle-estates.co.uk
Contact:
Ms Samantha Knight
Tel: 0870 839 2747
Fax: 0870 839 2728
franchise@castle-estates.co.uk

Certax Accounting Ltd
Accountancy and taxation services
47 Clarence Road
Chesterfield
Derbyshire, S40 1LQ
www.certaxaccounting.co.uk
Contact:
Mr Keith Bradshaw
Tel: 01246 200255
Fax: 01246 279403
CA@certax.co.uk

Chem-Dry Midlands & London
Carpet, upholstery and curtain
cleaning
Belprin Road
Beverley
East Yorkshire, HU17 0LP
www.chem-dry.co.uk
Contact:
Ms Claire Hostick
Tel: 01482 888195
Fax: 01482 888193
claire@cdns.co.uk

Chem-Dry Northern & Southern
Belprin Road
Beverley
East Yorkshire, HU17 0LP
www.chemdry.co.uk
Contact:
Mrs Claire Hostick
Tel: 01482 888195
Fax: 01482 888193
claire@cdns.co.uk

Chemex International
Hygiene, cleaning and
maintenance chemicals
Spring Road
Smethwick
West Midlands, B66 1PT
Tel: 0121 525 4040
Fax: 0121 525 4922
www.chemexinter.com
Contact:
Mr Richard Sarjent
Tel: 0121 525 4040
Fax: 0121 525 4922
**richard.sarjent@chemicalexpress.
co.uk**

ChipsAway International Ltd
Paint repair system for automobiles
ChipsAway House
Arthur Drive
Hoo Farm Trading Estate

Kidderminster, Worcestershire,
DY11 7RA
www.chipsaway.co.uk
Contact:
Mr Nick Bicknell
Tel: 01562 825599
Fax: 01562 864969
carolyn@chipsaway.co.uk

Clarks Shoes
Retail shoe shops
40 High Street
Street
Somerset, BA16 OYA
Contact:
Mr R Marsden
Tel: 01458 443131
roger.marsden@clarks.com

Complete Weed Control
Amenity and industrial weed
control services
Hackling House
Bourton Industrial Park
Bourton-on-the-Water
Gloucestershire, GL54 2EN
Tel: 01451 822897
Fax: 01451 822587
Contact:
Mr Richard Minton
Tel: 01451 822897
Fax: 01451 822587
**cwc.ho@completeweedcontrol.co.
uk**

**Cookerburra Oven Cleaning
Services**
Domestic oven cleaning service
5/9 Berkeley Avenue
Reading
Berkshire, RG1 6EL
www.Cookerburra.co.uk
Contact:
Mr Michael Holloway
Tel: 0118 9599922

Fax: 0118 9595554
Mike@cookerburra.co.uk

Cottage Industries
Distribution of greeting cards and
confectionery
399A Harrogate Road
Bradford
Yorkshire, BD2 3TF
Contact:
Mr A Cheetham
Tel: 01274 626556
info@cottageindustries.co.uk

Countrywide Franchising Ltd
Estate agency
Century House
Rosemount Avenue
West Byfleet
Surrey, KT14 6LB
Tel: 01932 350314
www.cafl.co.uk
Contact:
Mr Philip Dobson
Tel: 01932 350314
Fax: 01932 350587
enquiries@cafl.co.uk

**Countrywide Grounds
Maintenance**
Grounds maintenance contractors
Teejay Court
Alderley Road
Wilmslow
Cheshire, SK9 1NT
Tel: 01625 529000
Fax: 01625 527000
**www.countrywidegrounds.co.uk/
franchise**
Contact:
Mr Simon Stott
Tel: 01625 529000
Fax: 01625 527000
**franchise@countrywidegrounds.
co.uk**

Countrywide Lawn Doctor Ltd
Specialised lawn treatment
Teejay Court
Alderley Road
Wilmslow
Cheshire, SK9 1NT
**www.countrywidelawndoctor.com/
franchise**
Contact:
Mr Simon Stott
Tel: 01625 529000
Fax: 01625 527000
**franchise@countrywidelawndoctor.
com**

Dairy Crest
Distribution of milk, dairy products
and soft drinks
14/40 Victoria Road
Aldershot
Hampshire, GU1 1TH
www.unigate.plc.uk
Contact:
Mr Robert Fowler
Tel: 01252 366807
robert.fowler@dairycrest.co.uk

Domino's Pizza
Home delivery and takeaway pizza
Lasborough Road
Kingston
Milton Keynes, MK10 0AB
Contact:
Ms Dawn Power
Tel: 01908 580617
dawn.power@dominos.co.uk

DP Furniture Express
Specialist pine furniture retail
outlets
Colima Avenue
Sunderland Enterprise Park
Sunderland
Tyne & Wear, SR5 3XF
www.durhampine.com

Contact:
Mr Colin McQueen
Tel: 0191 5162603
Fax: 0191 5162613
colin.mcqueen@dp-fx.com

Drain Doctor Ltd
Plumbing
Franchise House
Adam Court
Newark Road
Peterborough, Cambridgeshire,
PE1 5PP
www.draindoctor.co.uk
Contact:
Mr F S Mitman
Tel: 01733 753939
jan.mitman@virgin.net

Driver Hire
Employment agency specializing in
blue-collar supply of temporary
workers
Progress House
Castlefields Lane
Bingley
West Yorkshire, BD16 2AB
www.driver-hire.co.uk
Contact:
Mr John Warren
Tel: 01274 551166
john.warren@driver-hire.co.uk

Dyno-Locks
Lock fitting and security
installations
Zockoll House
143 Maple Road
Surbiton
Surrey, KT6 4BJ
www.dyno.com
Contact:
Franchise Recruitment Department
Tel: 0500 456267
franchiserecruitment@dyno.com

Dyno-Rod
Drain cleaning inspection and
repair
Zockoll House
143 Maple Road
Surbiton
Surrey, KT6 4BJ
www.dyno.com
Contact:
Franchise Recruitment Department
Tel: 0500 456267
franchiserecruitment@dyno.com

Ecocleen Limited
Commercial Cleaning
3 Northgate Street
Bury St Edmunds
Suffolk, IP33 1HQ
Contact:
Mr Peter Legge
Tel: 01284 703535
Fax: 01284 700180
atraher@ecocleen.co.uk

Expense Reduction Analysts Ltd
Cost management and value
improvement specialists
St Paul
Cross Street
Winchester
Hampshire, SO23 8SZ
www.era-auditel.net
Contact:
Mr Robert Allison
Tel: 01962 849444
n.tubb@erauk.net

Express Dairies
Distribution of dairy products
Fosse House
6 Smith Way
Grove Park
Leicester, LE9 5SX
Contact:
Mr Mike Grey

Tel: 0116 2823202
Fax: 0116 2821202
mike-grey@express-dairies.co.uk

Express Despatch
Parcel distribution
Unit 4
Fairview Industrial Estate
Kingsbury Road
Crudworth, B76 9EE
Contact:
Mr Louis John
Tel: 01675 475757
admin@hq.expressdespatch.co.uk

Fastsigns
Signage
Dunston Innovation Centre
Dunston Road
Chesterfield, S41 8NG
Contact:
Mr Garth Allison
Tel: 01246 456512
Fax: 01246 261604
garth.allison@fastsigns.com

Favorite Chicken & Ribs
Fast food
7 Davy Road
Gorse Lane
Clacton-on-Sea
Essex, CO15 4XD
Contact:
Mr Adrian Goody
Tel: 01255 222568
Fax: 01255 430423
mailroom@favorite.co.uk

Flowers Forever
Preservation of wedding bouquets
and other floral tributes
Sterling House
10G Buntsford Park Road
Bromsgrove
Worcestershire, B60 3DX UK

www.flowersforever.co.uk
Contact:
Ms Hilary Jones
Tel: 01527 880 200
Fax: 01527 880 201
franchising@flowersforever.co.uk

Francesco Group
Ladies' and gentlemen's
hairdressing
1 The Green
Stafford, ST17 4BH
Contact:
Mr Ben Dellicompagni
Tel: 01785 247175
Fax: 01785 216185
emmajohnson@francescogroup.co.uk

Freedom Group of Companies
Facilities management
Freedom House
Bradford Road
Tingley
Wakefield, WF3 1SD
www.freedom-group.co.uk
Contact:
Ms Michele Glover
Tel: 01924 887785
michele.glover@freedom-group.co.uk

Furniture Medic
On-site furniture repair
Tigers Road
Wigston
Leicestershire, LE18 4WS
Contact:
Mr Ken Dennis
Tel: 0116 2759000
Fax: 0116 2759002
kendennis@servicemaster.co.uk

Greenthumb UK Ltd
Domestic lawn treatment service
Integra
St Asaph Business Park
St Asaph
Denbighshire, LL17 OLJ
www.greenthumb.co.uk
Contact:
Mr Stephen Waring
Tel: 01745 586062
info@greenthumb.co.uk

Guardian Homecare UK Ltd
Domiciliary Care Services
Hamilton House
2 Station Road
Epping
Essex, CM16 4HA
Contact:
Ms Anne Keene
Tel: 01992 575666
Fax: 01992 575152
jan.guardian@rya-online.net

Hire Intelligence UK
Short-term rental of personal
computers
Ilmer Meadows
Ilmer
Princes Risborough
Buckinghamshire, HP27 9RD
www.hire-intelligence.co.uk
Contact:
Mr Wolf-Rüdiger Feiler
Tel: 01844 342862
Fax: 01844 342862
wrfeiler@hire-intelligence.co.uk

Initial City Link
Same day and overnight parcel
service
Wellington House
61/73 Staines Road West
Sudbury on Thames
Middlesex, TW16 7AH
www.city-link.co.uk

Contact:
Ms Jane Roberts
Tel: 01932 822622
Fax: 01932 785560
linda.brown@city-link.co.uk

Interlink Express Parcels Ltd
Overnight parcels collection and
delivery
PO Box 6979
Roebuck Lane
Smethwick, Warley
West Midlands, B66 1BY
Contact:
Mr Mike Noad
Tel: 01562 881002
Fax: 01562 881001
jane.hodgkinson@geopostuk.com

In-Toto Ltd
Retailing of kitchens and bathroom
furniture and appliances
Shaw Cross Court
Shaw Cross Business Park
Dewsbury
West Yorkshire, WF12 7RF
www.intotofranchise.co.uk
Contact:
Mr D Watts
Tel: 01937 841483,
Mob: 07785 552541
david.watts@intoto.co.uk

Jo Jingles Ltd
Music and singing club for
pre-school children
1 Bois Moor Road
Chesham
Buckinghamshire, HP5 1SH
Contact:
Mrs Gill Thomas
Tel: 01494 778989
Fax: 01494 719361
headoffice@jojingles.co.uk

Kall-Kwik Printing (UK) Ltd
Quick printing and design
Artemis
Odyssey Business Park
West End Road, South Ruislip
Middlesex, HA4 6QF
www.kallkwik.co.uk
Contact:
Ms Caroline Joyce
Tel: 01895 872000
Fax: 01895 872110
caroline.joyce@kallkwik.co.uk

Kumon Educational UK
After-school teaching of maths and
English
Ground Floor
Landmark House
Station Road
Cheadle Hulme
Cheshire, SK8 7GE
Tel: 020 8447 9010
Fax: 020 8447 9030
Contact:
Mr Terry Kelly
Tel: 020 8447 9010
Fax: 020 8447 9030
terry.kelly@kumon.co.uk

Leadership Management (UK) Ltd
Management training
15 Grange Gardens
Farnham Common
Bucks, SL2 3HL
Tel: 01753 669358
Fax: 01753 669458
Contact:
Mr Ray King
Tel: 01753 669358
Fax: 01753 669458
jointheteam@lmi-uk.com

Mail Boxes Etc
Business, postal and
communications services

Unit 9, The Alfold Business Centre
Loxwood Road
Surrey, GU6 8HP
www.mbe.co.uk
Contact:
Mr Chris Gillam
Tel: 01403 759300
Fax: 01403 753820
cgillam@mbe.co.uk

Martin & Co
Property management and
lettings
182 Old Christchurch Road
Bournemouth, BH1 1NU
www.propertyfranchise.co.uk
Contact:
Franchise enquiries
Tel: 01202 292829
propertyfranchise@martinco.com

McDonald's
Quick service food
3 Cross Lane
Salford
Manchester, M5 4BN
Contact:
Franchising Team
Tel: 0161 2534116
Fax: 0161 2534148
franchise@uk.mcd.com

Merry Maids
Domestic cleaning
Tigers Road
Wigston
Leicester, LE18 4WS
Contact:
Mr Ken Dennis
Tel: 0116 2759000
Fax: 0116 2759002
kendennis@servicemaster.co.uk

Metro Rod
Drain care and repair
Metro House
Churchill Way
Macclesfield
Cheshire, SK11 6AY
Tel: 01625 888131
Fax: 01625 616687
www.metrorod.co.uk
Contact:
Mrs Wendy Drennan
Tel: 01625 888131
Fax: 01625 616687
wendy.drennan@metrorod.co.uk

Minster Services Group UK
Contract office cleaning
Minster House
948–952 Kingsbury Road
Erdington
Birmingham, B24 9PZ
Tel: 0121 386 1722
Fax: 0121 386 1191
www.minstergroup.co.uk
Contact:
Mr Mark Huckle
Tel: 0121 386 1722
mark.huckle@minstergroup.co.uk

Molly Maid UK Limited
Domestic cleaning
Bishop House South
The Bishop Centre
Bath Road
Taplow
Maidenhead
Berkshire, SL6 ONY
www.mollymaid.co.uk/franchise
Contact:
Mr Andrew Parsons
Tel: 01628 663500
Fax: 01628 663700
aparsons@mollymaid.co.uk

Money Shop
Cheque cashing, loans and related
financial services
46 Brook Street
Chester
Cheshire, CH1 3DZ
Tel: 0845 345 4705
Fax: 0845 345 4715
Contact:
Mr Courtney Vaughan
Tel: 0845 345 4705
Fax: 0845 345 4715
marie.roberts@dfguk.com

Monkey Music
Music and singing classes for
pre-school children
Unit 3
Thrales End Farm
Thrales End Lane
Harpenden, AL5 3NS
www.monkeymusic.co.uk
Contact:
Mrs Angie Davies
Tel: 01582 469242
Fax: 01582 469600
jointheteam@monkeymusic.co.uk

Mr Clutch
Fast fit of clutches, gearboxes and
brakes
2 Priory Road
Stroud
Rochester
Kent, ME2 2EG
Contact:
Mr Joe Yussuf
Tel: 01634 717747
Fax: 01634 731115
j.yussuf@mrclutch.com

Mr Electric UK
Electrical installation and repair
Five Mile House
128 Hanbury Road

Bromsgrove
Worcestershire, B60 4JZ
Contact:
Mr Clive Houlston
Tel: 01527 574343
Fax: 01527 874031
enquiries@mr-electric.co.uk

MRI Worldwide
Executive recruitment
MRI House
5 Victoria Street
Windsor
Berkshire, SL4 1HB
www.mriww.com
Contact:
Ms Carol Davids
Tel: 0870 777 3900
Fax: 0870 777 3910
cdavids@mriww.com

National Schoolwear Centres plc
Schoolwear retail
Ketteringham Hall
Church Road
Wymondham
Norfolk, NR18 9RS
Tel: 01603 819966
Fax: 01603 819977
Contact:
Mr Ian Masson
Tel: 01603 819966
Fax: 01603 819977
ianm@n-sc.co.uk

**Nationwide Investigations Group
Limited**
Private investigations bureau
141 Western Road
Haywards Heath
West Sussex, RH16 3LH
Tel: 01444 416004
Fax: 01444 441663
www.investigationfranchise.co.uk

Contact:
Mr S Withers
Tel: 01444 416004
Fax: 01444 441663
franchise@nig.co.uk

Nevada Bob UK Ltd
Golf Retail
The Rotunda
Broadgate Circle
Broadgate
London, EC2M 2BN
Contact:
Mr Jamie Goral
Tel: 020 7628 4999
Fax: 020 7628 7999
info@nevadabobs.co.uk

Northcliffe Retail Ltd
Newsagency
St George Street
Leicester, LE1 9FQ
Contact:
Mr Vance Potter
Tel: 0116 222 4801
Fax: 0116 251 6802
taramistry@northclifferetail.co.uk

Northwood GB Ltd
Residential lettings
1 Bellevue Road
Southampton, SO15 2AW
Tel: 02380 336677
Fax: 02380 333789
www.northwoodfranchises.co.uk
Contact:
Mr Andrew Goodson
Tel: 02380 336677
Fax: 02380 333789
sales@northwoodfranchises.co.uk

O'Briens Irish Sandwich Bars
Sandwich café
2 Elsinore House
77 Fulham Palace Road
London, W6 8JA

www.obriens.ie
Contact:
Mr Paul Stanton
Tel: 0208 741 7777
Fax: 0208 741 7788
info@obriens.ie

Ovenu
Domestic oven valeting
67 Barkham Ride
Wokingham
Berkshire, RG40 4HA
Contact:
Mr Rik Hallewell
Tel: 01189 736739
Fax: 01189 731876
rik.ovenu@ukonline.co.uk

PDC Copyprint
Print, design and communicate
1 Church Lane
East Grinstead
West Sussex , RH19 3AZ
Tel: 01342 315321
Fax: 01342 327117
www.pdccopyprint.co.uk
Contact:
Mr Stephen Ricketts
Tel: 01342 315321
Fax: 01342 327117
intl@pdccopyprint.com

Perfect Pizza
Restaurants and take-away units
Units 5 & 6, The Forum
Hanworth Lane
Chertsey
Surrey, KT16 9JX
www.perfectpizza.co.uk
Contact:
Ms Armanda Jarvis
Tel: 01932 568000
armanda_jarvis@papajohns.co.uk

Pirtek Europe plc
Hydraulic and industrial hose
35 Acton Park Estate
The Vale
Acton
London, W3 7QE
Contact:
Mr John Chaplin
Tel: 020 8749 8444
info@pirtek.co.uk

Pitman Training Group
IT and business skills training
centres
Sandown House
Sandbeck Way
Wetherby
West Yorkshire, LS22 7DN
www.pitman-training.co.uk
Contact:
Mr M Cressey
Tel: 01937 548562
**franchising-
opportunities@pitman-
training.com**

Post Office Ltd
Retail and post office products
Franchise Opportunities
1st Floor
130 Old Street
London, EC1V 9PQ
Contact:
Miss Stephanie Lawrie
Tel: 020 7320 7219
Fax: 020 7320 7230
**POL_Franchise_Opportunities@
postoffice.co.uk**

Prontaprint Ltd
Fast print centre
Artemis
Odyssey Business Park
West End Road, South Ruislip
Middlesex, HA4 6QF

www.prontaprint.com
Contact:
Rosh Majithia
Tel: 01895 872064
Fax: 01895 872110
rosh.majithia@adareodc.com

Pronuptia Bridal & Mens Formal Wear
Sale and hire of wedding dresses and menswear
PO Box 2478
Hove, BN3 6AG
Tel: 01273 563006
Fax: 01273 563006
Contact:
Mr Robert Devlin
Tel: 01273 563006
Fax: 01273 563006
pronuptia@btopenworld.com

Rainbow International Carpet Care and Restoration Specialist
Soft furnishings and disaster restoration
Spectrum House
Lower Oakham Way
Oakham Business Park
Mansfield, NG18 5BY
Tel: 01623 675100
Fax: 01623 422466
www.rainbow-int.co.uk
Contact:
Mr Ron Hutton
Tel: 01623 675100
Fax: 01623 422466
ron@rainbow-int.co.uk

Recognition Express Ltd
Name badges, signage, vehicle livery, trophies and awards
Wheatfield Way
Hinckley Fields
Hinckley
Leicestershire, LE10 1YG

www.recognition-express.com/franchise/
Contact:
Mr N Toplis
Tel: 01455 445555
Fax: 01455 445566
ntoplis@recognition-express.com

Revive! Auto Innovations (UK) Ltd
Automotive paint repairs
25 Somers Road
Rugby
Warwickshire, CV21 7DG
Tel: 01788 569999
Fax: 01788 570080
Contact:
Mrs Terry Nicholson
Tel: 0800 9174379
Fax: 01788 570080
enquiries@revive-uk.com

Riverford Organic Vegetables Ltd
Home delivery of organic vegetable boxes
Wash Barn
Buckfastleigh
Devon, TQ11 0LD
Tel: 01803 762720
Fax: 01803 762718
www.riverford.co.uk
Contact:
Mr Ian Bradley
Tel: 01803 762720
Fax: 01803 762718
franchise@riverford.co.uk

Rosemary Conley Diet and Fitness Clubs
Diet and fitness clubs
Quorn House
Meeting Street
Quorn
Loughborough, Leicestershire, LE12 8EX
www.rosemary-conley.co.uk

Contact:
Ms Heather Shaw
Tel: 01509 620222
heather.shaw@rosemary-conley.co.uk

Safeclean
Furniture care and stain removal
152 Milton Park
Abingdon
Oxfordshire, OX14 4SD
Contact:
Mr Paul Roberts
Tel: 01235 444757
safeclean@valspar.com

Saks Hair & Beauty
Hair and beauty salons
Saks Franchise Services Ltd
Saks HQ
55–59 Duke Street
Darlington, DL3 7SD
www.sakshairandbeauty.com
Contact:
Ms Jennifer Evans
Tel: 01325 380333
Fax: 01325 360228
franchise@sakshairandbeauty.com

Scottish & Newcastle Pub Enterprises
Public house retailing
2–4 Broadway Place
South Gyle Broadway
Edinburgh, EH12 9JZ
Tel: 0131 528 2713
Fax: 0131 528 2889
www.pub-enterprises.co.uk
Contact:
Ms Sophie Baker
Tel: Freephone 0500 94 95 96
Fax: 0191 224 6357
sophie.baker@pub-enterprises.co.uk

Select Appointments plc
Recruitment consultancy
Regent Court
Laporte Way
Beds, LU4 8SB
www.select.co.uk
Contact:
Debbie Smith
Tel: 01582 811600
Fax: 01582 811611
franchise@select.co.uk

ServiceMaster Ltd
Cleaning services, furniture and
carpet repairs and restoration
ServiceMaster House
Tigers Road
Wigston
Leicestershire, LE18 4WS
Tel: 0116 275 9000
Fax: 0116 275 9002
Contact:
Mr Ken Dennis
Tel: 0116 275 9000
Fax: 0116 275 9002
kendennis@servicemaster.co.uk

Sevenoaks Sound & Vision
Electrical retail
109–113 London Road
Sevenoaks
Kent, TN13 1BH
Tel: 01732 466215
www.sevenoaksfranchising.co.uk
Contact:
Mr Malcolm Blockley
Tel: 01494 431290
Fax: 01732 743981
m.blockley@btconnect.com

Signs Express
Sign makers
Franchise Head Office,
The Old Church
St Matthews Road

Norwich
Norfolk, NR1 1SP
Tel: 0800 731 2255
Fax: 01603 613136
www.signsexpress.co.uk
Contact:
Mr D Corbett
Tel: 0800 731 2255
Fax: 01603 613136
fran@signsexpress.co.uk

Sliderobes
Fitted bedroom furniture
Sliderobes House
61 Boucher Crescent
Belfast, BT12 6HU
Tel: 028 90 681034
Fax: 028 90 661032
www.sliderobes.com
Contact:
Mr Rodney Jess
Tel: 028 90 681034
Fax: 028 90 661032
**franchise.enquiries@sliderobes.
com**

Snack in the Box
Snack delivery to businesses
Belvedere Point
Penner Road
Havant
Hampshire, PO9 1QY
Contact:
Mr Matthew O'Neil
Tel: 0239 241 5000
Fax: 0239 247 5005
matt@sitb.co.uk

Snack in the Box Vending Services
Deliver snacks to the workplace
Belvedere Point
Penner Road
Havant
Hampshire, PO9 1QY

Contact:
Mr Matthew O'Neil
Tel: 0239 241 5000
Fax: 0239 247 5005
matt@sitb.co.uk

Snap-on-Tools
Distribution of automotive hand
tools
Telford Way
Kettering
Northants, NN16 8SN
www.snapon.com
Contact:
Mr Seán Derrig
Tel: 01536 413800
Fax: 01536 413900
ukweb@snapon.com

Snappy Snaps Franchises Ltd
One hour developing and printing
Glenthorne Mews
Glenthorne Road
Hammersmith
London, W6 OLJ
www.snappysnaps.com
Contact:
Mr T MacAndrews
Tel: 020 8741 7474
info@snappysnaps.co.uk

Sportscoach
Sports schools for children
The Courthouse
Elm Grove
Walton-on-Thames
Surrey, KT12 1LZ
Contact:
Mr Manzoor Ishani
Tel: 01932 256264
Fax: 01932 256210
info@scoach.co.uk

Spud U Like Ltd
Fast food restaurant
9 Central Business Centre
Great Central Way
London, NW10 0UR
Contact:
Mr T Schleisinger
Tel: 020 8830 2424
headoffice@spudulike.com

Stagecoach Theatre Arts
Part-time theatre schools for
children
The Courthouse
Elm Grove
Walton-on-Thames
Surrey, KT12 1LZ
www.stagecoach.co.uk
Contact:
Mr Manzoor Ishani
Tel: 01932 254333
Fax: 01932 256227
mail@stagecoach.co.uk

Stainbusters Ltd
Floor, carpet and upholstery
cleaning
15 Windmill Avenue
Woolpit Business Park
Woolpit
Bury St Edmunds, Suffolk,
IP30 9UP
www.stainbusters.co.uk
Contact:
Ms Christine Gooch
Tel: 0800 137772
franchise@stainbusters.co.uk

Stumpbusters UK Ltd
Tree stump grinding
Hill House
Brimmers Road
Princes Risborough
Bucks, HP27 0LE
Contact:
Mr A Broom

Tel: 01844 342851
stump@globalnet.co.uk

Subway
Fast food sandwich outlets
3 Market Place
Carrickfergus
County Antrim
Northern Ireland, BT38 7AW
www.subway.co.uk
Contact:
Mr Paul Heyes
Tel: 0800 085 5058 (UK), 0044 2893
359 080 (Eire)
Fax: 028 93 359102
sharp.pencil@dnet.co.uk

Swisher
Washroom cleaning and sanitation
9 Churchill Court
33 Palmerston Road
Bournemouth, BH1 4HN
Tel: 01202 303333
Fax: 01202 303232
www.swisher.co.uk
Contact:
Mrs Marilyn Keen
Tel: 01202 303333
Fax: 01202 303232
franchise@swisher.co.uk

TaxAssist Accountants
General accountancy services
TaxAssist House
112–114 Thorpe Road
Norwich, NR1 1RT
Tel: 01603 611811
Fax: 01603 619992
www.taxassistdirect.info
Contact:
Mr Neil Mason
Tel: 01603 447414
Fax: 01603 619992
hannah.westgarth@taxassist.co.uk

Techclean
Cleaning of computer equipment
Techclean plc
VDU House
Old Kiln Lane
Churt, Farnham
Surrey, GU10 2JH
Tel: 01428 713713
Fax: 01428 713798
Contact:
Mr Nick Zarach
Tel: 01428 713713
Fax: 01428 713798
info@techclean.co.uk

The Flat Roof Company
Refurbishment of flat roofs
Unit 7, Guardian Park
Station Industrial Estate
Tadcaster
North Yorkshire, LS24 9SG
www.flatroof.co.uk
Contact:
Mr Kevin Moody
Tel: 01937 530788
franchiseinfo@flatroof.co.uk

The Original Poster Company
Distribution of greeting cards
Elephant House
28 Lyon Road
Walton-on-Thames
Surrey, KT12 3PU
www.originalposter.com
Contact:
Mr Jeremy Webster
Tel: 01932 267300
Fax: 01932 267333
fionar@originalposter.com

The Property Search Group
Personal searches for the legal
sector
142 Trinity Street
Huddersfield

West Yorkshire, HD1 4DT
Contact:
Mr Gary Hester
Tel: 01484 311649
Fax: 01484 311539
info@propertysearchgroup.co.uk

The Village Green Team Ltd
Home and lifestyle maintenance
The Oak Business Centre
79–93 Ratcliffe Road
Sileby
Leicestershire, LE12 7PU
Tel: 01509 812424
Fax: 01509 812425
www.vgteam.com
Contact:
Colleen Denby
Tel: 01509 812424
info@vgteam.com

Thorntons
Chocolate and sugar confectionery
Franchise/JV Co-ordinator
Thornton Park
Somercotes
Derby, DE55 4XJ
Contact:
Miss Fiona Radford / Han Van Reen
Tel: 01773 542454
Fax: 01773 540757
fiona.radford@thorntons.co.uk

Thrifty Car Rental
Car and van rental
Flightform House
Halifax Road, Cressex Business Park
High Wycombe
Buckinghamshire, HP12 3SN
www.thrifty.co.uk
Contact:
Mr Ian Saxon
Tel: 01494 751500
Fax: 01494 751503
ian.saxon@thrifty.co.uk

Toni & Guy
Hairdressing
Innovia House
Marish Wharf
St. Mary's Road
Langley, SL3 6DA
Contact:
Mr John Murphy
Tel: 01753 612 040
Fax: 01753 612 051
amber.etherington@innovia.co.uk

Travail Employment Group Ltd
Business employment agency
24 Southgate Street
Gloucester, GL1 2DP
www.travail.co.uk
Contact:
Mr Bill Hendrie
Tel: 01452 420700
franchise@travail.co.uk

Tumble Tots (UK) Limited
Physical play for pre-school children
Bluebird Park
Bromsgrove Road
Hunnington
Halesowen, West Midlands, B62 0TT
www.tumbletots.com
Contact:
Mr David Hunt
Tel: 0121 585 7003
Fax: 0121 585 6891
david.hunt@tumbletots.com

Urban Planters Franchise Ltd
Indoor plants rental, sale and
maintenance
The Tack Room, The Stables
Mudgley Road
Rooks Bridge
Somerset, BS26 2TH
www.urbanplanters.co.uk
Contact:
Mr Alan Page

Tel: 01934 751188 or 0800 358 2245
Fax: 01934 751199
info@urbanplanters.co.uk

Vendo plc
Commercial vehicle power washing
215 East Lane
Wembley
Middlesex, HA0 3NG
Contact:
Mr I Calhoun
Tel: 020 8908 1234

Ventrolla Ltd
11 Hornbeam Square South
South Harrogate
North Yorkshire, HG2 8NB
Tel: 01423 870011
www.ventrolla.co.uk
Contact:
Mr S C Emmerson
Tel: 01423 859323
Fax: 01423 859321
info@ventrolla.co.uk

Viewplus
Home delivery rental of DVD +
VHS movies, PlayStation games
The Forum
277 London Road
Burgess Hill
West Sussex, RH15 9QU
Tel: 01444 240250
Fax: 01444 240251
Contact:
Ms Helen Monteiro
Tel: 01444 240250
Fax: 01444 240251
sales@viewplus.co.uk

Vision Express
Retail opticians
Abbeyfield Road
Lenton
Nottingham, NG7 2SP

Contact:
Mrs Hilary Hann
Tel: 0115 988 2109
Fax: 0115 988 2175
hilary.hann@visionexpress.com

Wiltshire Farm Foods
Private home meals delivery service
Apetito Ltd
Canal Road
Trowbridge
Wiltshire, BA14 8RJ
www.wiltshirefarmfoods.com
Contact:
Mr Ben Haynes
Tel: 01225 756015
Fax: 01225 756069
ben.haynes@apetito.co.uk

Wimpy International Ltd
Family hamburger restaurant
2 The Listons

Liston Road
Marlow
Buckinghamshire, SL7 1FD
www.wimpyburgers.co.uk
Contact:
Mr Chris Woolfenden
Tel: 01628 891655
info@wimpyburgers.co.uk

Xperience
Estate agents
68 School Road
Tilehurst
Reading
Berkshire, RG31 5AW
www.xperience.co.uk
Contact:
Mr Michael Stoop
Tel: 0118 945 9900
Fax: 0118 945 9901
admin@lgfl.co.uk

Associate members

Companies with a growing franchise network with evidence of successful franchising for a period of one year with a least one franchisee.
To become an associate member of the BFA, franchisors are required to submit a completed application form, including disclosure document, franchise agreement, prospectus, accounts, etc and provide proof of a correctly constituted pilot scheme successfully operated for at least one year, financed and managed by the applicant company (as for full membership) but with evidence of successful franchising for a period of one year with at least one franchisee.

24 Self Video
Video rental of films and games
12 Wolfe Close
Parkgate Industrial Estate
Knutsford, Cheshire, WA16 8XJ
Tel: 08708 505070
Contact:
Mrs Tessa Howard-Vyse
Tel: 08708 505070
Fax: 01565 633759
info@24selfvideo.co.uk

Alliance Preservation
Building preservation services
Seaton Hall
Staithes, TS13 5AT
Tel: 0800 096 9390
www.alliance-preservation.com
Contact:
Mr David Brice
Tel: 0800 0969390
david.brice@blueyonder.co.uk

Antal International Network
Executive recruitment
Regent House
24–25 Nutford Place
London, W1H 5YN
www.antalfranchising.com
Contact:
Mr Kevin Cox
Tel: 0870 774 5464
Fax: 0870 774 5465
franchise@antal.com

Barrett & Coe
Training in wedding and portrait
photography
79A Thorpe Road
Norwich
Norfolk, NR1 1UA
www.barrettandcoe.co.uk
Contact:
Mr Andrew Coe
Tel: 01603 629739
enquires@barrettandcoe.co.uk

Benjys Group Limited
Mobile catering vans
8th Floor, Thames Tower
Princess House
1 Suffolk Lane
London, EC4X 0AX
Tel: 0845 330 0126
Fax: 020 7743 7501
Contact:
Franchise enquiries
Tel: 0845 330 0126
Fax: 020 7743 7501
franchise@benjys-sandwiches.com

bluemonday Recruitment
Recruitment
18 Soho Square
London, W1D 3QL
Tel: 020 7025 8747
Fax: 020 7025 8100
Contact:

Ms Debbie Whelan
Tel: 020 7025 8747
Fax: 020 7025 8100
dw@bluemondayrecruitment.com

Car Medic
Car refinishing
14 Firbank Way
Leighton Buzzard
Bedfordshire, LU7 4YP
Contact:
Mr Andrew Hack
Tel: 01525 375375
Fax: 01525 218007
andy@smartercars.fsnet.co.uk

Care@
Nursing and care staff agency
123–131 Brandford Court
Bradford Street
Digbeth
Birmingham, B12 0NS
Contact:
Mr Jon Tipper
Tel: 0121 693 2470
Fax: 0121 693 2469

Chips Franchise Ltd
Video games and accessories
63–65 Borough Road
Middlesbrough, TS1 3AA
Tel: 0870 013 0028
Fax: 01642 351477
www.chipsworld.co.uk
Contact:
Mrs Debra McCabe
Tel: 0870 013 0028
Fax: 01642 351477
franchise@chipsworld.co.uk

Clothes Aid Collections Ltd
Commercial collection of charity
bags
Leroy House
436–438 Essex Road
London, N13 QP

Contact:
Mr Laurie Hollande
Tel: 020 7226 4607
Fax: 020 7704 0737
paula@clothesaid.co.uk

CNA International
Executive recruitment and
management consultancy
4 Boundary Court
Willow Farm Business Park
Castle Donington
Derby, DE74 2UD
Tel: 01332 856200
Fax: 01332 856222
www.cnacareers.co.uk
Contact:
Ms Paula Reed
Tel: 01332 856200
Fax: 01332 856222
info@cnainternational.co.uk
Mr Alan Tarant
Tel: 01332 856200
Fax: 01332 856222
info@cnainternational.co.uk

Consol Suncenter (Franchise) Ltd
Automated tanning salons
42 Old Market Street
Bristol, BS2 OE2
Tel: 0117 925 7722
Fax: 0117 925 5233
Contact:
Mr Poul Nymann
Tel: 0117 925 7722
Fax: 0117 925 5233
consol@consol.uk.com

Costa Ltd
Coffee retail
Whitbread Court
PO Box 777
Dunstable
Bedfordshire, LU5 5XG
Contact:

Ms Vivien Dunn
Tel: 020 8956 2250
vmd@away2be.com

Countrywide Signs Limited
Estate agency board suppliers and
contractors
105 Wyberton West Road
Boston
Lincolnshire, PE21 7JU
Tel: 01205 363909
Fax: 01205 364640
www.countrywide-signs.com
Contact:
Mr Martin Baker
Tel: 01205 363909
Fax: 01205 364640
sales@countrywide-signs.com

Dancia International
Retail dancewear
Crown House
Crown Road
Portslade
Brighton, BN41 1SH
www.dancia.co.uk/franchise
Contact:
Ms Beverly Kirkup
Tel: 01273 414455, ext 20
franchise@dancia.co.uk
Mr T Kirkup
Tel: 01273 414455
franchise@dancia.co.uk

Davis Coleman Ltd
Banking and legal agents
PO Box 5498
Ongar
Essex, CM5 0TJ
Contact:
Mr Harry Varney
Tel: 01277 364333
Fax: 01277 364773
h.varney@daviscoleman.com

Devonshire Art Publishers
Supply greeting cards to retailers
7 Park Royal Metro Centre
Britannia Way
Coronation Road
London, NW10 7PA
Contact:
Ms Marcella Rowan
Tel: 020 8691 6611
Fax: 020 86919169
devonshirecards@btinternet.com

Dream Doors Limited
Kitchen door replacement
Unit D22, Heritage Business Park
Heritage Way
Gosport
Hampshire, PO12 4BG
Contact:
Mr John Dyer
Tel: 02392 604630
Fax: 02392 586317
franchising@dreamdoorsltd.co.uk

DTT (Franchising) Ltd
Driver transport training
Unit 2
Shepherds Grove Industrial Estate
East
Stanton
Bury St Edmunds
Suffolk, IP31 2BG
Tel: 01359 251717
Fax: 01359 253601
Contact:
Mr Paul Van Der Hulks
Tel: 01359 251717
Fax: 01359 253601
paul@d-t-t.co.uk

Dublcheck Cleaning Ltd
Cleaning
Padeswood Hall
Padeswood
Mold

Flintshire, CH7 4JF
Tel: 01244 550150
Fax: 01244 550250
Contact:
Mr Mark Sansom
Tel: 01244 550150
Fax: 01244 550250
mark@dublcheck.co.uk

Esquires Coffee Houses
Coffee retail
Ground Floor
54A Clerkenwell Road
London, EC1M 5PS
Contact:
Mr Peter Kirton
Tel: 020 7251 5166
Fax: 020 7251 5177
peterk@esquirescoffee.com

Filta Group
Purification of cooking oils
The Locks
Hillmorton
Rugby, CV21 4PP
Contact:
Mr J Urosevic
Tel: 01788 550100
Fax: 01788 551839
enquiries@filtagroup.com

**Franchise Development Services
(FDS)**
International franchise consultancy
Franchise House
56 Surrey Street
Norwich, NR1 3FD
www.franchise-group.com
Contact:
Mr Roy Seaman
Tel: 01603 620301
Fax: 01603 630174
enquiries@fdsltd.com

Granite Transformations
Kitchen worktop resurfacing
Unit L3, 52 Morley Road
Deacon Trading Estate
Tonbridge
Kent, TN9 1RA
www.granitetransformations.com
Contact:
Mr Bob Boynton
Tel: 01732 365836
Fax: 01732 366536
**bob@granite-
transformations.co.uk**

Green Cleen (UK) Ltd
Wheeled bin washing
18 Ladfordfields Industrial Park
Seighford
Staffordshire, ST18 9QE
Contact:
Marius Coulon
Tel: 01785 282855
Fax: 01785 281300
info@greencleen.com

Greensleeves Lawn Care
Domestic lawncare service
York House
198 Barnsley Road
Denby Dale
Huddersfield, HD8 8TS
Contact:
Mr David Truby
Tel: 01484 866566 or 0808 100 1413
david@greensleeves.uk.com

Helen O'Grady Drama Academy
Self-development for children
Helen O'Grady (CI) Ltd
North Side
Vale
Guernsey, GY3 5TX
Tel: 01481 200250
Fax: 01481 200247
www.helenogrady.co.uk

Contact:
Mr N Le Page
Tel: 01481 200250
Fax: 01481 200247
headoffice@helenogrady.co.uk

Hydro-Dynamix Ltd
Domestic, contract and commercial
cleaning
Greenwich House
Peel Street
Maidstone
Kent, ME14 2BP
Tel: 01622 664993
Fax: 01622 695170
Contact:
Mr James Every
Tel: 01622 664993
Fax: 01622 695170
james.every@hydro-dynamix.com

Ivory Tower Cards Ltd
Greetings cards
13A Waldeck House
Waldeck Road
Maidenhead
Berkshire, SL6 8BR
Contact:
Ms Suzanne Ivory
Tel: 01628 626866
Fax: 01628 626861
enquiries@ivorytowercards.com

Jani King
Contract cleaning
150 London Road
Kingston-upon-Thames
Surrey, KT2 6QL
Contact:
Mr P Howarth
Tel: 020 8481 4300
Fax: 020 8481 4343
jessicaa561@janikinggb.co.uk

Jim's Mowing
Home service gardening
Unit 4
Lakeview Stables
St Clere Estate
Sevenoaks, Kent, TH15 6HL
Contact:
Mr Jason Jaap or Richard Harrison
Tel: 0845 009 5467
Fax: 01732 763949
info@jimsmowing.co.uk

Kids Klub Franchising
Children's entertainment videos
Shunters Yard
Station Road
Semley
Nr Shaftesbury
Dorset, SP7 9AH
www.kids-klub.co.uk
Contact:
Mr G Thomas
Tel: 01747 853999
Fax: 01747 853888
info@kids-klub.co.uk

Kwiklite (Franchising) Ltd
Lighting maintenance
Longueville House
Orton Longueville
Peterborough, PE2 7DN
Contact:
Mr Peter Hurford
Tel: 01733 704771
Fax: 01733 704711
peter.hurford@kwiklite.co.uk

La Baguette Du Jour Ltd
Sandwich café and espresso bar
F18 Ashmount Business Park
Upper Forest Way
Swansea Enterprise Park
Swansea, SA6 8QR
Contact:
Mr Mark Meadon

Tel: 01792 790701
Fax: 01792 791006
enquiries@la-baguette.co.uk

Lasertech UK Limited
Sales and distribution of printer
consumables
Wharfside Ind Estate
Wharf St
Howley
Warrington
Cheshire, WA1 2HT
Contact:
Miss Ruth Brown
Tel: 0870 787 2323
Fax: 0870 787 0708
franchise@lasertech.co.uk

Link Up Properties Franchising Ltd
Estate agency
Sterling House
20 Victoria Way
Burgess Hill
West Sussex, RH15 0NF
www.linkupproperties.co.uk
Contact:
Mrs Cherie Matthews
Tel: 01444 257222
Fax: 01444 257333
cherie@linkprop.co.uk

Maid2Clean
Domestic house cleaning and
ironing
Caiden House
Canal Road
Timperley, Altrincham
Cheshire, WA14 1TD
Tel: 01606 836080
Contact:
Mr Mike Hanrahan
Tel: 01606 836080
Fax: 01606 835366
sales@maid2clean.co.uk

Minuteman Press International Inc
Design, print and copying
Heatley Court, Mill Lane
Heatley
Lymm
Cheshire, WA13 9SD
Contact:
Mr George Holzmacher
Tel: 01925 757794
Fax: 01925 757783
info@mpihq.com

**Mitchells And Butlers Business
Franchise**
Pub retail
27 Fleet Street
Birmingham, B3 1JP
Contact:
Mr Simon Higginbottom
Tel: 0121 498 4463
Fax: 0121 233 2246
franchise.services@mbplc.com

Mixamate Concrete
Concrete delivery
The Corner House
Old Weston Road
Staffordshire, ST19 9AG
www.mixamate.co.uk
Contact:
Alan Gibson
Tel: 0800 288 8001
information@mixamate.co.uk

Provisional listing companies

Companies new to franchising,
developing their franchise concept
and taking BFA accredited advice
on its structure

0800handyman Ltd
Professional handyman service
Shakespeare House
168 Lavender Hill
London, SW11 5TG
Tel: 0800 426 396
Contact:
Mr Bruce Greig
Tel: 020 7801 6247
bruce@0800handyman.co.uk

1/2 Price Ink Cartridges
Printer consumables
Unit 1
Fernhill Court, Fernhill
Almondsbury, Bristol
Avon, BS32 4LX
Contact:
Ms Claire Mayes
Tel: 0845 129 8702
Fax: 0845 129 8703
claire@12ink.com

1st 4 Tops Ltd
Granite worktop
Haugh Lane
Addison Industrial Estate
Blaydon
Tyne & Wear, NE21 4TE
Contact:
Mr Paul Maguire
Tel: 0191 414 6463
Fax: 0191 414 2497
ask@1st4tops.co.uk

247Staff
Recruitment
Granby Chambers
1 Halford Street
Leicester, LE1 1JA
Contact:
The Franchise Team
Tel: 0845 225 5025
Fax: 07043 301684
info@247staff.net

4max Visual Impact
Wide format printing
3 Rivergate
Rivermead Drive
Swindon
Wiltshire, SN5 7ET
www.4max.co.uk
Contact:
Mr Martin Watts
Tel: 0870 402 4444
Fax: 0870 382 4444
enquiries@4maxltd.co.uk

Action International
Business Coaching
3–5 Richmond Hill
Richmond
Surrey, TW10 6RE
Contact:
Mr Ian Johnstone
Tel: 01284 711648
**ianjohnstone@action-
international.com**

Advanced Protection Systems
Monitored security systems
Building 24
BRE, Bucknalls Lane
Watford
Hertfordshire, WD25 9XX
Tel: 01923 677577
Fax: 01923 677588
Contact:
Mr Steve Sheen
Tel: 01923 677577
Fax: 01923 677588
info@advancedprotection.co.uk

All Trades Network
Property insurance repairs
Capricorn House
Capricorn Park
Blakewater Road
Blackburn
Lancashire, BB1 5QR

Contact:
Mr Keith Roberts
Tel: 01254 269677
Fax: 01254 269661
info@alltradesnetwork.biz

Animals at Home
Pet taxi, ambulance and pet care
services
Cale Oak Farm
Aston Road
Bampton
Oxfordshire, OX18 2BW
Contact:
Mr Mark Booty
Tel: 07970 0163364
Fax: 01993 851033
mark@animalsathome.co.uk

Aqua-lec
Plumbing, heating and energy
saving
Brooklyn House
Money Lane
The Green
West Drayton
Middlesex, UB7 7PQ
Contact:
Ms Carol Otway
Tel: 01845 420777
Fax: 01895 438737
carol.otway@aqua-lec.com

Armaplate UK Ltd
Vehicle lock protection systems
Central Workshops
off Longworth Rd
Horwich
Bolton, BL6 7DB
Contact:
Mr Tom McQuiggan
Tel: 01204 468295
Fax: 01204 468356
sales@armaplate.com

Ashton Burkinshaw
Lettings and property management
5 Clarendon Place
King Street
Maidstone
Kent, ME14 1BQ
www.aboutletting.co.uk
Contact:
Mr Graham Harrison
Tel: 01622 350601
Fax: 01622 350611
graham@ashtonburkinshaw.co.uk

Ask The Workpoint
Recruitment agency
98 Bradshawgate
Bolton
Lancashire, BL1 1QJ
Tel: 01204 532711
Fax: 01204 364461
Contact:
Mr Malcolm Hughes
Tel: 01204 532711
Fax: 01204 364461
m.hughes@theworkpoint.com

Attiva Franchising Ltd
Health and fitness clubs
Farringford House
Montford Bridge
Shrewsbury, SY4 1EB
Contact:
Mr Craig Farman
Tel: 0845 230365
Fax: 01743 851458
craig.farman@attivaUK.com

Automate
Automatic doors and shopfronts
Unit 9
Hill Lane Industrial Estate
Markfield
Leicestershire, LE67 9PN
Contact:
Ms Gemma Larter

Tel: 01530 249 500
Fax: 01530 249 444
gemmalarter@automateuk.com

Autoshine Express
Vehicle wash and car care
84 Whitburn Road
Birniehill
Bathgate
West Lothian, EH48 2HR
www.autoshine-express.co.uk
Contact:
Mr James Allison
Tel: 01506 650959
Fax: 01506 634968
info@autoshine-express.co.uk

Babyprints
Castings of children's hands and feet
The Orchard
Station Road
Elsenham, nr Bishops Stortford
Hertfordshire, CM22 6LG
Contact:
Mr Colin Hart
Tel: 01279 817169
Fax: 01279 816565
colinhart@babyprints.co.uk

Bartercard UK Plc
Trade exchange
Bartercard House
Brooklands Close
Sunbury
Middlesex, TW16 7DY
www.bartercard.co.uk
Contact:
Ms Sandi Miller
Tel: 0870 920 5000
Fax: 0870 920 2255
sandi.miller@bartercard.com

Bin Masters
Repair and maintenance of waste
containers
Municipal House
4 Telford Road
Ferndown Industrial Estate
Wimborne
Dorset, BH21 7QL
Tel: 01202 872526
Fax: 01202 870306
www.binmasters.co.uk
Contact:
Ms Janet Twining
Tel: 01202 872526
Fax: 01202 870306
janett@binmasters.co.uk

Business for Breakfast
Private members business club
31 Peel Street
Manchester, M30 0NG
Contact:
Mr John Fisher
Tel: 0871 097 1180
Fax: 0871 433 8333
john@bforb.co.uk

Chamberlains Security Ltd
Security business
28 Hamilton Terrace
Leamington Spa
Warwickshire, CV32 4LY
Contact:
Mr Graham Venn
Tel: 01926 886780
Fax: 01926 337875
info@chamberlainssecurity.com

Chameleon NCF Ltd
Telecommunications installation
Brunel Way
Severalls Business Park
Colchester
Essex, CO4 4QX

Contact:
Ms Rachel Havers
Tel: 01206 500880
Fax: 01206 500810
rhavers@chameleondirect.co.uk

Charisnack
Healthier snacks
3 Providence Court
Pynes Hill
Exeter
Devon, EX2 5JL
Tel: 0845 123 1132
Fax: 01392 360395
Contact:
Mr Gordon Blood
Tel: 0845 123 1132
Fax: 01392 360395
gordon@charisnack.co.uk

Clairol Professional
Sale of professional hair products
Bessemer Road
Basingstoke
Hampshire, RG22 4AF
www.clairolprofessional.co.uk
Contact:
Mr Paul Green
Tel: 01256 490888
**enquiries@clairolprofessional.co.
uk**

**Clive's Easylearn Pop Music
Schools**
Music tuition
Clive's Franchise Ltd
PO Box 305
Brockenhurst, SO42 7XX
www.clivesmusic.com
Contact:
Mr Clive Brooks
Tel: 02380 477433
franchise@clivesmusic.com

Coffee Republic
Coffee/food
109/123 Clifton Street
London, EC2A 4LD
Contact:
Mr Brian Carroll
Tel: 020 7033 0613
Fax: 08701 400112
briancarroll@coffeerepublic.co.uk

ComputerXplorers
Children's classes in IT
Wheatfield Way
Hinckley Field Industrial Estate
Hinckley
Leicestershire, LE10 1YG
Contact:
Mr Jon Owen
Tel: 01455 45572
Fax: 01455 445520
jowen@computerxplorers.co.uk

Concept Building Solutions
Building insurance claims
management
4 The Printworks
Hey Road
Clitheroe, BB7 9WA
Tel: 0800 783 2818
Fax: 01254 825251
Contact:
Mr Darren Griffin
Tel: 01254 825250
Fax: 01254 825251
**info@conceptbuildingsolutions.co.
uk**

Connect 2 (franchising) Ltd
Promotional merchandise
Bawdon Lodge Farm
Charley Road, Nanpanton
Loughborough
Leicestershire, LE12 4XJ

Contact:
Mr Nick Pigott
Tel: 01530 242 601
Fax: 01530 245 357
sales@connect2franchising.com

Contours Express
Fitness and weight loss
53 Benedictine Place
25 London Road
St Albans
Hertfordshire, AL1 1LB
Contact:
Mr Jason Chong
Tel: 0845 606 6139
Fax: 0845 706 4499
jason@contoursexpress.com

Cuticles Ltd
Nail and beauty studio
The Garden Studio
Eynsham Park
North Leigh
Oxfordshire, OX29 6PN
Contact:
Ms Ros Lewis
Tel: 01993 883925
Fax: 01993 886605
ros.lewis@cuticles.ltd.uk

Direct Workwear (UK) Ltd
Personal Protective Workwear
Mountsorrel Hall
No 2 Loughborough Road
Mountsorrel, Loughborough
Leicestershire, LE12 7AT
www.directworkwear.co.uk
Contact:
Mr Paul Venn
Tel: 07970 464222,
Office: 0845 351 9969
paul@directworkwear.co.uk

Doorstep Holidays
Tour operator
Medway Quay
36 Riverside
Sir Thomas Longley Road
Rochester, ME2 4DP
Tel: 0870 027 5200
Fax: 0870 027 5201
Contact:
Mr Mick Crawford
Tel: 0870 027 5200
Fax: 0870 027 5201
mick@doorstepholidays.co.uk

Drive Doctor (UK) Ltd
Driveway restoration
3 Colville Court
Winwick Quay
Warrington
Cheshire, WA2 8QT
Contact:
Mr Michael Palin
Tel: 0800 169 4469
Fax: 01942 606681
info@drivedoctor.uk.com

easyInternetCafé
Internet cafés
42/43 Gloucester Crescent
London, NW1 7DL
Tel: 020 7241 9166
Fax: 020 7482 2857
Contact:
The Franchise Team
Tel: 020 7241 9000
franchising@easygroup.co.uk

Eleclocal
Electrical installation and
maintenance
Essex House
High Street
Dunmow, CM6 1AE
Contact:
Mr Matt Moakes

Tel: 0808 0000000
admin@localgroup.co.uk

Energie Fitness Clubs
Energie House
Tongwell Street
Fox Milne
Milton Keynes, MK15 0YA
Contact:
The Franchise Team
Tel: 01908 607605
Fax: 01908 670597
info@energiehq.com

Essential Healthcare International
Healthcare products and services
Parkhouse
Bradford Road
Birstall, Batley
West Yorkshire, WF17 9PH
www.essential-healthcare.com
Contact:
Mr Graham Mylchreest
Tel: 0845 344 1900
Fax: 0845 344 1901
gm@essential-healthcare.com

Euro Talk-World Languages
Language learning system
9 Park Royal Metro Centre
Britannia Way
London, NW10 7PA
Contact:
Mr Michael Matthews
Tel: 020 8965 9988
Fax: 020 8965 8777
info.wls@btconnect.com

Fit 'N' Fun Kids
Physical development classes for
children
Unit 10
Tregoniggie Industrial Estate
Falmouth
Cornwall, TR11 4SN

Tel: 01326 379428
www.fitnfunkids.co.uk
Contact:
Ms Rachel Jones
Tel: 01326 379428
Fax: 01326 379428
info@fitnfunkids.co.uk

Fit-ex Ltd
Curtain and blind fitting
6 Craddocks Parade
Craddocks Avenue
Ashstead
Surrey, KT21 1QL
Tel: 01372 275037
Fax: 01372 271500
www.fit-ex.com
Contact:
Mr David Hinwood-Jones
Tel: 01372 275037
Fax: 01372 271500
info@fit-ex.com

Frère Jacques Patisserie
Retail French patisserie
Unit 25, Cotteswold Dairy Site
Northway Lane
Tewkesbury
Gloucestershire, GL20 8JG
Tel: 01684 295030
Fax: 01684 295084
Contact:
Ms Helen Dangreaux
Tel: 07967 6758014
Fax: 01684 295084
frere.jacques@btinternet.com

Furniture Pro
Furniture repair
Valspar Industries Ltd
152 Milton Park
Abingdon
Oxfordshire, OX14 4SD

Contact:
Mr Craig Henthorn
Tel: 01235 444749
Fax: 01235 862730
chenthorn@valspar.com

Gas-Elec Safety Systems Ltd
Safety inspection
Brooklyn House
Money Lane
The Green
West Drayton
Middlesex, UB7 7PQ
Contact:
Ms Carol Otway
Tel: 01895 420777
carol.otway@gas-elec.co.uk

Globalink International
Business telecommunications
Globalink House
Honeybridge Lane
Dial Post
Horsham
West Sussex, RH13 8NX
Contact:
Mr Phil Gaffer
Tel: 0870 845 5655
Fax: 0870 845 5656
phil@globalinkgroup.com

Go Cruise
Sale of cruises
Crown House
Crown Street
Ipswich, IP1 3HS
Tel: 0121 445 7121
www.cruisefranchise.co.uk
Contact:
Mr Steve Williams
Tel: 01473 292 016
steve.williams@fredolsen.co.uk

Hair on Broadway
Hairdressing
333 Watling Street
Radlett
Hertfordshire, WD7 7LB
Contact:
Mr David Twyman
Tel: 01923 854100
Fax: 01923 850565
hob@btconnect.com

Harvey World Travel (UK) Ltd
Travel agency
Harvey House
Lakeside Plaza, Walkmill Lane
Bridgtown
Cannock
Staffordshire, WS11 0XE
Contact:
Ms Natalie Turner
Tel: 08712 080525
**franchising@harveyworldtravel.
co.uk**

Hudson's Coffee House
Coffee bars
Office at rear of Cleave House
Sticklepath
Okehampton
Devon, EX20 2NL
Contact:
Mr Tim Penrose
Tel: 0121 236 9009
Fax: 0121 236 3008
tim@hudsonsfood.com

Increase Decrease
Ironing service
Unit 4, Venture Court
Bedwas Housr Ind Estate
Bedwas
Caerphilly, CF83 8DW
Contact:
Mr M Clarke
Tel: 02920 887768

Fax: 02920 884281
**andy@increasedecrease.demon.co.
uk**

Ink World
Inkjet Cartridges
143A Queen's Road
Nuneaton
Warwickshire, CV11 5LD
Tel: 0800 011 2011
Fax: 0800 011 2022
Contact:
Mr Mark Reid
Tel: 0800 011 2011
Fax: 0800 011 2022
mail@ink-world.co.uk

Ink Xpress
Inkjet cartridges
36–40 Grimwade Street
Ipswich
Suffolk, IP4 1LP
Contact:
Mr Nicholas Reid
Tel: 01473 242720
franchisesales@inkxpress.com

IQ Media Limited
Media and communications
The Coach House, Sundial House
Altrincham Road, Styal
Wilmslow
Cheshire, SK9 4JE
Contact:
Mr Simon Poyser
Tel: 01625 418666
Fax: 01625 522253
simonpoyser@iqmedia-uk.com
**katherinelivingstone@iqmedia-uk.
com**

Jacks of London
Men's barber shop
15 Wimbledon Bridge
Wimbledon
London, SW19 7NH

Tel: 020 8971 2038
www.jacksoflondon.co.uk
Contact:
Ms Sue Whitehead
Tel: 020 8971 2038
Fax: 020 8971 2038
info@jacksoflondon.co.uk

Jordans Residential
Lettings and property management
10 Alderley Road
Wilmslow
Cheshire, SK9 1JX
Contact:
Ms Jayne Dowse
Tel: 0870 703 9013
Fax: 01625 250005
jayne.dowse@jordansrentals.com

Just Lets Property Management Ltd
Residential property management
142 Oundle Road
Peterborough, PE2 9PJ
Contact:
Mr Steven Heron
Tel: 0870 748 9569
Fax: 0870 133 9476
franchise@justlets.com

KA International
Interior decoration retailer
793 Fulham Road
London, SW6 6HD
Tel: 020 7736 5208
Fax: 020 7751 9737
Contact:
Mr Chris Tillin
ctillin@ka-international.com

Kaleidoscope Events Ltd
Event management and team
building
PO Box 2679
Faringdon, SN7 7ZP
Contact:
Mr Mike Mallett

Tel: 08703 506061
mike@keml.co.uk

Keytek UK Limited
Locksmith Services
6 Acorn Business Park
Ling Road
Poole
Dorset, BH12 4NZ
Contact:
Ms Emma Darby
Tel: 01202 245004
Fax: 01202 245001
emma.darby@keytekuk.com

Little Impressions Ltd
Plaster casts of children's feet and
hands
7 Bulkington Avenue
Worthing
West Sussex, BN14 7HH
Tel: 01903 230515
Fax: 01903 603120
Contact:
Mr Tony Franks
Tel: 01903 230515
Fax: 01903 603120
info@little-impressions.com

Local Life Ltd
Website directory and design
Bergerco House
6 Nelson Street
Southend-on-Sea, SS1 1EF
Contact:
Mr Tony Martin
Tel: 01702 343411
Fax: 01702 391040
tony.martin@locallife.co.uk

matrix-direct-recycle
Electrical and electronic equipment
Unit 17
Yorkshire IT Park
Huddersfield, HD4 7NR
www.m-d-recycle.co.uk

Contact:
Mr Craig Thompson
Tel: 01484 353777
Fax: 01484 353778
info@m-d-recycle.co.uk

Medics on the Move
Home finders
Bridge House
8 Avon Vale
Stoke Bishop
Bristol, BS9 1TR
Contact:
Ms Vickie Knighton
Tel: 0870 350 1858
Fax: 01179 044683
vickie@medicsonthemove.co.uk

Microsport
Teaching sport to pre-school children
The Cow Shed
Bard Hill
Salthouse
Norfolk, NR25 7XB
Contact:
Ms Jane Waters
Tel: 020 7623 3195
Fax: 020 7623 3195
info@micro-sport.co.uk

Mobile Car Valeting
MCV House, Redcomb Business Park
Desford Road
Enderby
Leicestershire, LE19 4AD
Contact:
Mr T Smith
Tel: 0116 230 3040
Fax: 0116 230 3935
terry@mobilecarvaleting.co.uk

Monk Marketing
Promotional merchandise
63a Brighton Road
Shoreham by Sea
West Sussex, BN43 6RE

Contact:
Mr Michael Monk
Tel: 01273 464010
Fax: 01273 464131
mike@monkmarketing.com

Monkey Puzzle Day Nurseries
Child care
Aldbury House
Dower Mews, High Street
Berkhampstead
Hertfordshire, HP4 2BL
Contact:
Mr Mark Crosby
Tel: 01442 825558
**mark@monkeypuzzledaynurseries.
com**

Morris Pasties Ltd
Cornish pasties
60 East Street
Newquay
Cornwall, TR7 1BE
Contact:
Mr Chris Morris
Tel: 01637 873405
Fax: 01637 875319
info@morrispasties.co.uk

Mortgage and Property Services Ltd
Mortgage broker
Lingfield Park
Darlington
Co Durham, DL1 1RW
Tel: 01325 487324
Fax: 01325 489973
Contact:
Mr Paul Welch
Tel: 01325 487324
Fax: 01325 489973
paul.welch@mandps.com

Moshulu
Footwear retail
Coastgard Road Ltd
Devonshire Road
Heathpark
Honiton, Devon, EX14 1SD
Contact:
Mr Daryl Fulls
Tel: 01404 540770
Fax: 01404 540771
franchise@moshulu.co.uk

NBC Bird Solutions (franchising) Ltd
Bird and pest control
The Heritage Centre
Banham Zoo
Banham
Norfolk, NR16 2HE
Tel: 0800 108 8026
Fax: 01953 888890
Contact:
Mr John Dickson
Tel: 01953 888090
Fax: 01953 888890
enquiries@birdsolutions.co.uk

New Age Kurling
Sports products and event
5 Lower Sands
Dymchurch
Kent, TN29 0NE
Contact:
Mr John Bennett
Tel: 01303 873270
Fax: 01303 873271
info@kurling.co.uk

Oakleaf Sales Limited
Interior decoration
Unit A
Melbourne Mills
Chesham Street
Keighley
West Yorkshire, BD21 4LG

Contact:
Mr Jonathan Banister
Tel: 01535 663274
Fax: 01535 662031
sales@oakleaf.co.uk

Ology
Business advisers
Yarmouth House
Trident Business Park
Daten Avenue
Warrington, WA3 6BX
Tel: 0870 241 8191
Fax: 0870 241 9017
www.ologybusiness.com
Contact:
Mr David Pike
Tel: 0870 241 8191
Fax: 0870 240 9017
info@ologybusiness.com

PAPERfix Ltd
Binders, laminators and paper
handling equipment
Unit 1
Elmfield Business Park
Lotherton Way
Garford
Leeds, LS25 2JY
www.paperfix.co.uk
Contact:
Mr Ted Girtchen
Tel: 0845 601 7376
Fax: 0845 601 8536
ted.girtchen@paperfix.co.uk

Pareto Law
Graduate assessment, placement
and training
Barfield House
Alderly Road
Wilmslow
Cheshire, SK9 1PL
Contact:
Miss Sally Price

Tel: 01625 255255
Fax: 01625 255256
sprice@paretolaw.co.uk

PC Friend
Retail of PC consumables
Unit 10
Woodhouse Business Centre
Wakefield Road
West Yorkshire, WF6 1BB
Contact:
Mr Peter Tantram
Tel: 01924 899567
Fax: 01924 898177
franchise@pcfriend-online.com

Petpals (UK) Ltd
Pet care services
Phoenix House, Basepoint
Caxton Close, East Portway
Andover
Hampshire, SP10 3FG
Tel: 0870 300 9020
Fax: 01264 326361
www.petpals.com
Contact:
Ms Tracey Eden
Tel: 0870 300 9020
Fax: 01264 326361
franchise@petpals.com

Pierre Lang
Designer jewellery
Peter Southgate
PO Box 3324
Wokingham
Berkshire, RG41 5QV
www.pierrelang.com
Contact:
Mr Pierre Lang
Tel: 0118 978 2851
Fax: 0118 978 2876
plang777@aol.com

Pinnacle Chauffeur Transport Ltd
Luxury chauffeur business
Unit 5
Crown Business Centre
George Street
Failsworth, Manchester, M35 9BW
Tel: 0800 783 4107
Fax: 0161 683 3189
www.wedriveyou.co.uk
Contact:
Mr Christopher Brown
Tel: 0870 752 3377
Fax: 0161 683 3189
chrisbrown@wedriveyou.co.uk

Pizza Hut UK Ltd
Pizza delivery, take-away outlets
1 Imperial Place
Elstree Way
Borehamwood
Hertfordshire, WD6 1JN
Contact:
Enterprising Futures Ltd
Tel: 020 8956 9000
Fax: 020 8956 2211
cgarside@tdatransitions.co.uk

Popping Tins Ltd
Vending Pringles products
20b Picton House
Hussar Court
Waterlooville, PO7 7SQ
Contact:
Mr Brett Merchant
Tel: 0239 2711781
brett@poppingtins.co.uk

Protex UK Sales Ltd
Tyre sealant installation
Walkford Farm Offices
Walkford Lane
New Milton
Hampshire, BH25 5NH
Contact:
Ms Rachel Fisher

Tel: 0845 658 2820
Fax: 0700 395 5955
franchiseenquiry@protex.uk.net

Punctureseal International Ltd
Tyre sealant
St Brandons House
29 Great George Street
Bristol, BS1 5QT
Contact:
Mr Tony Robinson
Tel: 0117 920 0047
Fax: 0117 920 0001

Razzamataz Theatre Schools
Children's singing drama and
dance school
Head Office, 2nd Floor
Atlas Works, Nelson Street
Denton Holme
Carlisle, CA2 5NB
Contact:
Ms Denise Hutton
Tel: 01228 550129
Fax: 01228 525830
franchise@razzamataz.co.uk

Reactfast Plumbing
Emergency plumbing services
Unit 113
Jubilee Trade Centre
130 Pershore Street
Birmingham, B5 6ND
Tel: 0121 666 4086
Fax: 0121 666 4091
www.reactfastfranchises.co.uk
Contact:
Mr Andy Staveley
Tel: 0121 666 4086
Fax: 0121 666 4091
franchises@reactfast.co.uk

Rings by Design Franchising
Bespoke jewellery
B8 Houghton Enterprise Centre
Lake Road

Houghton Le Spring, DH5 8BJ
Contact:
Mr Ian Ward
Tel: 0800 083 7746
info@ringsbydesign.com

Sandler Sales Institute
Sales and sales management
training
20 Cheriton House
Cromwell Business Park
Chipping Norton
Oxfordshire, OX7 5SR
Contact:
Mr Shaun Thomson
Tel: 0870 770 2642
Fax: 0870 770 2643
shaun@sandler.com

Skillfix
Plumbing, heating and drainage
4 Fairfield Close
Christchurch
Dorset, BH23 1QZ
Contact:
Mr Steve Old
Tel: 01202 588993
Fax: 01202 588999
franchise@skillfix.com

Smiffy's
Party shops
Peckett Plaza
Heapham Road Industrial Estate
Gainsborough
Lincolnshire, DN21 1FJ
www.smiffys.com
Contact:
Ms Carolyn O'Hare
Tel: 01427 619721
Fax: 01427 619744
marketing@smiffys.com

Soapycar.com
Visiting car wash
Unit 14
Link House
Leat Street
Tiverton
Devon, EX16 5LG
Contact:
Mr David Simmonds
Tel: 01884 252928
Fax: 01884 253028
info@soapycar.com

Star Brite Chemicals
Industrial cleaning chemicals and
supplies
XL House
Rutherford Way
Crawley
West Sussex, RH10 2PB
Contact:
Mr Simon White
Tel: 01293 434250
Fax: 01293 434252
enquiries@starbrite.co.uk

Success Photography
Special events photography
Moleside, 9 Reigate Road
Sidlow
Reigate
Surrey, RH2 8QH
Contact:
Ms Kate Bell
Tel: 01293 822211
Fax: 01293 820642
kate@successphotography.com

Sunbelt Business Brokers
Business transfer agents
11 Henrietta Street
Covent Garden
London, WC2E 8PY
Tel: 020 7836 4900
Fax: 020 7836 4904

Contact:
Mr Stuart Montgomery
Tel: 020 7836 4900
Fax: 020 7836 4904
**smontgomery@sunbeltnetwork.
com**

Superseal International
Puncture protection
Maghery Business Centre
Maghery Rd
Dungannon
Co Tyrone, BT71 6PA
Contact:
Mr John Lavery
Tel: 0870 744 3750
Fax: 0870 744 3740
info@punctureproof.com

Surelet
Residential lettings and property
management
3 Tuffley Park
Lower Tuffley Lane
Gloucester, GL2 5DP
Contact:
Miss Clare Crisp
Tel: 01452 317657
Fax: 01452 305302
info@surelet-franchise.co.uk

Sureslim
Retail sale of eating programmes
23–25 Bell Street
Reigate
Surrey, RH2 7AD
Tel: 0870 321 4014
Fax: 0870 321 4015
Contact:
Mr Daryl Taylor
Tel: 01737 229761
Fax: 01737 229769
daryl@sureslimuk.com

Survair Franchising Ltd
Protective coatings for property
maintenance
Caolila
Glendevon
Perthshire, FK14 7JY
Tel: 0845 458 5364
Fax: 01259 781291
Contact:
Mr Damian McConnell
Tel: 0845 458 5364
Fax: 01259 781291
damian@survair-franchising.com

Talent Management
Talent agency
27/28 Tombland
Norwich, NR3 1RE
Contact:
Ms Suzy O'Connor
Tel: 0700 4 TALENT (825368), ext. 223
Fax: 01603 666102
suzy@talentmanagement.com

The Asbestos Group
Safety/inspection services
Senate House
Saxon Business Park
Stoke Prior, Bromsgrove
Worcestershire, B60 4AD
Tel: 0800 376 1933
Fax: 0800 376 1930
www.theasbestosgroup.co.uk
Contact:
Ms Becci Pugh
Tel: 0800 376 1933
Fax: 0800 376 1930
info@theasbestosgroup.co.uk

The Brampton Pie Company
Retail pies/foods
46a High Street
Brampton
Huntingdon, PE28 4TH
www.thebramptonpiecompany.com

Contact:
Ms Emma Talic
Tel: 01480 414558
info@bramptonpies.co.uk

**The Camping and Caravanning
Club (franchising) Ltd**
Camping and caravanning sites
and products
Greenfields House
Westwood Way
Westwood Business Park
Coventry, CV4 8JH
Contact:
Mr Gary Fletcher
Tel: 02476 694995
Fax: 02476 694886
**huw.rees@campingandcaravanning
club.co.uk**

The Inkdrop
Printer consumables
2A Newton Court
Pendeford Business Park
Wolverhampton, WV9 5HB
Tel: 01902 787200
Fax: 01902 787300
Contact:
Mr Justin Kyriakou
Tel: 01902 787200
Fax: 01902 787300
info@the-inkdrop.co.uk

The Little Gym
Physical fitness for children
Itaca International SA
44 Highview Avenue
Edgware
Middlesex, HA8 9AU
www.thelittlegym.com
Contact:
Mrs Bev Regan
Tel: 020 8958 7373
Fax: 020 8357 8860
bevregan@thelittlegym.co.uk

The Mattress Doctor
Cleaning and sanitizing of
mattresses
8 Mountbatten Drive
Ringstead
Northants, NN14 4TX
Tel: 0845 330 6607
Fax: 0845 458 8181
Contact:
Mr Bryan Walters / Bruce King
Tel: 0845 330 6607
Fax: 0845 458 8181
mail@matdoc.co.uk

The Original Chocolate Fountain
Hire of chocolate fountains
Unit A37–42
New Covent Garden Market
Nine Elms Lane
London, SW8 5EE
Contact:
Ms Helen Harper
Tel: 020 7627 6425
Fax: 020 7627 6381
info@theoriginalchocolatefountain.
com

The Penn Group
Management consultancy
Central Boulevard
Blythe Valley Park
Solihull, B90 8AG
Tel: 01564 711230
Fax: 01564 711330
www.thepenngroup.co.uk/
franchising
Contact:
Mr Philip Wright
Tel: 01564 711230
Fax: 01564 711330
philip@thepenngroup.co.uk

The Phone Works
Mobile communications
Holy Oak Farm
Upton Snodsbury
Worcester, WR7 4NH
www.thephoneworks.co.uk
Contact:
Mr Phil Guest
Tel: 0845 050 0545
Fax: 01905 381177
info@thephoneworks.co.uk

**The Plastic Surgeon (Franchising)
Ltd**
Surface repairs for wood, metal and
plastic
Blue Waters House
Pottery Road
Bovey Tracey
Devon, TQ13 9DS
Tel: 01626 833001
Fax: 01626 833008
Contact:
Mr Stephen Lear
Tel: 01626 833001
Fax: 01626 833008
slear@the-plastic-surgeon.co.uk

The Platinum Academy
Training of beauty therapists
Unit 3
Erskine Trading Estate
Liverpool, L6 1NA
Contact:
Ms Jan Myers
Tel: 0151 266767
shaina@beautycourses.co.uk

The Platinum Limo Company
Stretched limo hire/sales
30 Edison Street
Hillington Park
Glasgow, G52 4JW
Tel: 08700 13 5466
Fax: 0141 891 4888

www.platinumlimo.co.uk
Contact:
Mr Jackie Farrell
Tel: 08700 13 5466
Fax: 0141 891 4888
jackie.farrell@platinumlimo.co.uk

The Rangers Shop
Football merchandise shops
Retail Dept
Argyle House, Ibrox Stadium
Edmiston Drive
Glasgow, G51 2XD
Contact:
Ms Julie Waites
Tel: 01325 251 455
Fax: 01325 251 466
gerrycarey@rangers.co.uk

The Sales Recruitment Network Ltd
Sales recruitment consultancy
1–2 North End
Swineshead
Boston
Lincolnshire, PE20 3LR
www.tsrn.co.uk
Contact:
Ms Teresa Darnell
Tel: 0870 350 1071
Fax: 0870 350 1072
td@tsrn.co.uk

The Sweet Partnership
Confectionery distribution
Units 4 & 5, Metana House
Priestley Way
Crawley, RH10 9NT
Contact:
Mr Rob Kerridge
Tel: 01293 551599
Fax: 01293 552620
rob@tspf.co.uk

The Townends Group
Estate agents
Latour House
Chertsey Boulevard
Hanworth, Chertsey
Surrey, KT16 9JX
Tel: 01932 736500
Fax: 01932 736599
www.townends.co.uk
Contact:
Mr Keith Young
Tel: 01932 736500, ext 291
Fax: 01932 736599
kyoung@townends.co.uk

Trimage (Scotland) Ltd
3D effect sculptures on acrylic
Bruach
Spittal
Carnwath
Lanarkshire, ML11 8LY
Tel: 01555 841073
www.trimagescotland.co.uk
Contact:
Mr Nigel Ward
Tel: 01555 841073
nigel@trimagescotland.co.uk

Trugreen
Lawn care
Tigers Road
Wieston
Leicester, LE15 4WS
Tel: 0116 275 9000
Fax: 0116 275 9002
Contact:
Mr Ken Dennis
Tel: 0116 275 9000
Fax: 0116 275 9002
kendennis@servicemaster.co.uk

UNZE (Franchising) Ltd
Own-label footwear
The Movement House,
Ajax Works, Hertford Road
Barking
Essex, IG11 8DY
Contact:
Mr Kamran Saleem
Tel: 020 8591 7111
Fax: 020 8591 6694
info@unzefranchise.co.uk

Vantana Ltd
Window blinds
Starlaw Road
Starlaw Business Park
Livingston, EH54 8SF
Tel: 01506 466444
Fax: 01506 460872
Contact:
Mr Scott Murray
Tel: 01506 466444
Fax: 01506 460872
franchise@vantana.co.uk

West End Training
Training and outplacement services
Temple Court
Cathedral Road
Cardiff, CF11 9HA
Tel: 029 2078 6429
Fax: 029 2078 6666
Contact:
Mr Clive Sherer
info@westendtraining.co.uk

World Property Centre Franchising
Property sales
Phoenix House
Christopher Martin Road
Basildon
Essex, SS14 3HG
Tel: 01268 286500
Fax: 01268 286555

Contact:
Ms Karen Hammond
Tel: 01268 286500
Fax: 01268 286555
karen@worldpropertycentre.com

WPA Franchise
Private medical insurance
Rivergate House
Blackbrook Park
Taunton
Somerset, TA1 2PE
Contact:
Mr Adrian Humphreys
Tel: 01823 625272
adrian.humphreys@wpa.org

Affiliated professional advisers

Solicitors

Addleshaw Goddard
100 Barbirolli Square
Manchester, M2 3AB
Contact:
Mr G Lindrup
Tel: 0161 934 6255
Fax: 0161 934 6060
garth.lindrup@addleshawgoddard.com

Beachcroft Wansbroughs
St Ann's House
St Ann Street
Manchester, M2 7LP
Contact:
Mrs Pauline Cowie
Tel: 0161 934 3111
Fax: 0161 934 3288
pcowie@bwlaw.co.uk

Biggart Baillie & Gifford
Dalmore House
310 St Vincent Street
Glasgow, G2 5QR
Contact:
Mr C Miller
Tel: 0141 228 8000
info@biggartbaillie.co.uk
Fax: 020 7760 1111
john.sipling@blplaw.com

Blake Lapthorn Linnell
Kings Court
21 Brunswick Place
Southampton
Hampshire, SO15 2AQ
Tel: 023 8063 1823
Fax: 023 8022 6294
www.bllaw.co.uk
Contact:
Mr Geoffrey Sturgess
Tel: 023 8072 0124
Fax: 023 8022 6294
geoffrey.sturgess@bllaw.co.uk

Brodies LLP
15 Atholl Crescent
Edinburgh, EH3 8HA
Contact:
Mr J C A Voge
Tel: 0131 228 3777
julian.voge@brodies.co.uk

Chambers & Co
Jonathan Scott Hall
Thorpe Road
Norwich, NR1 1UH
Contact:
Mr J Chambers
Tel: 01603 616155
chambers@paston.co.uk

Clairmonts
9 Clairmont Gardens
Glasgow, G3 7LW

Contact:
Mr D S Kaye
Tel: 0141 331 4000
info@clairmonts.co.uk

David Bigmore & Co
Thornton Grange
Chester Road
Gresford, LL12 8NU
www.dbigmore.co.uk
Contact:
Mr David Bigmore
Tel: 01978 855058
Fax: 01978 854623
db@dbigmore.co.uk

Eversheds
Cloth Hall Court
Infirmary Street
Leeds, LS1 2JB
Contact:
Ms R Connorton
Tel: 0113 243 0391
ruthconnorton@eversheds.com

Eversheds
Senator House
85 Queen Victoria Street
London, EC4V 4JL
Contact:
Mr M Mendelsohn or Chris
Wormald
Tel: 020 7919 4862
chriswormald@eversheds.com

Eversheds
Eversheds House
70 Great Bridgewater Street
Manchester, M1 5ES
Contact:
Ms R Connorton
Tel: 0161 831 8000
Fax: 0161 832 5337
ruthconnorton@eversheds.com

Eversheds
Central Square South
Orchard Street
Newcastle Upon Tyne, NE1 3XX
Contact:
Ms R Connorton
Tel: 0191 241 6000
Fax: 0191 241 6499
ruthconnorton@eversheds.com

EXB Legal
27 Seymour Street
Liverpool, L3 5PE
Contact:
Ms Elise Billy
Tel: 0845 094 0180
Fax: 0870 133 2884
law@exblegal.com

Field Fisher Waterhouse
35 Vine Street
London, EC3N 2AA
Tel: 020 7861 4000
Fax: 020 7488 0084
Contact:
Mr Mark Abell
Tel: 020 7861 4000
mark.abell@ffw.com

Fraser Brown Solicitors
84 Friar Lane
Nottingham, NG1 6ED
Contact:
Mr Sam Lodh
Tel: 0115 947 2541
Fax: 0115 947 3636
slodh@fraserbrown.com

Goodman Derrick
90 Fetter Lane
London, EC4A 1PT
Contact:
Mr Matthew Wanford
Tel: 020 7404 0606
Fax: 020 7831 6407
mwanford@gdlaw.co.uk

Halliwell Landau
St James' Court
Brown Street
Manchester, M2 2JF
Contact:
Mr John Burns
Tel: 0161 831 2932
Fax: 0161 835 2994
john.burns@halliwells.com

Hamilton Pratt
120 Edmund Street
Birmingham, B3 2ES
Contact:
Mr John Pratt
Tel: 0870 351 4900
Fax: 0870 351 4905
john.pratt@hplaw.co.uk

Hill Dickinson
Pearl Assurance House
2 Derby Square
Liverpool, L2 9XL
Tel: 0151 236 5400
Fax: 0151 236 2175
Contact:
Mr Stephen Lansdown
Tel: 0151 243 2348
Fax: 0151 243 2301
stephen.lansdown@hilldickinson. com

HJ Walker Sibia Solicitors
603/614 The Cotton Exchange
Old Hall Street
Liverpool, L3 9LQ
Contact:
Mr G Howard Jones
Tel: 0151 227 2600
Fax: 0151 225 1551
law@hjws.com

Keeble Hawson
Protection House
16–17 East Parade
Leeds, LS1 2BR

Contact:
Mr H D McKillop
Tel: 0113 244 3121
postroom@keeblehawson.co.uk

Leathes Prior
74 The Close
Norwich
Norfolk, NR1 4DR
www.leathesprior.co.uk
Contact:
Mr R J Chadd
Tel: 01603 610911
jchadd@leathesprior.co.uk

Maclay Murray & Spens
151 St Vincent Street
Glasgow, G2 5NJ
www.maclaymurrayspens.co.uk
Contact:
Ms M Burnside
Tel: 0141 248 5011
mab@maclaymurrayspens.co.uk

Marshall Ross & Prevezer
4 Fredricks Place
London, EC2R 8AB
Contact:
Mr R Levitt
Tel: 020 7367 9000
Fax: 020 7367 9004
r.levitt@mrp-law.co.uk

Mills and Reeve
78–84 Colmore Row
Birmingham, B3 2AB
Contact:
Mr Peter Manford
Tel: 0121 454 4000
Fax: 0121 456 3631

Mundays
Cedar House
78 Portsmouth Road
Cobham
Surrey, KT11 1AN

Contact:
Mrs Nicola Broadhurst
Tel: 01932 590500
Fax: 01932 590220
nicola.broadhurst@mundays.co.uk

Nina Moran-Watson Solicitors
The Lodge House
Crow lane
Tendring
Essex, CO16 9AP
www.nmoran-watson.co.uk
Contact:
Ms Nina Moran Watson
Tel: 0870 241 5092,
Mob: 07968 445804
Fax: 0870 770 1623
nina@nmoran-watson.co.uk

Osborne Clarke
Apex Plaza
Forbury Road
Reading
Berkshire, RG1 1AX
www.osborne-clarke.co.uk
Contact:
Mr Mark Antingham
Tel: 01189 252042
Fax: 01189 252043
Mark.Antingham@osborneclarke.com

Owen White
Senate House
62–70 Bath Road
Slough
Berkshire, SL1 3SR
www.owenwhite.com
Contact:
Ms Jane Masih
Tel: 01753 876800
jane.masih@owenwhite.com

Parker Bullen
8 Newbury Street
Andover
Hampshire, SP10 1DW
Contact:
Mr Chris Gwinn
Tel: 01264 400500
Fax: 01264 333686
chris.gwinn@parkerbullen.com

Parker Bullen
45 Castle Street
Salisbury
Wiltshire, SP1 3SS
Contact:
Mr M Lello
Tel: 01722 412000
Fax: 01722 411822
mark.lello@parkerbullen.com

Shadbolt & Co LLP
Chatham Court
Lesbourne
Reigate
Surrey, RH2 7LD
www.shadboltlaw.com
Contact:
Ms Caroline Abrey
Tel: 01737 226277
Caroline_Abrey@Shadboltlaw.com

Shakespeares Solicitors
Somerset House
Temple Street
Birmingham, B2 SDJ
Contact:
Ms Jayne Lynn
Tel: 0121 632 4199
Fax: 0121 643 2257
jayne.lynn@shakespeares.co.uk

Sherrards
45 Grosvenor Road
St Albans, AL1 3AW
Contact:
Mr Manzoor Ishani

Tel: 01727 832830
Fax: 01727 832833
mgi@sherrards.com

Sylvester Amiel Lewin & Horne
Pearl Assurance House
319 Ballards Lane
London, N12 8LY
Contact:
Mr J Horne
Tel: 020 8446 4000
lawyers@sylvam.co.uk

Taylor Wessing
Carmelite
50 Victoria Embankment
Blackfriars
London, EC4Y 0DX
Contact:
Mr C Lloyd
Tel: 020 7300 7000
c.lloyd@taylorwessing.com

Thomas Eggar
75 Shoe Lane
London, EC4A 3JB
Contact:
Mr Richard Brown
Tel: 020 7842 0000
Fax: 020 7842 3900
richard.brown@thomaseggar.com

Thomas Eggar
Belmont House
Station Way
Crawley
West Sussex, RH10 1JA
Contact:
Mr M Crooks
Tel: 01293 742700
Fax: 01293 742999
michael.crooks@thomaseggar.com

Thorntons WS
50 Castle Street
Dundee, DD1 3RU
Contact:
Mr Stuart Brymer
Tel: 01382 229111
Fax: 01382 202288
dundee@thorntonsws.co.uk

TLT Solicitors
One Redcliffe Street
Bristol, BS1 6TP
www.TLTsolicitors.com
Contact:
Mr William Hull
Tel: 0117 917 7777
whull@tltsolicitors.com

Wragge & Co
55 Colmore Row
Birmingham, B3 2AS
Contact:
Mr Michael Luckman
Tel: 0121 233 1000
michael_luckman@wragge.com

Wright Johnston & Mackenzie LLP
302 St Vincent Street
Glasgow, G2 5RZ
www.wjm.co.uk
Contact:
Angus MacLeod
Tel: 0141 248 3434
Fax: 0141 221 1226
enquiries@wjm.co.uk

Business services

Overview Mapping
Mapping, demographic
information to franchisors
Tithe Barn
Blisworth Hill Farm
Blisworth
Northants, NN7 3DB
www.overviewmapping.com

Contact:
Mr Andrew Overton
Tel: 0871 223 0442
Fax: 0871 223 0443
info@overmap.co.uk

EK Williams Ltd
Accountancy products and
associated business services
No 1 Pavilion Square
Cricketers Way
Westhoughton
Bolton
Lancashire, BL5 3AJ
Contact:
Customer Care
Tel: 0800 587 0498
Fax: 01942 814636
customer.care@ekwgroup.co.uk

Exhibition organizers

Venture Marketing Group Ltd
Carlton Plaza
111 Upper Richmond Road
Putney
London, SW15 2TJ
Contact:
Mr D Tuck
Tel: 020 8394 5230
david.tuck@vmgl.com

Financial services

Franchise Finance
105 Briar Avenue
Norbury
London, SW16 3AG
Contact:
Mr Nicholas Potter
Tel: 020 8679 0126
Fax: 020 8679 0126
potterpef@hotmail.com

Franchise manual publishing consultants

Horwath Franchising Ltd (Manual Preparation and Review)
London and York
www.horwathfranchising.co.uk
Contact:
Ms Sarah Richards
Tel: 0870 458 6682
manual@horwathfranchising.co.uk

Manual Writers International
The Garden House
Norton Grange
Little Kineton
Warwickshire, CV35 0DP
www.manual-writers.com
Contact:
Mrs Penny Hopkinson
Tel: 01926 641402,
Mob: 07956 315750
penny@manual-writers.com

Insurance brokers

Barnett & Barnett Ltd
650 London Road
Isleworth
Middlesex, TW7 4EG
Contact:
Mr Craig Kitchen
Tel: 020 8568 2021
Fax: 020 8560 7044
craig.kitchen@barnett-and-barnett.co.uk

Media and communications

Business Franchise Magazine
2nd Floor
83–84 George Street
Richmond
Surrey, TW9 1HE

Contact:
Natalie Hoare
Tel: 020 8332 9995
Fax: 020 8332 9307
editor@circlepublishing.net

Daily Express
The Northern & Shell Building
10 Lower Thames Street
London, EC3R 6EN
Contact:
Ms Danni Christie
Tel: 0871 520 2882
danielle.christie@express.co.uk

Daily Mail
4th Floor
Northcliffe House
2 Derry Street
Kensington
London, W8 5TT
Contact:
Ms Geraldine Haenow
Tel: 020 7938 6433
Fax: 020 7937 7755
geraldine.haenow@dailymail.co.uk

Daltons Weekly
Link House
West Street
Poole
Dorset, BH15 1LL
Tel: 020 8329 0150
Fax: 020 8329 0101
www.DaltonsBusiness.com
Contact:
Mr Steve Croucher
Tel: 020 8329 0279
Fax: 020 8329 0101
steve.croucher@daltons.co.uk

Franchise World
Highlands House
165 The Broadway
Wimbledon
London, SW19 1NE

Contact:
Mr Robert Riding
Tel: 020 8605 2555
Fax: 020 8605 2556
info@franchiseworld.co.uk

Q Media Limited
The Coach House, Sundial House
Altrincham Road, Styal
Wilmslow
Cheshire, SK9 4JE
Contact:
Mr Simon Poyser
Tel: 01625 418666
Fax: 01625 522253
simonpoyser@iqmedia-uk.com
katherinelivingstone@iqmedia-uk.com

Sunday Express
The Northern & Shell Building
10 Lower Thames Street
London, EC3R 6EN
Contact:
Ms Yvette Taylor
Tel: 0871 520 2864
yvette.taylor@express.co.uk

The Franchise Magazine
Franchise House
56 Surrey Street
Norwich, NR3 1FD
Contact:
Mr Simon Carpenter-Foster
Tel: 01603 620301
enquiries@fdsltd.com

The Mail on Sunday
2 Derry St
London, W8 5TS
Contact:
Ms Joanne Beeney
Tel: 020 7938 7312
joanne.beeney@mailonsunday.co.uk

The Scotsman Publications Ltd
108 Holyrood Road
Edinburgh, EH8 8AS
Contact:
Mr Ken Mowbray
Tel: 0131 620 8620
kmowbray@scotsman.com

whichfranchise.com
78 Carlton Place
Glasgow, G5 9TH
www.whichfranchise.com
Contact:
Mr J Sellyn
Tel: 0141 429 5900
enquiry@whichfranchise.com

Bankers

Bank of Scotland
City of London
Corporate Centre 6th Floor
155 Bishopsgate
London, EC2M 3YB
Contact:
Mr Daryll Windsor
Tel: 020 7012 8199
Fax: 020 8012 8210
franchising@bankofscotland.co.uk

HSBC
Franchise Unit
12 Calthorpe Road
Birmingham, B15 1QZ
www.ukbusiness.hsbc.com
Contact:
Cathryn Hayes
Tel: 0121 455 3438
franchiseunit@hsbc.com

Lloyds TSB
Business Banking
Canon's House PO Box 112
Canon's Way
Bristol, BS99 7LB

www.lloydstsbbusiness.com
Contact:
Mr Richard Holden
Tel: 0117 943 3089
franchising@lloydstsb.co.uk

NatWest
NatWest Franchise Section
Level 2, 2 Waterhouse Square
138–142 Holborn
London, EC1N 2TH
Tel: 020 7427 8405
Fax: 020 7427 8502
www.natwest.com
Contact:
Mr Mark Scott
Tel: 020 7427 8405
Fax: 020 7427 8502
**franchise.retailbanking@natwest.
com**

The Royal Bank of Scotland
Franchise Department
PO Box 20000, The Younger
Building
Drummond House
3 Redheughs Avenue
Edinburgh, EH12 9RB
www.rbs.co.uk/franchise
Contact:
Mr Alan Smart – National Franchise
Manager
Tel: 0131 556 8555
Fax: 0131 523 5059
alan.smart@rbs.co.uk

Chartered accountants

Beresfords
Castle House
Castle Hill Avenue
Folkestone
Kent, CT20 2TQ
Contact:
Mr T C Hindle

Tel: 01303 850992
Fax: 01303 850979
mail@beresfordsaccountants.com

FranAccounts
ALB House
4 Brighton Road
Horsham
West Sussex, RH13 5BA
www.franaccounts.co.uk
Contact:
Mr James Harmey
Tel: 01403 255788
Fax: 01403 255704
dtomsett@albaccountancy.co.uk

Morris & Co
Ashton House
Chadwick Street
Moreton
Wirral
Cheshire, CH46 7TE
Tel: 0151 678 7979
Fax: 0151 606 0909
www.moco.co.uk
Contact:
Mr Phil Harrison
Tel: 0151 678 7979
Fax: 0151 606 0909
franchise@moco.co.uk

Rees Pollock
35 New Bridge Street
London, EC4V 6BW
www.reespollock.co.uk
Contact:
Mr Michael Day
Tel: 020 7778 7200
Fax: 020 7329 6408
michael@reespollock.co.uk

WDM Associates
Oakfield House
378 Brandon Street
Motherwell, ML1 1XA
Contact:

Mr Terry Dunne
Tel: 01698 250251
Fax: 01698 250261
terry@wdmassocs.co.uk

Development agencies

Scottish Enterprise
150 Broomielaw
Atlantic Quay
Glasgow, G2 8LU
Contact:
Mr Brian Smail
Tel: 0141 228 2730
Fax: 0141 228 2559
brian.smail@scotent.co.uk

Franchise consultants

Acheson Franchise Advisors
14 Royena Palace
Marcus Beach
Queensland, 4573, Australia
Tel: 00 61 74 481 774
Fax: 00 61 74 481 775
Contact:
Mr David Acheson
Tel: 00 61 74 481 774
Fax: 00 61 74 481 775
achesons@email.tc

AMO Consulting
74 Kirk Street
Strathaven, ML10 6BA
www.amoconsulting.com
Contact:
Mr Euan Fraser
Tel: 01357 523308
Fax: 01357 523308
euanfraser@bun.com

BDO Stoy Hayward Management Consultants
8 Baker Street
London, W1U 3LL

www.mchardy.biz
Contact:
Mr Max McHardy
Tel: 020 7486 5888
max.mchardy@bdo.co.uk

Business Options
High Curley House
Frith End Road
Frith End
Hampshire, GU35 0RA
www.businessoptions.biz
Contact:
Mr Clive Sawyer
Tel: 01420 479995
Fax: 07970 067724
clive.sawyer@businessoptions.biz

Enterprising Futures Ltd
(London Office)
500 Chiswick High Road
London, W4 5RG
Contact:
Mr Chris Dunn
Tel: 020 8956 2200

F.D.S. Midlands Ltd
28 Footherley Road
Shenstone
Lichfield
Staffordshire, WS14 0NJ
Tel: 01543 483509
Fax: 01543 481029
Contact:
Mr Ken Young
Tel: 01543 483509
Fax: 01543 481029
fdsmids@supanet.com

First Franchise Limited
17 Pine Grove
Church Crookham
Hampshire, GU52 6BD
Contact:
Mr Keith McIntyre
Tel: 01252 404559

Fax: 01252 404559
info@firstfranchise.com

The Franchise Company
Gateway House
55 Coiscliffe Road
Darlington
Co. Durham, DL3 7EH
www.franchisecompany.co.uk
Contact:
Ken Rostron
Tel: 01325 251455
Fax: 01325 251466
info@franchisecompany.co.uk

Useful website addresses

uk.betheboss.com
uk.franchiseopportunities.com
www.british-franchising.org
www.findafranchise.co.uk
www.franchisebusiness.co.uk
www.FranchiseDirect.co.uk
www.franchise-group.com
www.franchisesales.com
www.franchiseuk.co.uk
www.franchiseworld.co.uk
www.franinfo.co.uk
www.whichfranchise.com

Tips on selling

If there is one thing that makes the British squirm it is being sold to. It's so embarrassing. You don't want to hurt the salesman's feelings, but oh, don't you wish he'd go away and pick on someone else. Imagine, then, the soul-freezing horror that strikes a Briton when he is asked not to be sold to, but to do the selling! To sell, you have to shed your diffidence, steady your nerves for the possibility of rejection, and assume the resilience of a rubber ball. Far better to do something easy, like wrestle with an alligator.

Well, for the tyro franchisee there is bad news and good. The bad is that you will almost certainly have to sell (though if you are fortunate your franchisor will do the donkey work and pass on sales leads to you, and he – or, of course, she – may give you some coaching in how to maximize your sales). The good is that selling is not half so daunting as you might at first imagine. Simply being polite is half the battle. Even better news: if you recoil from the very thought of foot-in-the-door tactics, you almost certainly value the opposite characteristics of courtesy, politeness, consideration and an appreciation of the other person's point of view – all great attributes when it comes to promoting your business, winning new customers and keeping existing ones. An open, honest and friendly attitude is a natural form of salesmanship possessed by people who would shrink from the idea of themselves as sellers. So the first rule of selling is to remember that it is part of everything you do in your business. To be prompt, to be polite, to smile, to answer the phone in a friendly welcoming way, to deal quickly with inquiries and efficiently with complaints, these are all effective sales techniques. You must adopt them, and if you employ staff, you should ensure that they, too, know the meaning of service and customer satisfaction.

What follows is a brief guide. As you will see, I am assuming that you are running a business-to-business franchise. If you are selling to the public, broadly the same principles apply.

A basic rule of selling is to know your product or service and, if necessary, be able to demonstrate it. The more knowledgeable and enthusiastic you are about what it is you are selling and the benefits it confers, the more you will discover the natural salesperson that slept unsuspected within you. You must constantly be mindful of what it is that your business has to offer; who your likely customers are; the nature and strength of the competition you face; and the best ways of getting your product or service known.

Nationwide advertising will probably be carried out by the franchisor at the expense of all the franchisees. But that still leaves you with local advertising and promotion in your territory. The *Yellow Pages* and leafleting are well-used and successful means of getting a local business known.

As for approaching customers direct – either in person or on the phone – again the franchisor should be able to help, often by example. It is not unusual for new franchisees to be accompanied by experienced sales people. You can learn more about selling by being with a professional for a week than reading about it for a month.

Here are some broad guidelines to selling direct over the phone:

▮ Find a quite place where you can talk without interruption. If possible, use a hands-free phone to allow you to make notes.

▮ Compile a list of prospects, their names and job titles. There are a number of ways to find out who makes the buying decisions in a target business. **The internet** – companies often give contact details for key members of staff on their websites. **Telephone** the company and ask who's responsible for purchasing your particular product or service. **The trade press** – articles about companies often quote senior management. Make a note of their names. **Trade fairs and exhibitions** – good sources of information about key personnel in exhibiting companies.

▮ Rehearse your opening line. Say who you are and why you are calling. Establish quickly if there is an interest in your product or service.

▮ Have all the facts at your fingertips – how much your goods or services cost; how many have already been sold; why they are better than your competitors'; their specifications and availability; delivery times, and so on. Have your fax and mobile phone numbers, e-mail addresses and postcodes to hand and your diary at your elbow.

▮ Sell the benefits, not the features. Look at your product or service through the eyes of a potential customer. What features would make them want to buy?

▮ Match benefits to the customers' needs. This is the essence of marketing. Always bear in mind that your business should be 'customer-led', not 'product-led'. In other words, you are in business to meet the needs of your customers, not to suit your own convenience.

▮ In talking to customers find out what they're hoping to achieve from the purchase. Encourage them to ask lots of questions.

▮ Ask more general questions, too. The answers may give you clues to unexpected benefits that you can offer.

▮ Do your homework so you can ask informed questions. Analyse your product and identify what factors are most likely to make the customer buy. Quantify any customer benefits in terms of money or time saved by using your product. Show how other businesses have benefited from buying your product or service.

▮ Sales methods. Selling wouldn't earn its place in the art of management without an acronym, so it has one all of its own – AIDA, concocted as follows:
 – Get the customer's Attention.
 – Stimulate the customer's Interest.

- Create the **D**esire to buy.
- Confirm the **A**ction to be taken.

▌ Looked at another way, getting the customer's **attention** is the same as preventing him from losing his attention. To stop him switching off or putting the phone down straight away, hold his attention with an eye-catching brochure or a thought-provoking statement. To arouse his **interest** explain the benefits your product can bestow. Prompt him into **action** with an inducement such as a time-limited offer. Always leave your telephone number, address, e-mail address or order form.

▌ Confirm **action** by repeating what has been agreed and stating the next steps, such as delivery times. Send a confirmatory e-mail or letter.

▌ Close a sale. Don't be afraid to push things along if the conversation is stalling. Sound positive and create a sense of urgency. Convince the customer that he needs your product and would be on to a good thing if he bought sooner rather than later. A bold 'Could I take your order now?' often works. Giving the customer alternatives such as a choice of specifications or materials can be an effective way of closing a sale.

▌ If the customer has one remaining objection, you can often clinch the deal by making a solution to the problem a condition of the sale. For example: 'If I guarantee early delivery, will you place your order now?'

▌ Try to get something out of the call, even if it's only striking that particular prospect from your list. Things to aim for are a face-to-face meeting, a request for a brochure, or an agreement to call again at a future date.

▌ If a sale is agreed, confirm the terms. Make sure the customer is happy and follow up with further confirmation in writing or with a telephone call.

▌ If the customer says no, don't argue, accept the decision and say you will be happy to help if he changes his mind or needs further information.

▌ If a customer shows some interest, follow through. Make a note of the conversation and be sure to deliver what you promised, and quickly. Get the brochure in the post. Send any information requested.

Other rules about selling are organizational and mainly a matter of common sense. For example, you should keep a record of your customers, stay in touch with them, and listen to what they have to say. The closer you can get to them without being pushy, the better chance you stand of winning repeat orders and getting word-of-mouth recommendation, of which there is no better form of advertising.

You should also forecast and plan your sales. A month-by-month sales forecast can help you avoid cash-flow problems and manage your business more effectively. In combination with a sales plan, it will free up time for developing your business rather than responding to day-to-day developments in sales and marketing.

Index

Index of advertisers